THE
SERVANT-DRIVEN
CHURCH

RELEASING EVERY MEMBER FOR MINISTRY

RAY FULENWIDER

 COLLEGE PRESS
PUBLISHING COMPANY
Joplin, Missouri

Cover Design by Mark A. Cole

Library of Congress Cataloging-in-Publication Data

Fulenwider, Ray, 1939–
    The servant-driven church: releasing every member for ministry /
Ray Fulenwider.
        p.   cm.
    ISBN 0-89900-793-7 (pbk.)
    1. Lay ministry. I. Title.
BV677.F86 1998
253—dc21   98-22257
                                                        CIP

I dedicate this book

to thousands of God's servants around the world: These men and women faithfully serve, although most of them are unknown outside their local churches. We need a tomb of the unknown church servants to honor them. But they will have something far better in heaven.

I dedicate this book

to Christian universities, schools of preaching and seminary educators who are preparing servants for the next generation. What an exciting and important task you have!

I dedicate this book

to shepherds, ministers and Christian leaders who are not afraid to dream and face criticism as they implement needed change to meet the needs of all the people in the church community.

I dedicate this book

to the shepherds, deacons, teachers, ministers and secretaries at the Central Church of Christ, Richland Hills Church of Christ and Broadway Church of Christ. I love you deeply. It's been a great journey of faith.

I dedicate this book

to my wife, Ann, and my four children, Deana, Jeana, Joel and Jana. They all have a servant spirit and would do anything for anybody.

I dedicate this book

last of all, to my 81-year-old Dad. Dad has a limited public education, but he has served as an elder for many years. He is the one who modeled and taught me to work as a servant.

TABLE OF CONTENTS

Preface

"The greatest among you will be your servant" (Matt. 23:11). Since teaching at Pepperdine University almost ten years ago, Rick Warren and the "Purpose-Driven Church" at Mission Viejo have profoundly affected my ministry. I made several trips to Mission Viejo and was tremendously impressed with their biblical message and mission. I highly recommend Rick Warren's recent book called *The Purpose-Driven Church*. I believe his book will be one of the greatest influences in the religious world in the 21st century.

In some small ways, my prayer is for *The Servant-Driven Church* to be a companion book on the shelves with *The Purpose-Driven Church*. After more than four decades in ministry, I have discovered we can have the right Scriptures, the right purposes, and unlimited opportunities — but God has tremendous difficulty working in churches which are not servant driven. God will not call all of us to build 10,000 member churches, but he does call all of us to be servants. My prayer is that each one of us will empty his cup so God can fill it with his servant spirit. To God be the glory as we approach each day with the servant attitude: "Lord, here am I, use me."

THE SERVANT'S PRAYER FOR THE 21ST CENTURY

Lord, there will be times when I don't have enough time
— help me to make the time to serve.
Lord, there will be times when I have enough cares of my own
— help me to tenderly care for others as you do.
Lord, there will be times when I've given all I had to give
— help me to keep on giving more.

For All of God's Servants,
Ray Fulenwider

Introduction

"A new command I give you: Love one another" (John 13:34). With these words Jesus gave us the foundation stone on which we are to build our life in obedience to him. But he did not just come down from heaven, issue this command, and leave; he gave us a lifetime of examples of daily living. Among these examples were clear and pointed teachings about serving each other. Would it be possible to love others without serving them? Certainly not!

> ## The attitude of being a servant is to pervade our thinking in all that we do.

During our time on this earth as God's children our first love and desire should be to become more like Jesus. This means learning to put people first before anything or anyone except God. In order to do this the attitude of being a servant is to pervade our thinking in all that we do. However, we cannot just teach people and expect them to go forth and serve. When most of us accept Christ, we are faced with the daunting task of trying to overcome a lifetime of selfishness and self-centeredness. It takes practice and training, learning and growing, loving and caring to develop a strong servant spirit.

In order to provide training and opportunities for practice, situations in which the members of our congregations can learn and grow, we must first have a leadership which has already learned these lessons and put them into practice. Our ministers, elders, deacons, Bible school superintendents, worship leaders, missions committee members, women's leaders, etc. must be teachers and role models in servanthood for the rest of the congregation. The ultimate goal is to have such a strong servant attitude instilled in every member of the congregation that they are driven by their love for Jesus to seek out new opportunities for serving their fellow Christians, their unbelieving friends and relatives, and the community at large. This is a lofty goal, but where do we begin?

This book is a blueprint for preparing and training the church's leaders, those already committed to service within the church, to establish the framework of organization which will allow every member to find a place of service and pursue it with a whole heart. Jesus said, "You know that the rulers of the Gentiles lord it over them, and their high officials exercise authority over them. Not so with you. Instead, whoever wants to be great among you must be your servant, and whoever wants to be first must be your slave. . ." (Matt. 20:25-27). When the leaders have learned to be servants, they have become like the Chief Shepherd and Servant, Jesus Christ. This servant spirit produces a servant-driven church which prospers spiritually and numerically.

The world was not ready for the servant teaching of Jesus when he came into the world. They were looking for a king!

> He doesn't come riding in a Mercedes convertible — but he comes with the spirit of one riding on a donkey.

This servant concept is just as revolutionary as we approach the 21st century. It's his way to lead and change the world. He doesn't come riding in a Mercedes convertible — but he comes with the spirit of one who rides a donkey, the spirit of one who carries a towel and a wash basin. Don't read this book unless you are willing to wash feet as a servant, get your fingernails dirty serving people, have your heart broken with cares for your people and be burdened to reach the lost with the gospel!!!

The Servant's Dream

Violence! Murder! Robbery! Rape! Lying! Anger! Divorce! Juvenile delinquents! Abused children! Loss of Christian values! No prayers in school! How did our world get in such a mess? God's servant in the midst of all this change and turmoil believes that God has called him to the Kingdom for "such a time as this." With a childlike faith, the servant believes God can use him to make a significant difference in today's world. He has eight basic dreams.

1. *The servant's dream is to be chosen to serve.* "I urge you to live a life worthy of the calling you have received" (Eph. 4:1). He wants to feel the exhilaration of being called by God as the verse indicates. He is not interested in money, fame, power or fortune. He is interested in doing God's work in God's way for God's glory.

> ### The servant wants to do God's work in God's way for God's glory.

He also wants to be chosen to serve by the congregation. Many people are frustrated because they are never given the opportunity to serve in ministry. Many congregations have the annual selection of deacons and ministry leaders by members to help overcome this problem. Servants also want to be chosen by the elders and church leaders. It means a lot to a servant when a shepherd personally meets with him and asks him to serve in specific areas.

The servant feels chosen by God to serve for such a time as this. He is deeply influenced by Ephesians 4.

Do you feel called to serve?

Who:	God chose you to be his people (v.1).
What:	Christ gave each one of us a special gift (v. 7).
Why:	Christ gave these gifts to prepare God's holy people for the work of serving (v. 12).
When:	Each part does its own work (v. 12).
Results:	This makes the whole body grow and be filled with love (v. 16).
Message:	Say what people need — words that will help others become stronger (v. 29).

Don't leave God out of your planning.

The servant believes very strongly in the providence of God. He believes that God has providentially called the church family together. Providence is the hand of God in the glove of history. He believes that each person in the local church has been called together for "such a time as this" (Esther 4:14). Although the servant may make ten-year growth plans and projections, he does not leave God out of the planning. He realizes that God is the one responsible for the growth and he enjoys giving God the glory. The servant enjoys having God's providence demonstrated through seeing responses to questions put to the congregation which prove the dynamic workings of God in the growth of a local congregation. Those questions would proceed like this.

"How many of you were members of this congregation twenty years ago?" Or, "how many of you were members when this facility was built?"

Usually only a small number of people are present when these things happened. The servant likes it when these people stand and the congregation applauds them. He is thankful for their faith, sacrifice and perseverance. They usually have stories to share of the difficulty of building the facilities. The servant likes to have it pointed out that the older group had a lot of faith and needed a lot of help. And, God has provided the increase! Otherwise, we would be sitting in a nearly vacant auditorium.

The next question is: "How many of you have moved here from another state or country?" A large group usually stands and all applaud them. God knew that the local church needed them!

The next question is: "How many came here from another congregation within the state?" An even larger number of people usually stands and everyone applauds.

Next comes the question: "How many have been taught the gospel and been led to Christ by someone in this congregation?" A fairly large number usually stands and everyone applauds.

Finally the people are asked: "How many of you who have come to this congregation planned to be here ten or twenty years ago?" There is usually not a single person who stands! People learn an incredible lesson about the providence of God from this congregational testimony. Many of the people move from one place to another "kicking and screaming." They didn't want to move! This is the story of thousands of people who move each year. But, the servant realizes that God has called many different people from all over the world with incredible gifts, talents and abilities. The servant never leaves God out of the planning. Since God has called this great volunteer army together in the local church, he expects great things to happen!

What can you learn about God's providence from your congregation's testimony?

Why does God call a great volunteer army to the local church?

2. *The servant's dream is to use the gifts God has given him.* Romans 12:6 teaches "we have different gifts according to the grace given us." God did not make us all alike and he did not create us with equal gifts. Some have five talents, some two talents, and some one talent. The servant wants to use his God-given gift to serve. Some people can sing like angels. Others can hardly carry a tune in the shower. Some are great encouragers of people when they visit the hospitals. Others cause the patients to be so discouraged and frustrated, they are almost ready to call the undertaker! Some are great teachers, but others put the class to sleep.

3. *The servant's dream is to know what is expected of him.* He is not afraid to get his hands dirty and he doesn't mind serving long hours. But, he gets frustrated if he does not know what the local church wants him to do. He needs written communication

concerning his specific areas of responsibility. And, he needs to know what kind of training and help the church will provide him so he can fulfill these expectations.

> # The servant's dream is to keep dreaming.

4. *The servant's dream is to involve people in his ministry and equip them so the church will be built up.* Ephesians 4:11-12 teaches us that God gave us different leaders and gifts to "prepare God's people for works of service so that the body of Christ may be built up." First Corinthians 12:22 points out "those parts of the body that seem to be weaker (or less important) are indispensable." Everybody is somebody in the kingdom of God. All are made in the image of God and are provided gifts by him.

5. *The servant's dream is to become more and more like Jesus.* Ephesians 4:13 gives us a unique definition of maturity — "attaining to the whole measure of the fullness of Christ." The servant leader wants to do everything that Jesus would do. He also wants to do everything with the spirit and attitude of Jesus. He realizes that where "two or three are gathered together," Jesus is there!

What's your dream for the local church?

What are some ways Satan attacks the church today?

6. *The servant's dream is to keep dreaming.* He realizes that all great movements begin with a dream or vision. He knows that "young men shall see visions, and old men shall dream dreams" (Acts 2:17, NASB). He understands that a church family without a dream or vision is a sinking ship. He believes that Satan is constantly striving to torpedo his dreams. If Satan can do this, he can always stop a church from moving forward. The servant leader knows that dreams lead to what a congregation stands for — the faith to make the dreams come true. This faith is more caught than taught at the beginning point. It's not so much an in-depth theology as it is an explanation of how God is working in the lives of the people. The servant knows that dreams turn into deeds and congregational priorities. He knows the impor-

tance of an organization or structure to implement the priorities and achieve goals. The servant leader wants every member involved and using their gifts to implement the dream. The servant leader is not naive. He knows that Satan attacks the hardest when great things are happening in a local congregation. He knows Satan will strive to divide the leaders and the congregation. Satan will do his best to raise up a group who are opposed to change, long for the good old days, question every good idea and divide a congregation into two separate camps. Thus, the servant leader realizes the tremendous importance of a dream or vision which will unite the congregation to fulfill the great dreams that God had for his local church when he sacrificed his most precious gift, his Son, as an example of the value of his dream for the church.

7. *The servant's dream is to fulfill the kingdom dream of Jesus.* Every great movement begins with a dream. Jesus spoke of his kingdom dream over eighty times! The kingdom dream is a great commission and not a limited commission. God wants his message taken to all people. There are at least four major points in the great commission of Matthew 28:16-20.
   a. Reach nonmembers (OUTREACH).
   b. Teach and make disciples (LOVING MEMBERS OF THE FAMILY OF GOD).
   c. Train and equip for active service (INVOLVEMENT).
   d. Motivate the new member to reach the nonmember (MULTIPLICATION).

> The servant's dream is to reproduce
> the faith of the first century church
> for the twenty-first century.

8. *The servant's dream is to reproduce the faith of the first century church for the twenty-first century.* We are given the seemingly impossible task of carrying the gospel all over the world. The early church had an even more difficult task in the first century, but they "turned the world upside down." There is an incredible

receptivity to the gospel today. The Bible and its teachings have been put back in the prisons in Texas. There were more than five thousand baptisms in Texas prisons through Christ's Prison Fellowship Ministry in 1995! The wall has fallen in Berlin. The Iron Curtain has come down in Russia. According to a Gallup poll, 40% of the adults in today's world are willing to change religions to honestly seek what they believe is the way, truth and need for their family. The wall of prejudice has greatly dissolved. Over one-fifth of all adults move each year and over half of them will change religions when they move. Although these statistics scare many people because so many are leaving the church in which they were reared — it lets us know that a majority of the people are unprejudiced people seeking the truth and servant involvement as we approach the twenty-first century.

What are
the servant's
8 basic dreams?
Are they your
dreams?

God has created his church and led it to become all that it is today. He has called his family together for "such a time as this" (Esther 4:14) to make a real impact on the world in the 21st century. To do this, we must follow ten basic commandments for the 21st century.

1. *God commands us to lift up Christ in our community* (John 12:32). We need to lift the cross so high that it says to the thousands in our area that there is. . . . . .

a LIGHT that never goes out,

a HEART that never grows cold,

a MESSAGE that never grows old,

an EAR that is never closed.

God commands us to lift up Christ in our community.

The church has to be so much more than just a church building located in a certain section of a community. Churches of Christ launched a daring mission plan in the late 1940s. The plan was to build a church building strategically located in every county or precinct in the United States. The building of church buildings throughout the United States was fairly successful as the total exceeded 13,000! However, the plan as a whole was a major failure as very few of these congregations made a significant impact on the surrounding community. The average size of the congregations ended up being around 75 members. The church in the 21st century must get involved in the lives of people in the community. The members must exhibit a caring attitude as they find out the needs of the people and they must lift up a risen Savior as the answer. They must use every available means in every available way to touch every soul in the community. We must do much more than meet at a church building two or three times a week where we conduct services and classes which cater primarily to our interests!

2. *God commands us to be a caring church* (Luke 10:25-37). We need to find human needs and with God's help take care of them. Each person in the community should know that we are vitally interested in their needs. We must develop holistic programs which demonstrate to the people in the community our love, care and concern for them. Programs are needed such as grief recovery, divorce recovery, parenting help, premarital and postmarital counseling and groups formulated to meet the major needs of the people in the community. We should develop close relationships and be deeply interested in home and family. We need to develop "life-time marriages" and "heaven-time relationships." We should also offer to the community a "God of the second chance." All of us make mistakes and every one of us needs to have the opportunity to start over. The caring church will teach a message of grace and forgiveness.

How do church leaders best implement these 10 commandments of servants?

3. *God commands us to be in the people business* (Matt. 25:31-46). We need to reach out to all kinds of people — hungry, lonely, troubled, wealthy, poor, single, married, remarried, black, white, yellow, educated, uneducated, healthy, sick and

> 80% of the churches go after
> the same 20% of the people.

the handicapped. I've often said that 80% of the churches go after the same 20% of the people. The target audience for most churches is the middle class or upper middle class, first-time married group. More than one-third of the adults over the age of 18 in the United States today are single! If we add the remarried to this group, we find that the singles and remarried represent the majority in today's world. There is nothing wrong with trying to reach the first-time married, but there is another very large group who are very receptive to the gospel. Many changes must be made by the typical church to reach this receptive audience. It will be a difficult task for many churches, but it can be done. There are thousands of young children who are products of broken homes. Many churches will not have open, welcome arms for this group because these children can be quite disruptive to the normal Sunday morning class. However, as changes are made in the local church program, a caring congregation will be able to successfully change many lives in this group.

> We should offer the community
> a "God of the second chance."

Joe Almanza was a member of the Texas Mafia. In fact, he was scheduled to become the head of the Mafia in Texas. This did not happen because he became addicted to heroin and ended up in a Texas prison. While he was in prison, he found a gospel tract in a trash can and this led to his conversion. He is now a Gospel preacher in the Dallas area. Although he has not been out of prison many years, he has led over 2,000 to Jesus Christ. He especially enjoys speaking in prisons because he knows how to best meet their needs. Joe has a lovely family today and his wife works in a Christian school.

Several summers ago I was preaching in a congregation close to the Pacific Ocean. As I was about to begin my sermon, I noticed there were two beach "bums" in the audience. There was no one seated within ten feet of them! It looked like they were being treated like visitors from a leper colony. I recognized these two beach "bums" as two young men who had been reached in a drug rehabilitation program at the Richland Hills Church of Christ in Fort Worth, Texas. They were so enthused from their conversion that they decided to spend the entire summer along the California beach teaching people the gospel. They had a lot of success with a group of people that most of the coastal churches neglected. Our ministries should be used by God to change people's lives because people matter to God and we are in the people business.

Can God use formerly dysfuncional family members in mighty ways as servants?

4. *God commands us to be a grace-centered church* (Eph. 2:8). We need to accept people responding to Jesus where they are and pray that God will help us as his servants to help them become all that he wants them to be. We need to be patient with these new people and remember that they are "newborn babes" in Christ. We should not expect them to be fully mature the day they become a Christian. We should also not expect them to be like us when they come from different cultures and backgrounds.

> We need to accept people where they are and lead them to where God wants them to be.

I'll never forget the Sunday when a young college student responded to the invitation. He had long hair which reached all the way down to his knees. He definitely did not look like the rest of the people in the audience. He wanted to become a child of God. It was so quiet you could almost hear a pin drop. I took the young man to the baptistery where he confessed that Jesus Christ was the Son of God. I had an irate deacon waiting for me in my office. He was so upset he had not even watched the baptism! He asked me what I did with the young man and I said that I just pushed him a little further down into the water. I gave this answer because I knew he was referring to the young man's long hair. He could not believe that I had baptized the young

Should we expect new Christians to be fully mature?

19

man without making him first get a haircut. The deacon probably would not have baptized Jesus because of the length of his
hair. The young man became a leader in our college program.
He reached people at Texas Tech that no one else was reaching.
Within three months he had led several dozen college students
to Jesus Christ.

The Sunday after the young man with the long hair
responded, I got an even greater shock. A college girl responded
from the back of the balcony with the shortest, brightest hot
pink pants I have ever seen at a church service. The young girl
was a cheerleader at Texas Tech and had recently broken up
with her boyfriend. Some of the Christian college students at
the Broadway Church of Christ Bible Chair had reached out to
her during these difficult times. They not only helped her cope
with a problem — they had also introduced her to Jesus Christ.
She came forward desiring to be a Christian that morning. Her
lifestyle changed as she grew toward spiritual maturity over the
next several months. She also taught more than two dozen
Texas Tech students about Jesus Christ.

5. *God commands us to learn and share "His Story"* (Matt. 28:16-
20). We should be committed to excellence in our potential and
become a productive servant as well as a lifelong learner. The
KAA educational plan is a good model for us to follow in
regard to this principle. The K stands for Knowledge. Every
student needs to have knowledge of the Bible. We cannot share
a message we do not know. One of the frustrations in the normal Bible school program is that the apex of our Bible knowledge is somewhere around the sixth grade level. This conclusion is drawn when we give a test to both children and adults in
our Bible School program. If the test has about three-fourths of
the questions from the Old Testament and one-fourth of the
questions from the New Testament, the highest grades will usually be made by the sixth graders. One of the reasons for this is
that youth and adults usually do not study the Old Testament as

What do you
think about
the KAA
educational
model?

God commands us to share "His Story."

20

much as the children do. However, it is still perplexing to know that our highest grades are made by the sixth graders. We must develop programs and motivations in the 21st century church which encourage us to be lifelong learners.

The first A in KAA stands for Attitude. We need to develop servant students with Christlike attitudes. We may have all the right answers, but have an attitude which drives people away from Jesus Christ. Employers tell us that more jobs are lost because of poor attitudes than because of poor job skills. The last A stands for Action. We must motivate our people to action. We need to develop a large, volunteer army of servants marching for the Master. We cannot continue to have only ten to twenty percent of our members actively involved.

> The gospel is "caught as well as taught."

The gospel is "caught as well as taught." We are the only Bible that some will originally read. It is imperative to practice what we preach to a very skeptical world. Priscilla is a good illustration of this principle. Priscilla moved from Wichita Falls to Fort Worth, Texas, when she was nineteen years old. She was a very beautiful girl and had been asked to pose for *Playboy* magazine. She moved to Fort Worth looking for money, fame, fortune, and an exciting, worldly lifestyle. Within six months Priscilla had achieved all her goals. She had moved in with a divorced lawyer to live in his mansion. He had given her a high paying job as his secretary. He also bought her a mink coat and a new convertible, but something was still missing in Priscilla's life. She walked over to the booth at a mall where Community Bible Class was giving away Bibles in a drawing for people who registered. She said that she had been given a Bible when she graduated from high school, but she had never even opened it up. Since she already had a Bible that she had never used, she was not going to register for another Bible. She also let the people at the booth know that she wasn't interested in the Bible. As she walked away, the Bible booth attendant named Alvin

Jennings told Priscilla to read the Bible because it would make her a better person. As she walked briskly away, Alvin doubted that she would ever read her Bible. To the surprise of everyone, Priscilla was back at the Bible booth at the mall the very next Sunday. She said that she had read the first eleven chapters in the book of Genesis. She also asked that someone teach her the Bible. During the next three months, Alvin Jennings spent many hours studying the Bible with Priscilla. Late one Saturday night she called Alvin and told him she wanted to become a Christian. On Sunday, she became a servant child of the King. She lost her job, her lawyer relationship, her mink coat, her car and the mansion in which she lived. Sometimes we forget today how powerful the gospel is!

Several months later Priscilla went with the youth group on a mission trip to the Bahamas. She was a coteacher with my daughter, Deana. They taught thirty teenage girls in a Vacation Bible School each day. Deana is an exceptional Bible student and she taught thorough, in-depth lessons for the first four days. Despite the excellent teaching from the Word of God, there had not been a single response. On the last day Priscilla shared her story about why she became a Christian and what she gave up. The girls really responded to her testimony and 25 of the girls made decisions to become Christians. It's important that we "have a ready answer for the hope that is in us" from the word of God, but it is also important for us to share why we became a Christian in our own words. This is one of the most useful ways to reach people in the world today. I have encouraged parents for years to share with their children first why they became a Christian. The story needs to be shared in a very personal way with deep feelings. After the story has been shared with children and mates, it should be shared with other family members. Then we can share the story with friends and neighbors.

Have each person share in their own words why they became a Christian.

There are millions of people throughout the world who are uneducated and others who are highly educated. Therefore, we should use every available means in every available way to introduce Jesus to every available soul.

6. *God commands us to have committed, prayerful spiritual leaders* (Acts 20:28-38). Churches rise and fall because of spiritual

> ## Churches rise and fall because of spiritual leadership.

leadership. I've been a resource person for over 350 elders' retreats. Most of our leaders are in need of encouragement because their job as volunteer servant leaders is very difficult. I like to begin the retreats with a time of affirmation because most of these men have been deeply hurt by criticism.

The elders at the Central Church of Christ in Amarillo recently participated with the congregation in a "50 Day Spiritual Walk." (See Appendix I for this material.) All of the congregation used a daily devotional guide which gave answers to the question: "What do you do when you don't know what to do?" Each of the elders shared their testimony before the congregation on Sunday morning. All of the men made themselves vulnerable and shared how they had coped with some very difficult situations. One shared how he had coped when his only daughter died with leukemia; another, how he had handled marital problems; and still others were dealing with bankruptcy, agony over the divorce of a child or coping with cancer. It was an incredible eight weeks as a different testimony was shared each Sunday. Attendance jumped by 150 and contributions increased by $3,000 a Sunday. The men went before the congregation to see if the congregation wanted them to continue to serve as elders. They received a 98% affirmation with more than 1000 votes turned in! Congregations are looking for servant leaders today who make themselves vulnerable and identify with the needs of the congregation.

What do you do when you don't know what to do?

Many of the same elders had learned a great lesson some five years earlier. The church had been devastated financially because of a huge downturn in the economy. They were trying to make payments on a six million dollar loan to pay for new facilities. Payments were $22,000 a week and the contribution was $21,000 a week. The church had lost 800 in attendance in the last eight years! Everything looked hopeless. It was at this point that these great men of faith turned their problem over to

When do you usually pray the most?

God. They realized that they could not handle this problem. They began each elders meeting on their knees in prayer. They prayed from 30 minutes to an hour without ceasing. They totally emptied themselves of any pride or fear and let God fill them up spiritually. And God provided a miracle! The church gave an immediate special contribution of $175,000, the building was refinanced and payments were lowered to $10,250 a week, and the church began to grow again. However, none of this would have been possible without the elders getting on their knees and turning the problem over to God, delegating the financial problem out to a group that God would use in a special way to provide solutions, and getting back to their main role of being spiritual shepherds of the flock instead of being paralyzed by a very difficult financial crisis. These servant leaders never ask the congregation to commit to anything to which they are not committed. All decisions are "handled with prayer."

How important is prayer in the life of servant leaders?

> We should praise God for our talents.
> We shouldn't boast because
> they are gifts from him.

7. *God commands us to use our God-given talents to serve* (Eph. 4:11-15; 1 Pet. 4:10-11). Although some members are given more talents than others, each member has been given a talent. These are not talents which members should boast about because all of these talents come from God. The servant praises God for his talent and gives God the glory. There needs to be a place for each servant to use his talent to the glory of God. We need to be committed to equipping and training people for ministry. The strength of the church for tomorrow depends upon the church of today training and mobilizing volunteers for action.

What is your congregation doing to train and equip people to serve?

Later on in this book, we will carefully describe how to recruit, train, equip, motivate and involve volunteers. We will carefully describe the role of eldership and other leadership to foster the climate essential for fulfilling this great principle. We will share a plan of how to involve every member. We will discuss the importance of the annual selection of deacons, a spiritual clustering plan to coordinate all of these servant-driven programs, and a way to keep both the newer member and the older member involved. For now, we simply want to stress that everybody is somebody in the kingdom of God. God has given each person a talent to be used to the glory of God in building up the body.

> # Everybody is somebody in the kingdom of God.

8. *God commands us to be a community of love as God's extended family in the world* (John 3:16). We need to love, praise and adore God, our Father, because God first loved us. We have good news to share:

*There is forgiveness — a Savior has come.
*There is hope — we can be made new again.
*There is salvation — we can focus on the cross.
*There is light — at the end of the tunnel.

Servant members must model this example of love to the community. When they do this, "friendship evangelism" becomes the natural tool to bring friends, relatives and neighbors to Christ.

Special events which involve many members are a great way to reach out to a community with love. We have used the annual Community Teachers Appreciation Night in Fort Worth, Nashville and Amarillo. Some of these Wednesday nights have an attendance as high as 1200! We sometimes forget how low the morale of teachers in a community can be. Many feel unappreciated and like political pawns at times. We put invitations in every teacher's box in the public schools. In Amarillo, that's more than 3200 teachers. The invitations are all delivered to the schools by church volunteers who love to do this. We get hundreds of notes, calls and letters from teachers who cannot come sharing how much they appreciate the invitations. Then, we

Are you using special events to reach people in the community?

always have a tremendous attendance for the free meal for the teachers and their families as well as the appreciation program which follows. We use our children's chorus, special adult singing chorus and special solos in our appreciation program. We always have a short message geared for the teachers and give each teacher an appreciation parchment.

We also reach out to the community with love when we have our Police and Fireman's Appreciation Program on Sunday night. The format is very similar to the Teacher's Appreciation Program. Since some of the policemen and firemen always have to be on duty, we use our teenagers to deliver food to them while they are on duty. The police and firemen are overwhelmed with this expression of love.

> # God commands us to dare to be different.

Other programs used to express love to the community include special events for judges, mothers, fathers, grandparents, nurses, parent of the year, etc. Anything which reinforces the major goals of a local church can be enhanced through the use of a special event. Special Easter, Thanksgiving and Christmas events can reach a community who are very receptive on these particular days.

The Meals on Wheels program, soup kitchen, and clothing room all say to the community, "We care." The youth have a major project each year to clean up and repair homes for the elderly and the poor. They especially try to do this with homes in close proximity to the church building.

9. *God commands us to dare to be different* (1 Cor. 12-14; Heb. 10:19-25). Our praise-filled celebration assemblies should offer a variety of ways for people to get in closer touch with God's Spirit and in closer love for one another. With the Bible as our guide, we should look for new biblical ways to focus all members of the church family and the community on the theology of Jesus as we approach the 21st century. Variety in our assemblies

and programs should meet the needs of people from all backgrounds and walks of life. People should feel welcome to use their varied God-given gifts to participate in inspirational services which bring each person closer to God and one another. This is tremendously difficult to do.

One of the greatest challenges facing us today is to be able to design programs and assemblies which meet the needs of all people. To do this, the following principles must be followed:

a. **We must objectively study the Bible.** We need to be dedicated to the fact that we will never do anything which would be in conflict with the Bible. If the Bible allows us the freedom to do some things differently which better meet the needs of the congregation and the community, then we should seriously consider making these changes.

b. **We should soberly look at our traditions and culture in the local church.** If it is a tradition, we should not present it as Bible. Traditions can be both good and bad — but they are not binding. If what we are doing is a tradition, then it can be changed as long as changing it would not be in conflict with the Bible.

> What changes could be made in your assemblies to better meet the needs of all the people?

> What are some good and bad traditions we have?

We should design biblical programs and worship assemblies to meet the needs of all.

---

c. **We should take out a blank page and design biblical programs and worship assemblies which best meet the needs of all the people.** We need to use every available means in every available way to bring every available soul into a closer relationship with Jesus Christ.

d. **We must develop a comfort zone so that each member will allow us to do what is best biblically to bring every person into a closer relationship with God.** This is the most difficult point of all. We must grow in spiritual maturity where we are more interested in others than we are in ourselves. We should not want the singing to be only the

How do we
develop a
spiritual
maturity which
allows us to
feed the entire
flock?

way we like it, or the preaching, prayers, communion, etc. We should have the tolerance to allow the elders and church leaders to design programs and services which will reach all people. Not only do we need to allow the tolerance to do this, but we should be highly supportive of a variety of programs and services which make this possible. If someone asks us how we feel about a service or how we feel about the singing, we might say, "That's not my favorite type of singing or service, but I'm thrilled that we have a leadership who best strive to serve biblical, spiritual food to all the people." That will silence the critics in a hurry.

e. **We need to build a congregation which our children and grandchildren will attend.** We need to challenge each parent and grandparent with this idea because it is not happening in numerous congregations. It is so frustrating to have a church made up primarily of older people when it does not have to be that way.

> The big question is not
> "Will our children have faith?"
> but "Will our faith have children?"

The question which concerns many of us is, "Will our children have faith?" That's a valid question. However, a more relevant question for many churches today is, "Will our faith have children?"

The Central Church of Christ in Amarillo, Texas is a 90-year-old downtown congregation in a low-income, high crime neighborhood. Most churches like this in the United States are either seriously struggling or have closed their doors and moved out to the suburbs. But, the Central Church continues to thrive and many young couples and young singles become new members of the church each year. Hundreds of other people from throughout the area visit the church. There are many reasons for this, but one of the reasons is the two different types of Sunday morning services offered by the congregation. The 8:30 a.m. service is a regular, traditional service. The older people and many other church members love it. Lee Kendle is an outstanding songleader and Dick Marcear always delivers a tremendous 25-minute message from the word of God. Most of the people who have grown up in this church and are over the age of forty love this service. We also have a Children's Bible Hour offered at the same time, and we usually have around thirty children from ages three to seven.

> What are the pros and cons of two different services on Sunday morning?

> May God give us bold leaders and spiritual followers who will implement what is needed to serve God and spread His kingdom!

The bold, caring elders also offer an 11:00 a.m. contemporary service. Instead of one songleader for this service, we have six different ones with microphones. We found as much Scripture in the Bible for six songleaders as we did for one. There is more singing in the second service. Most of the songs are new songs and they are projected on a screen rather than using songbooks. The people stand while they are singing the spirited songs. People feel free to clap or raise hands. The sermon uses the same outline as the first service, but the sermon is about ten minutes long. There are more testimonies and responses. The number of children in Children's Bible Hour runs between seventy and eighty. The audience is much younger in age although there are exceptions. The service is much less formal as few of the men wear suits. The vast majority of our visitors, nonmembers and responses are at the second service.

> Is it possible to implement changes like this in your local congregation?

Is one service better than the other one? No! That's like asking whether you like steak or pizza the best. The fact is that both services are needed and a spiritual menu is offered which brings everyone closer to God and one another. People are not forced to do one thing, but they are offered a spiritual choice. May God help us raise up choices like this all over the world. I will not tell you that it is easy, but I will tell you that it is needed. May God give us bold leaders and spiritual followers who will implement this as needed. The Central elders did this and went before the congregation a year later for reaffirmation or rejection. Over 1000 members voted on this and gave these elders a 98% affirmation!

> ## People are looking for "a place to call home."

10. *God commands us to be a "place to call home"* (1 Thess. 1:1-10; 1 Cor. 9:19-27). Surveys in the community constantly reveal that people are looking for " a place to call home" or "a belonging place" in today's world. Central's theme on every letterhead is "Central Church of Christ. . .a place to call home." Carlie Burdette, one of the members, even wrote a song by this title for us. (See illustration 1.)

There is so much mobility in today's world. The average young couple moves every two and one-half years and the average single moves every ninety days! Most husbands and wives both work. Children are in day care or school and have little time with their parents. People may be surrounded by hundreds of people, but may have no close friends. Most have also moved many miles away from parents and grandparents. No wonder, people are looking for a place to call home. The average person who moves to a new community today is not interested in doctrine. They are looking for "a place to call home" and a church which best meets the needs of each person in their family. Surveys also indicate that 50% of the new people who move into your community will change churches or religions! I know this concerns many whose children are leaving their former faith when they move — but the positive side is that we have a 50% chance to reach each new person who moves into our community. To do this, we must make biblical changes to reach these people. Every growing organism grows to maturity, levels off and dies unless there is new life. . .new

Why are people looking for a "place to call home"?

Central Church of Christ
A Place to call Home

Illustration 1

31

blood. . .new ideas. . .new dreams. . .and new activity. We need to be committed to change as it is needed. We should be committed to sharing the changeless message of the gospel with a changing world as we enter the 21st century. That's a difficult task, but members in The Servant-Driven Church know that this dream must be implemented.

The Servant's Philosophy and Purpose

"The greatest among you shall be your servant" (Matt. 23:11, NASB).

It was just before the Passover Feast. Jesus knew that the time had come for him to leave this world and go to the Father. Having loved his own who were in the world, he now showed them the full extent of his love. The evening meal was being served, and the devil had already prompted Judas Iscariot, son of Simon, to betray Jesus. Jesus knew that the Father had put all things under his power, and that he had come from God and was returning to God; so he got up from the meal, took off his outer clothing, and wrapped a towel around his waist. After that, he poured water into a basin and began to wash his disciples' feet, drying them with the towel that was wrapped around him (John 13:1-5).

How did Jesus show the full extent of his love?

The greatest person is the greatest servant!

These Scriptures form the foundation for the philosophy of The Servant-Driven Church. Notice the importance placed upon these Scriptures.

1. All the world today is looking for a hero and wants to know who is the greatest. Jesus very carefully explains in words which everyone can understand that the greatest person is the greatest servant!
2. Jesus was about to leave this world so he teaches his greatest lesson. He models what he had taught earlier.
3. He washed the disciples feet as a servant to show them "THE FULL EXTENT OF HIS LOVE." Jesus had taught earlier in Matthew 22:37-39 that the greatest commandment was to "LOVE the Lord your God with all your heart and with all your

33

soul and with all your mind. This is the first and the greatest commandment. And the second is like it: LOVE your neighbor as yourself." Now the GREATEST COMMANDMENTS which are about LOVE are connected to the GREATEST PERSON — a SERVANT to model "THE FULL EXTENT OF HIS LOVE."

> # There is nothing in leadership more powerful than a servant example.

We can teach the greatest commandments for years, but we will make little progress unless we have a group of dedicated, volunteer SERVANTS willing to march for the Master on a daily basis. These servants are not jealous or lazy. They do not care who gets the credit because they want to give honor and glory to their MASTER, Jesus Christ. They have learned to deny themselves and daily take up the cross of Jesus. They have reached a spiritual maturity where they are more interested in giving than in receiving — and more interested in what's best for the entire church than what they would individually want for themselves.

What are some servant examples leadership can demonstrate?

There is nothing in leadership more powerful than a servant example. I was speaking at a leadership retreat in Flint, Michigan several years ago and had this principle vividly demonstrated to me. This was an elders and deacons retreat, and they had invited the graduating senior boys to come to the retreat. As I spoke on Friday night, I noticed that most of the senior boys looked extremely bored. But, at the first break time, I witnessed one of the most astonishing scenes I have ever seen in my life. All of the elders went to the restroom, got a towel, filled up a wash basin, called the senior boys to the front row, and the elders washed the boys' feet. It was so quiet you could hear a pin drop. I have never seen such a change take place instantly in young men's lives. The boys divided up and sat by an elder for the rest of the seminar which lasted five more hours. They listened to every word and avidly participated. Their whole countenance had changed. They seemed now to have an incredible respect for the elders, for the church, for God, and for authority. Although this happened almost 2,000 years later than the time Jesus washed the apostles' feet, it was still just as effective. The Servant-Driven Church never forgets that the greatest among us is a servant.

WRITING PURPOSE OR MISSIONS STATEMENTS

Rick Warren's book entitled *The Purpose-Driven Church* is the best book available to show us how to use Scriptures to define the major purposes of the church. I highly recommend this book as it relates to the servant's philosophy and purpose.

1. *A purpose statement needs to be BIBLICAL.* The Bible contains God's marching orders to his servants and instructions for us to follow. If the purpose statement cannot be backed up by the word of God, we need to change our purpose statement.

2. *It needs to be specific.* There is a strong tendency to ramble and say many wonderful things in a purpose statement, but it needs to be simple, clear and narrowly defined.

   Does your congregation have a purpose statement?

3. *It needs to be manageable.* It needs to be short enough to be remembered by everyone. It should be in short enough, manageable terms that the entire congregation relates to it and can communicate it to others. The shorter the purpose statement, the better. We probably don't remember much of what Patrick Henry or Martin Luther King said, but we will never forget: "Give me liberty or give me death" or "I have a dream."

4. *It needs to be measurable.* It should help us evaluate whether or not we are fulfilling our purpose statement. If we cannot evaluate the church by our purpose statement, we need to change the purpose statement. It should help us review, revise, and improve everything we do.

5. *It is attainable.* It does not need to be a "pie in the sky" dream, but it needs to be something we can accomplish with the grace and power of God.

> The purpose statement provides a road map for the local congregation.

We also need to look at five other areas as we make our purpose statement. These are (1) Image, (2) Meeting the needs of members, (3) Leadership development, (4) Growth, and (5) Giving.

This is based upon a business model which companies use to develop their purpose or mission statements. While some of the categories may not be as exciting, these are absolute necessities for the church to be healthy and continue developing.

IMAGE

The image of the church in the community is very important. What kind of image do we want to have and how will this image be projected and interpreted? How will the community view our purpose statements? Will we be respected or will it build walls between us and the community? Will our members as well as community be excited about an organization which has this type of image? How will we be perceived by different groups in the community and church?

What kind of image in the community does your congregation have?

MEETING NEEDS OF MEMBERS

When people first look at a picture, they usually first look at themselves. As people in the congregation look at the purpose statement, what do they see in it as it relates to their needs? We want to have a purpose statement that commits us to meeting the needs of our members.

LEADERSHIP DEVELOPMENT

The purpose statement must reflect the importance of training leadership and members so that success can be achieved. We cannot just make a lot of purpose statements and set goals without showing a way that we can train and equip leadership and members to reach these goals.

> # A great commitment to the Great Commandment and the Great Commission will grow a great church!

GROWTH

Growth plans need to be projected because it is part of the GREAT COMMISSION, but growth should be at a rate where we can continue to meet needs of members and nonmembers so all can grow to spiritual maturity. The purpose statement should reflect both spiritual and numerical growth.

GIVING

Many people do not like to talk about giving, but this is one of the major topics in the Bible. Purpose statements are largely useless unless members will commit to giving their money, time and talent to fulfill these purposes. The purpose statement must address giving and commitment. See illustration 2 for an example of how the five major goals are presented and illustration 3 for an example of the detailing of one goal.

EXAMPLES OF PURPOSE STATEMENTS

Rick Warren gives a great purpose statement for the church in general. It is:

*A great commitment
to the Great Commandment
and the Great Commission
will grow a great church!*

What do you like or dislike about Warren's purpose statement?

This is based upon two great Scriptures:

"'Love the Lord your God with all your heart and with all your soul and with all your mind'. . . .'Love your neighbor as yourself.' All the Law and the Prophets hang on these two commandments" (Matt. 22:37-40).

"Go and make disciples of all nations, baptizing them in the name of the Father and of the Son and of the Holy Spirit, and teaching them to obey everything I have commanded you" (Matt. 28:19-20).

Purpose #1: Love the Lord with all your heart. (WORSHIP)
Purpose #2: Love your neighbor as yourself. (MINISTRY)
Purpose #3: Go and make disciples. (EVANGELISM)
Purpose #4: Baptizing them. (FELLOWSHIP OF BELIEVERS)
Purpose #5: Teaching them to obey. (DISCIPLESHIP)

Truitt Adair and the Sunset International Bible Institute in Lubbock, Texas developed their purpose statement by looking at values, mission and vision. They first got each person's input concerning values. What do you value? What eternal truths and values

GOALS IN FIVE MAJOR AREAS

I. IMAGE

To maintain an image that identifies us as a Christ-centered, progressive community who is warm, positive, serving, affirming, and well-rounded with a place for everyone.

II. MEETING NEEDS OF MEMBERS

To provide support and encouragement for each individual as they grow to be disciples of Christ. To be sensitive to the needs of one another and encourage each individual to grow towards achieving their potential in all areas of their lives — spiritual, mental, emotional, physical, family, social and financial.

III. LEADERSHIP DEVELOPMENT

To provide training and opportunity for members to serve effectively as leaders in our ministries. (See illustration 3 for sample detailing of one goal area.)

IV. GROWTH

Because we recognize the benefits of growth and the great needs of the unchurched, we want to maintain consistent growth and continue to provide ministries which are meaningful to people of all ages, ethnic and economic groups.

V. GIVING

To encourage individual members to give generously, in proportion to their potential, of their time, talent and money. Because we realize that giving is a reflection of spiritual maturity, we realize that gifts will grow as each individual grows spiritually.

Illustration 2

GOALS

Area: LEADERSHIP DEVELOPMENT

Type: Overall

1. Recruit and train teachers so that we have 30-40 extra who are qualified to serve.

2. Develop a school of ministry to equip leaders for each church ministry (Practicums).

3. Have weekly staff Bible study and prayer time.

4. Elders meet with deacons.

5. Have an elders/ministry/deacons retreat.

6. Write material and curriculum for school of ministry.

7. Ministry chairmen and ministers to seminar and other places for training.

8. Internship program for ministry; apprenticeship.

9. Church Growth and Involvement Seminar for training new members and ministries.

10. Work with one child and one adult — to reproduce yourself or ministry.

11. Annual elders retreat in September to choose new deacons.

12. To encourage spiritual growth among deacons — begin each ministry meeting with prayer and Bible study.

Illustration 3

do you always want to hold on to? Following this, they followed this three point outline.

1. Values—who we are.
2. Mission—what we do and what we are about.
3. Vision—where we are going.

This formula and much discussion provided the following statements:

What eternal truths and values do you always want the congregation to hold on to?

MISSION

To prepare whole persons
to preach the whole gospel
to the whole world
wholly to please God.

VALUES

We value God's Word.
We value the body of Christ.
We value service and a servant spirit.
We value excellence in all that we do.

VISION

Our vision is to be a ministry training institute uniquely suited
for the needs and challenges of the 21st century.
Therefore, we are prepared to make changes as necessary,
in keeping with our mission and values.

The Central Church of Christ in Amarillo prepared new vision, mission and values statements for 1997. They first got written input from all the congregation in these three areas. A retreat for elders and ministers looked at all this input, leaders prayed on their knees for God's wisdom, discussed what our real values are, and formulated the material in illustration 4 which we gave to the congregation in January of 1997.

The Richland Hills Church of Christ in Fort Worth, Texas did not have a purpose statement when they grew from 1000 members to 4100 members from 1978-1990. However, they did have a leadership retreat in early 1978 where they developed nine basic goals, three major priorities and suggested steps to meet these goals. This material was taken to every leadership meeting. Each thing which was done was evaluated as to whether we were fulfilling these goals and priorities. Programs were either added or deleted according to this leadership plan. A copy of these original goals and priorities is found at illustration 5 (a & b).

In 1990, we began working on a purpose statement and new goals and priorities for the Richland Hills Church of Christ. Out of this study and research a beautiful statement for a SERVANT-DRIVEN CHURCH was developed. The catalyst thought was: the Richland Hills Church exists because PEOPLE MATTER TO GOD. The complete purpose statement along with some training materials for this purpose statement and its implementation are located in Appendix A.

Can you take this material and prepare a values, mission and vision statement for your congregation?

CENTRAL CHURCH OF CHRIST
1997

Vision   (Where we're going)
    Our **VISION** is to be:
        "AN EXCITING PLACE TO CALL HOME"
Mission   (What we do.)
    Our **MISSION** is to:
        "ATTRACT ALL PEOPLE TO A RELATIONSHIP WITH JESUS"
Values   (Who we are.)
    We **BELIEVE:**

1. *The Bible is the inspired word of God and is our final authority in all matters.*
2. *Each member is to use their gifts for the glory of God.*
3. *Every soul is of immeasurable value to God.*
4. *We are to accept one another just as God has accepted us.*
5. *We are stewards of all God has given us.*
6. *God wants all believers to be one in Christ.*
7. *The "Great Commandment" defines our primary love.*
8. *The "Great Commission" is our charge from Jesus.*
9. *We are to have the "attitude of Christ."*
10. *God answers prayer.*
11. *We are saved by the grace of God.*
12. *The Trinity (Father, Son & Holy Spirit).*

Illustration 4

GOALS AND SUGGESTED STEPS TO ATTAIN

I. CREATE A GREATER DESIRE FOR THE WORD

A. Exemplified by leadership
  1. Assembly
  2. Bible classes
  3. Meetings, etc.
B. Provide opportunities for sharing the word in our assemblies, classes, care units.
C. More public reading of the Bible (some responsive readings).
D. More congregational prayer time (the more we speak to God, the more we desire for him to speak to us).
E. Periodical special emphasis (daily Bible reading, promote "quiet times," etc.).
F. Sermons more Bible oriented (expository preaching).
G. Special Bible camps.
H. Encourage participation in seminars, lectureships, etc.

II. BECOME MORE NUMERICAL-GROWTH ORIENTED

A. Set annual growth goals as well as longer term.
B. Leadership study church-growth principles and learn to apply them.
C. Preach, teach, and encourage growth in all aspects of our work.

III. INCREASE OUTREACH IN THE COMMUNITY

A. Discern community needs and develop ways and means of meeting these needs.
B. Plan special activities in family life center.
C. Emphasize friends and relatives evangelism.
D. Benevolence.

IV. CULTIVATE CHRIST-CENTERED FAMILIES

A. Continue to develop special emphasis series, sermons, classes, retreats.
B. Develop and train individuals and teams for counseling and instruction.
C. Provide regular and special printed materials.
D. Planned family activities.
E. Family Life Center.

V. HELP DEVELOP IN EACH MEMBER A GREATER SENSE OF BELONGING

A. Special sharing times in assemblies for nonprofessionals.
B. Prayer partner program.
C. Encourage and teach each one to discover, develop, and deploy their Spiritual Gifts.
D. More intensive care unit ministry.
E. Provide more opportunities to serve in existing and new ministries.
F. Provide more opportunities for congregational input.
G. Recognition of accomplishments.
H. Special opportunities to give financially.
I. Welcome home ministry.

VI. PRODUCE CONSISTENTLY EDIFYING ASSEMBLIES

A. Focal point should be members, not visitors.
B. More detailed planning and coordination of assemblies.
  1. special themes
  2. less formal

Illustration 5a

41

PRIORITIES

NUMBER ONE — COMMITMENT TO CHRIST

Matthew 6:33 says to seek Christ's kingdom and his righteousness and all else will be added. To know God and Christ as Savior is the first step in the Christian life. Until people really become new in Christ and realize they have his Spirit living in them, they are really not prepared to do much for family, church, or community.

NUMBER TWO — COMMITMENT TO THE BODY OF CHRIST

We are committed to each other in Christ. We are called the body of Christ. So we are connected and made to be dependent on each other in His body. That means we must love and care for each other (Gal. 6:10; John 13:35).

NUMBER THREE — COMMITMENT TO THE WORK OF CHRIST IN THE WORLD

The Bible not only instructs Christians as to how they should relate to one another, but it also gives them some commands as to how they should relate to those who are not yet Christians. These commands embrace two major areas.

A. Evangelism

The good news is that Christ came that *all* might be saved. We must share this with others (2 Cor. 5:20).

B. Social involvement

Jesus gave the example. He healed the sick. He touched lepers. He ate with publicans and sinners. He fed the hungry. He cast out demons. He identified with the poor and the outcast.

C. Opportunities for sharing from congregation (elders and others).

D. More emphasis on prayer.

E. Create a spirit of celebration.

VII. ENCOURAGE MOTIVATION BASED ON WHAT CHRIST HAS DONE FOR US

A. More public statements by leadership affirming this.

B. Continually stressed in all preaching and teaching.

VIII. DEVELOP SPIRITUAL LEADERSHIP AT ALL AGES

A. Acknowledgment by leadership of spiritual qualities of individuals.

B. Share responsibilities with more and more members.

C. Share in planning.

D. Cultivate potential leadership.

E. Motivate young men and women to go into full-time ministry.

1. Needs to be regularly presented in classes, meetings, etc.

2. Intern programs in several areas.

IX. SUPPORT GREATER MISSION EMPHASIS

A. Maintain better communication with missionaries.

B. Provide more opportunities for giving to mission needs.

C. Encourage members to consider going into mission work.

D. Provide special mission programs periodically.

E. Summer mission projects.

F. Special displays with mission information to keep our members updated on our missionaries and opportunities in other areas.

Illustration 5b

Servant Leaders

Servant leaders realize there are six major leadership problems in most local congregations. They must address these problems before a church can move forward.

> **Church leaders have an incredible workload and must delegate tasks to responsible people.**

1. *Workload of the elders and minister.* These leaders have an incredible workload and we sometimes forget that the vast majority of our elders are volunteers. Most congregations have unbelievable expectations of these volunteers and ministers. They expect these leaders to put every troubled marriage back together in a short time. They expect them to solve the problems of our youth and children. They are expected to be outstanding Bible school teachers and to know how to explain all the difficult passages of the Bible, and it helps if they know the Greek and Hebrew meaning of most words. They are expected to be at every church function and to always be available for every member's phone call or visit. Many people expect them to have a perfect home, perfect children and to live a perfect life. They may not receive much praise when things are going great at church, but they certainly get all of the criticism when something is wrong. They are also expected to make sure that every program and ministry functions at a 100% capacity and that there is always plenty of money in the bank to fund both regular programs and special requests of all the members.

   What are six major leadership problems in most congregations?

2. *Wasted talents of members.* The servant leader knows that he cannot do everything himself. He knows that there are many

43

talented members in the congregation and he is willing to delegate many responsibilities to these members. The servant leader does not have a pride problem where he has to do everything himself. He believes in his members that God has added to the church. He knows that God gave talents to each member and that each member should be given the opportunity to use his talents to the glory of God and to serve one another. The servant leader knows that his most important task is shepherding the flock. The more ministries and tasks which can be given to other members, the more time he has for shepherding. This also builds a tremendous team approach so that servant leaders and members are all working together.

What are some of the things which keep churches from growing?

3. *Lack of numerical growth.* The vast number of churches are not growing today. As long as we have a handful of leaders doing most of the work and making nearly all the decisions, it is impossible to have long-term church growth. Elders need to have time to shepherd the flock and tend to the needs of members. New people need to use their talents in the work of the church. New people are looking for a place to belong and get involved. Most will not be happy just attending services once or twice a week. I believe that God adds people to the church, he gives them their gifts and he expects these gifts to be used to build up the church. The servant leader knows this and does all he can to help them find a useful place in the local congregation.

All members need to work together as a TEAM for the glory of God.

---

4. *Programs seemingly more important than people.* Programs seem more important than people when members are left out of the communication and decision-making process. The servant leader will make sure that he receives vital input from the congregation before making decisions or starting new programs. He wants everyone involved in the process. He will regularly

devise ways to get the best input from the congregation. The servant leader wants to destroy the concept that a few leaders get together in a small room and make all the decisions for the congregation. He wants each member to know that every member in the congregation is important, everyone's input is needed, and all need to work together as a TEAM for the glory of God.

5. *Frustration.* There is tremendous frustration in many local churches today. Most of the members do not know which direction the church is heading. They either do not know the purpose statement of the church or they have been left entirely out of the process. They do not know what the goals are, where they are going, or how to get there. They do not know what is expected of them in this process. Even the deacons may not know what is expected of them. They may complain about the elders not giving them anything to do. The elders may complain about the deacons not doing anything. The servant leader wants to make changes to address these frustrations.

> One of the greatest leadership problems at a local church is poor communication.

6. *Lack of communication.* The servant leader knows that one of the greatest leadership problems at a local church is poor communication. He wants to use every available means in every available way to communicate what's going on. He also wants to use every available means to hear from the congregation and let the congregation communicate with the leadership. The church of today is so different than the church of the 1950s in this area of communication. In the 1950s an elder or minister might present some exciting new program on Sunday morning which he had just thought of. He may not have received any input from the congregation. In fact, this may have been the first time anyone in the congregation has even heard of it. But in the 1950s most of the people would have gone right ahead and supported the elders with this new program. That rarely

What are some good ways to get input from the congregation?

happens in today's church. People today want to give their input and they want to be involved in the decision-making process.

The servant leader wants to see the big picture and he wants to communicate what the big picture is after he has received massive input from the congregation.

(1) Where are we?

(2) Where are we going?

(3) How are we going to get there?

(4) How are we going to pay for it?

(5) How are we doing?

Servant leaders who want to get the congregation involved in a team relationship must exhibit eight major characteristics.

> # Jesus Christ died to save PEOPLE.
> # The church is not bricks and buildings,
> # but it is PEOPLE.

1. *People-centered.* Servant leaders realize that the most important thing in the world is PEOPLE. Jesus Christ died to save PEOPLE. The word of God is written for PEOPLE. The church is not bricks and buildings, but it is PEOPLE. Heaven is prepared for PEOPLE. Since PEOPLE matter so much to God, every program and work of the church is PEOPLE CENTERED.

2. *Compassionate.* Servant leaders spend much time with people because of the great love they have for them. They are interested in their victories and defeats. They will be there in their trials and even when they "walk through the valley of the shadow of death." Servant leaders want to know the members of the flock and they want the congregation to know them. Cards, calls, visits and prayers all let the people know how much the leadership cares for them.

How can church leaders demonstrate care for the church family?

One of the things which helped the elders so much at Richland Hills was that we hired a part-time secretary for them. She kept them on top of everything concerned with caring for the needs of the people. She let them know about members in the hospital, members with marital or parenting problems, members who were bereaved, and mailed cards for both regular birthdays, spiritual birthdays of the day they became a Christian and wedding anniversary cards. They all signed a card for the birth of a child to let the parents know that they wanted to work with the parents in every way possible to train that precious child for Jesus Christ.

Servant leaders need to be approachable.

---

3. *Approachable.* Servant leaders are always approachable. They do not try to run and hide from members and they do not duck controversy. They learned a long time ago that the best way to deal with a problem is right after it happens because time usually causes the situation to get worse. Servant leaders make themselves vulnerable and have developed tremendous listening skills. Members are not afraid to come to them because they will be prayerfully received. The communication from the members may be exactly the opposite of what they hope to hear, but they will carefully listen to each person anyway. They are also always ready to attend seminars and workshops which teach them better listening skills. Some of the better workshops center around the neuro-linguistic training taught by LEAD consultants out of Pittsford, New York. The telephone number is 716-586-8366.

4. *Sure of the direction of the church.* The servant leader knows the major goals of the church and the direction he is trying to lead it. He cannot work with people who are asking questions or serving in ministries unless he knows where he is going. People will not follow a blind, unmarked trail very far. He sees that printed purpose and goal statements are available to everyone in the congregation.

5. *Team-oriented.* The servant leader demonstrates mutual support for ministers and other leaders. He knows that there will always be complainers in the congregation who are upset with what is going on. While he will very carefully listen to all the com-

plaints, he will still demonstrate mutual support for other leaders in every way possible. He knows that God does not want any one-man-shows in leading the church, and he wants to work as a team member concerning what's best for the entire church. The servant leader has already learned that a church will never split unless Satan can divide the leadership! Once he has done this, it is easy for Satan to split a church. Nothing builds teamwork and morale more than all of the leadership supporting and encouraging each other.

What will keep a church from splitting?

6. *Accountable to God for use of time.* The servant leader has his Bible and his game plan book of current ministry priorities. He is not prone to "chase rabbits," but sticks to his major priorities. If someone asks him what he is trying to do, he will readily communicate his ministry priorities. The servant leader who has no major priorities tires easily as he is pulled many different directions and accomplishes very little. He is also a "sitting duck" for the complainers if he cannot explain the major reasons why the church is doing what it is doing.

7. *Servant-minded in leadership style.* The servant leader tries to demonstrate a servant attitude in every way possible. When there is a church event where tables and chairs need to be set up, he and his mate are the first ones to get involved. When clean-up crews are needed at the end of an event, you will see the servant leaders cleaning up the tables, cleaning the kitchen and putting up the tables and chairs. Nothing communicates more to a congregation or to other leaders than a servant example.

> ## A church will never split unless Satan can divide the leadership!

8. *Not petty.* Nothing turns off a congregation more than leaders who spend much of their time arguing over matters of opinion. The congregation wants to know what is biblical and what fits in with the goals and purposes of the local church. Ministry leaders want church leaders to delegate tasks out to them. They

do not want to get involved with a group of church leaders who are prone to argue over matters of opinion. Who cares if the carpet is blue or red or green if we have delegated this out? Who cares where we put the water fountains? Leaders sometimes spend hours arguing about the minor things, and it really discourages other volunteer workers from getting involved. May God help us to stop majoring in the minors.

> # The servant leader is not prone to argue over matters of opinion.

People will not get involved in the work of the congregation if they constantly receive mixed messages from the leadership. They will also not get involved if the leadership is constantly looking over their shoulder after a task has been delegated to them. They will not stay involved if the leadership is either constantly arguing about what has been recommended or regularly changing what has been recommended. Servant leaders do not have an ego problem so they are good at delegating tasks to others and having faith in God's people to complete the tasks. They realize that it may not be done exactly the way they would have done it, but they are still confident with this arrangement. They want the task done in the way which produces future leadership and best benefits the entire church. Rather than getting involved in the details, they are most interested in what glorifies God, builds up his people, benefits his people and builds a great volunteer army marching for the Master. The leader who cannot let go will never be a servant leader and God cannot work through him to build a great church.

What will help us stop majoring in the minors?

QUALITIES OF LEADERSHIP

We must look at qualities of leadership as we look at servant leaders. The normal definition for leadership is: Take a group or person from where they are to where YOU want them to be. If people are not following you, you are not a leader. A better definition of leadership for the servant leader is: Take a group or person from

> # If people are not following you, you are not a leader.

where they are to where GOD wants them to be. People may give you any title or office or job in the church — but if people are not following you, you are not a leader. Second Samuel 23 teaches us that David's whispered wish was to his men as a command. Three of his men risked their lives to get him a drink of water! They were willing to die for him because they knew he was willing to die for them. THAT'S LEADERSHIP!

What's the secret of building a great church?

What's the secret of building a great church?

(1) It's not the educational level of the people. Many people say we could have a great church if we had all of those smart people. We would like to have many teachers, principals, lawyers and doctors. While this group may be helpful as they use their gifts to the glory of God, this is not the secret to building a great church. Many churches have these types of people and continue to wallow in mediocrity.

(2) It's not the amount of money available. Many people say that they would have a great church if they just had an abundant supply of money. Many churches with large supplies of money are struggling. Most churches with large savings accounts are not growing. Most of the largest churches in America are regularly in debt, but launch out by faith anyway.

(3) It's not the location of the building or the beauty of the facilities. While this might help, I've found exactly the opposite many times. On three different occasions, I have visited the largest churches in America of all faiths or backgrounds. Some of these places look almost impossible to find because of their locations. Others are old downtown churches with the very worst location possible.

(4) The real secret to building a great church is VISION. If the leadership and the membership do not have VISION, there is no way God can work through you to build a great church.

Let's look now at some QUALITIES OF SERVANT LEADERSHIP.

ENCOURAGING

There are two kinds of people in every congregation: Impossibility Thinkers and Possibility Thinkers. Impossibility Thinkers scan quickly over a proposed idea, scanning it with a sharp negative eye, looking only at the problems. They look for reasons why something won't work instead of visualizing ways it can be made to work. They can think of a dozen reasons why a thing cannot be done. It doesn't take a sharp mind to do that. Impossibility Thinkers consider themselves keen analysts. They are not keen analysts — they are people with little faith in God, little faith in their own God-given abilities, and little faith in their fellow Christians. They are inclined to say "no" to a proposal without really giving it a fair hearing. And usually their clinching argument is: "It costs too much!" Their attitude produces doubt, stimulates fear, and generates a mental climate of pessimism and fatigue. The Possibility Thinker knows that it can be done if God wants it done. He will do everything he can to create a positive spiritual climate which keeps and builds morale.

What's the difference between a Possibility Thinker and an Impossibility Thinker?

> # The church is the most important business in the world.

CONFIDENT

The servant leader has confidence that the church is the most important business in the world. If he doesn't feel this way, he will get out of leadership. He has confidence in God's people at the church and confidence in God. He has the confidence to attempt great projects which could not be accomplished without God's help. One of his favorite Scriptures is Philippians 1:6: "Being confident in this one thing, that God who has begun a good work in you will complete it."

Why do church leaders need to read Phil. 1:6 often?

COURAGEOUS

The servant leader is not afraid to risk. Walt Disney's brother used to say to him, "Walt, you will never amount to anything; everything you dream of costs millions of dollars." Old Walt didn't do so badly. Do you know the name of Walt's brother? All I know is that he went to work for Walt! Walt's most daring adventure came when he was an old man and he suggested the building of Disneyland. He proposed this to his board and every single person was against it. Not one of the men in leadership thought Disneyland would be a financial success because of the tremendous cost. But it was! Walt said before he died, "As long as man has imagination, Disneyland will continue to grow." That's not a bad motto for a church.

> One of the greatest shortcomings in a local church is the inability to make a decision.

Servant leaders must have the courage to make a decision and to stick to that decision. One of the greatest shortcomings in church leadership is the inability to make a decision. The servant leader knows that one of the greatest mistakes he could ever make would be to fail to make a decision which allows the church to become all that God wants it to be! Servant leaders also have the courage to be responsible for the decisions they make. They never forget the sign on President Truman's desk: The buck stops here.

OPTIMISTIC

Servant leaders cannot be negative. They are servants of a Master who has told them that "with him, all things are possible." He is excited about things which have never been accomplished that he knows God wants accomplished. He knows that it is impossible for God to use a fearful person in leadership and that a pessimist cannot lead a person very far. If you are following a leader on a mountain climbing expedition who says, "The next mountain range is very difficult. Less than one out of a hundred ever survive! All of you follow very close behind me," most people will not follow!

Why is it impossible for God to use a fearful person in leadership?

PERSISTENT

The servant leader follows through to completion. He gets the plan off the paper and puts it into action. His credibility is high because he completes his task. We should never forget that famous speech of Winston Churchill: "Never, never, never, never, never give up!" I once saw a book which was entitled *57 Rules for Success*. Page one said, "Get Results!" The rest of the book was filled with blank pages. The servant leader knows that the difference between success and failure many times is persistence.

QUALITY

We need to outthink, outfaith, and outlead all others. Leadership is being out front with a good example. Some leaders are being pulled along by their followers. They are so out of touch as we approach the 21st century that they are being dragged along kicking and screaming. Some leaders have power brakes instead of power steering. The servant leader knows the importance of study and keeping up with the newest biblical ways which help the church become all God designed it for.

> Some leaders have power brakes instead of power steering.

DISCERNING

In John 10 Jesus promised, "I know my sheep and they know me." The primary role of an elder is to be a shepherd to the people. One of the biggest wastes in the church is not using the talents of the people and motivating them to active service. We must know our people before we can get them involved. We must know our people so we can appoint them to the right tasks. We must know our people so we will not appoint pessimists to lead and delay the church from moving forward.

Why does a shepherd need to know the people?

Let's look at a group of people with the eyes of church leaders. Do you know any of these people? Are any of these people members at your congregation? Shammua, Shaphat, Igal, Geuel, Palti, Gaddiel, Gaddi, Ammiel, Sethur, Nahbi—have you heard of any of these people? They were leaders of the children of Israel! They were the ten spies who said that the children of Israel could not conquer the promised land.

How about Joshua and Caleb? You have heard of them. They were the two spies who gave the minority report that said the promised land could be conquered with the help of God. In Numbers 13:30 Caleb encouraged, "Let us go up at once and possess it." The ten replied, "All the people there are giants, we're like grasshoppers compared to them." God called this an EVIL REPORT! The only thing evil about it was that it was a NEGATIVE REPORT! God had told them to conquer the promised land and the majority of the leadership said that it could not be done. Joshua promised, "The Lord will give us the land; the Lord is with us; don't be afraid." The congregation was actually ready to stone Joshua and Caleb for saying this. It's tough being a leader!

Why was the spies' report called an evil report?

God became very disturbed with the children of Israel for their pessimism and lack of faith. He caused them to wander almost forty years in the wilderness — forty wasted years before they could inhabit the promised land. God had to let an entire generation of pessimists die off before the children of Israel could conquer the promised land. This averaged out to something like 85 funerals a day! Each funeral was a testimony: "We are burying a pessimist today who kept God's people from moving forward!"

What was the testimony of each funeral?

> ## The children of Israel averaged 85 funerals a day for 40 years.

MOTIVATED

Servant leaders know that they must be self-starters. Procrastination is one of the devil's most powerful weapons. They realize the urgency of their task and will not put off until tomorrow what needs to be done today. Most of the largest churches in America today are premillenial and this gives them a tremendous sense of urgency because they believe that the Lord might come soon!

Walt Frederick was a flabby janitor who started on an exercise program when he was past the age of sixty. He ended up completing the 26-mile Boston Marathon race at the age of 65. When he was interviewed on national television and asked to define the most difficult part of his success story, he replied, "It was just getting started — the first step, the first block, and finally the first mile."

SELF-ASSURED

The servant leader knows that if you are not getting any criticism, you are not doing much. Keep that list of critics in your meeting room and look at it when you receive a criticism. That list will not normally contain the names of more than twenty people. You do not want minority rule, and you want to do what best spiritually feeds the entire congregation in a biblical way. I have been told by Southern Baptists in their surveys that the average Baptist pastor leaves because of three people! May God help us destroy this concept!

> **If you are not getting any criticism, you are not doing much.**

"They said" is a killer of things and a word for weaklings. Find out who "they" is. It is usually the one who said it, his wife and a friend.

There was an elders meeting once where they took three hours to decide whether or not to let the new punch bowl ever leave the building. By a split vote, they decided not to. The very next week a very influential lady cornered one of the elders and told them how unhappy she was with their decision. She said her daughter was getting married at her home and she wanted to borrow the church's punch bowl. The elders had a short aisle meeting and reversed a decision in ten seconds that had taken them over three hours to make! The issue is not whether or not the decision should have been reversed. The issue is how well we can take criticism and stand behind decisions.

It's amazing how God intervenes when leaders remain calm, treat the critics with love, listen to them to hear what they are really saying, get on their knees and pray with them, and carefully with a loving spirit explain why they are doing what they are doing. May

What are good ways servant leaders can deal with critics?

55

God grant us more servant leaders with this beautiful Christlike attitude and more followers with whom we can disagree in an agreeable way where we are still friends with the Lord and one another.

EMPOWERING

A good leader inspires men with confidence in him. A SERVANT LEADER inspires men with confidence in themselves. Servant leaders surround themselves with people who know more than they do in specific areas. Insecure people do not make good leaders. The servant leader is secure in his relationship with God and has no ego problem about surrounding himself with people who know more than he does. He doesn't surround himself with yes-men. He doesn't give responsibility to people without giving them the authority to carry it out. And, he is not constantly looking over the shoulder of those to whom he has delegated a task. The servant leader knows these are imperatives in the building of a team. He constantly encourages and gives team members credit for what they have accomplished. He knows that people need encouragement the most when they are discouraged or have made a mistake. He knows how important this principle is in team building.

> People need encouragement the most when they are discouraged or have made a mistake.

A young couple's class in Fort Worth wanted to be responsible for the new church directory. They wanted it to be a perpetual directory in notebook binders which could always be updated. They bought black notebook binders with the name of the church embossed in gold. They bought their own cameras and took all of the pictures. It was a massive effort by the young couples class and it took hundreds of hours before completion. The day finally came to assemble the notebooks. The notebooks were laid out along with the pictorial directory sheets. Each person started down the long line to gather material to assemble their own church directory. About three-fourths of the way down the line, everything suddenly stopped. The church had been undergoing a tremendous growth explosion and there was no way to get any more sheets in the note-book. The whole enterprise was a complete failure at a cost of $7200. I'm sure some of the elders wanted to go up to them and say, "You wasted $7200 which could have been used to preach the gospel in our missions program. But the Richland Hills Church elders did not say a word about money. They put their arms around the ones who had been responsible for the project and told them how much they appreciated them. They thanked them for their ded-ication and for the hundreds of hours they devoted to the project. They didn't say a word about failure or money! That's what it takes to build a team. To this day, the people who are the most dedicated and loyal in that church are the ones the elders encouraged after that failed project!

Can we learn great lessons from mistakes?

> # A good leader inspires men with confidence in him. A SERVANT LEADER inspires men with confidence in themselves.

This leadership principle is true in every aspect of life. If you come home and the house is a mess — that's not the time to ask, "Didn't you do anything today?" That's really a cry for help when your mate really needs encouragement. The servant leader will especially be a sensitive encourager in every area of church work.

The servant leader is striving to build two important Bible principles in his team. These principles are taken from Exodus 18 and Numbers 11. In Exodus 18 Jethro, the father-in-law of Moses, sees him at work judging the people. Jethro tells Moses that he is working too hard and needs to delegate the work out. He tells Moses to put leaders over groups of a thousand, a hundred, fifty and ten. The principle of delegation was valid, but the whole endeavor was a complete failure. About a year later Moses is so frustrated in Numbers 11 that he is asking God to take his life! We sometimes forget in church leadership and organization that the first plan was the plan of Moses and the second plan was GOD'S PLAN! God's plan was to choose 70 of Israel's elders to lead the people. They were to be men who were known as leaders among the people. They had to have two leadership qualities which were a necessity in order to lead the people. (1) They would be full of God's Spirit just as Moses was, and (2) they would share the burden for the entire congregation. These are two great principles of leadership. People who have the Spirit of God living within them can lead and work out problems. People who share the entire burden will all work together instead of just being interested in one little area. They get the big picture and all work together to do what is best for the entire congregation.

What's the difference in God's plan and the plan of Moses?

ORGANIZED

We need to eliminate as much red tape as possible in today's world and make organization simple and clear. However, we must carefully organize so that efforts can be coordinated to fulfill our goals and purposes. We will have a complete chapter on organizational principles later in this book.

Sir George Smith in his book on Isaiah calls our attention to the word ambiguously translated "judgment." The word means method, order, system, and law. So when Isaiah says, "the LORD is a God of judgment" (30:18), he means that God is a God of method and order, and his creation is superbly organized. First Corinthians 14:40 teaches us that everything should be done in a decent and orderly way.

HUMBLE

This is such an important quality of the servant leader. People do not like to be around know-it-alls. Paul grew in the grace of humility with the passing of years.

How did Paul grow in humility?

(1) Early in his ministry he said, "I am the least of the apostles" (1 Cor. 15:9, NKJV).

(2) Sometime later he volunteered, "I am less than the least of all saints" (Eph. 3:8, NKJV)

(3) When his life was drawing to a close and he was preparing to meet his Lord, he mourned, "I am the chief of sinners" (1 Tim. 1:15, KJV, reordered).

TACTFUL AND DIPLOMATIC

There are so many hurting people in today's world, the servant leader knows how important it is to speak the right word with the right spirit. He prays daily for wisdom in this area. We will have a later chapter in this book about how to handle change and conflict. Each leader needs to have skill in reconciling opposing viewpoints without giving offense and compromising his principles. This is not easy to do.

> Each leader needs to have skill in reconciling opposing viewpoints without giving offense and compromising his principles.

There was one shoe salesman who said to a lady, "I'm sorry, madam, but your foot is too large for this shoe." The lady was irate. Another shoe salesman in the store next door said, "I'm sorry, madam, but this shoe is too small for your foot." The salesman had a satisfied customer who came back. Tact and diplomacy are such important qualities in church leadership.

THE MISSING LINK IN CHURCH LEADERSHIP

"When the Pharisees heard how he had tested the Sadducees, they gathered their forces for an assault. One of the religious scholars spoke for them, posing a question they hoped would show him up: 'Teacher, which command in God's law is the most important?'

"Jesus said, 'Love the Lord your God with all your passion and prayer and intelligence.' This is the most important, the first on any list. But there is a second one to set alongside it: 'Love others as well as you love yourself.' These two commands are pegs; everything in God's Law and the Prophets hangs from them" (Matt. 22:36-40, *The Message*).

There are three great lessons for servant leaders in this passage.

(1) Love God with all your passion (heart), prayer (soul), and intelligence (mind).

(2) Love others as shepherds of the flock in the same way as the Good Shepherd who laid down his life for the flock.

(3) Love self with godly self-esteem.

What are the three great lessons for servant leaders in Matt. 22?

LOVE GOD

The servant leader loves God with all of his passion or heart. There are some serious questions every leader needs to ponder.

1. How do you really feel about God?
2. What is your congregation's perception about your passion for God?
3. Does it make you uncomfortable to talk about this?

Central Church of Christ had a theme one year which was JOURNEY TO THE HEART OF GOD. Thirty-five 3-foot pictures were posted throughout the building to describe what it was like to go on a journey to the heart of God. It was both an awesome and a humbling experience.

People today remember slogans and perceive people by slogans. Examples would be:

1. Roosevelt: "All we have to fear is fear itself."
2. Kennedy: "Ask not what your country can do for you; ask what you can do for your country."
3. Johnson: "We need a great society."
4. Nixon: "I am not a crook."
5. Bush: "Read my lips!"
6. Clinton: "I didn't inhale."

Leaders need to take the church family on a JOURNEY TO THE HEART OF GOD.

What's the unwritten slogan about the local church leadership?

What's the perceived slogan for your passion for God? What's the unwritten slogan about the local church leadership?

The servant leader loves God with all of his soul or prayer life. This also raises some difficult questions.

1. How often do you talk to God?
2. What do you usually talk to him about?
3. Are you known as a praying leadership?

I've always been touched by Jim Bill McInteer getting on his knees in church every time a prayer is offered to God. I'm impressed at the way the Central Church elders spend hours on their knees in prayer in the elders meeting room. I'm also impressed when I go to a Promise Keepers Business Meeting and they spend one and a half hours in prayer and thirty minutes conducting a business meeting. Yet, they always seem to get finished with the business.

> ## Servant leaders keep learning.

The servant leader should love God with all of his intelligence or mind. This elicits some sobering questions:

1. How often do you study the Bible?
2. How well do you know the Bible?
3. How would you describe your quiet times with God?
4. What workshops, classes or seminars have you attended to improve your leadership skills?
5. What books, tapes or magazines have you recently used to help you?

Continuing education for all of us is essential. I recently attended a seminar where Dr. Criswell was present. He is the 80-year-old minister from the large First Baptist Church in Dallas, Texas. Dr. Criswell was there as a learner, and he was taking down every note he could to help him be a better church leader.

LOVE OTHERS

As we were preparing to add new elders at Central, we recently taught a "They Smell Like Sheep" series which was taught by Dr. Lynn Anderson. It's a tremendous series about the great love that the shepherd needs to have for the sheep. We actually brought real live sheep into the auditorium and our classrooms. Needless to say, people really got the message.

Leaders need to ask if they are addressing the five basic needs of the people in their congregation:

Are we meeting the five basic needs of the people?

1. Are we giving our people a purpose to live for?
2. Are we giving them a power to live on?
3. Are we providing them people to live with?
4. Are we teaching them principles to live by?
5. Are we providing them a profession to live out?

61

Leaders must have the capacity to love a great diversity of people from many different backgrounds. Mike Armour's book entitled *Systems-Sensitive Leadership* describes eight different groups of people in our congregations. As shepherds we need to meet their basic needs with a heart of love, take these people where they are and lead them to where God wants them to be.

1. *Survival* — This group has been devastated and they are just living one day at a time. They may be divorced, out of a job, spiritually dry, or have marital, physical or emotional problems.

2. *Safety* — This group wants to be part of something that lets them feel safe. They want to be part of something that is routine and predictable. Their motto is "Don't change things!"

How would you design worship assemblies to meet the needs of these groups?

3. *Strength* — This group looks for security in strength and they will follow strong leadership. They are primarily interested in themselves and they are not great team players. They want services, classes and programs which primarily meet their needs.

4. *Truth* — This group likes everything black or white. They deal in absolutes and believe everything is either right or wrong. They believe in stability, steadiness and conformity. They believe there is only one way to do something and it is either right or wrong.

5. *Diversity* — This group grows spiritually when they are allowed to do things many different ways. They like change for change's sake. They like new songs and freedom to innovate many changes in a local church.

6. *Relationships* — This group is people centered and they like close bonds of intimacy with other members. They like to have a close support system for each other. They like family closeness and are very sensitive to the needs of other members. They are very grace oriented and like to provide healing to those who have been beaten down by the rules.

7. *Adaptability* — This group is constantly changing. They don't get locked into certain ways of doing things unless the Bible

> God doesn't make junk!
> But he has made eight different groups.

says that is the only way to do it. They don't force people to conform to their changes, but they do believe in change when circumstances demonstrate a need for it. They thrive on education, research and much information to provide ways to change and better adapt to people's needs.

8. *World Community* — This group does not want to be judgmental about any religious group. They will work with everything good in a community which will help it develop spiritually or improve community morals.

It is imperative that the servant leader love all of these people in these groups. It seems impossible because there is such diversity. However, love and servanthood can be the spiritual bond to mold these groups into a volunteer army marching the same direction for Jesus Christ. It is not an easy task. This is the reason the information in this chapter about servant leaders is so very important.

> Church leaders need encouragement.
> One elder told me that all their members
> were active. "Half work with us
> and half work against us!"

LOVE SELF WITH GODLY SELF-ESTEEM

I have conducted over 350 elders retreats and this is a major problem for many elders. They do not feel adequate for the job, and they are going through tremendous struggles. They get so much criticism and are frustrated because they cannot please everyone. One new member asked an elder in a local church if every member was active. "Yes," replied the elder, "all the members are active. Half work with us and half work against us!"

These men always need an affirmation time on each retreat. When fellow elders and ministers share their appreciation for each other, the tears always begin to flow. These servant leaders need to know that God only made them a little lower than the angels. They need to know that God made them for such a time as this to lead his people. They need to know that God doesn't make junk, and they are in the most important position on this earth. When James Garfield became President of the United States, he resigned as an elder. He said that he had just stepped down to a lower position as President of the United States.

How important is godly self-esteem for church leaders?

Servant leaders cannot really love others unless they have godly self-esteem. They will get caught up in power struggles unless they have godly self-esteem. You can't have close relationships and take criticism without godly self-esteem. You cannot emotionally take the losing of members to other congregations unless you have godly self-esteem. And, it's going to happen—every shepherd is going to have some of the flock leave and this is very difficult to accept.

Judges 7 illustrates a group of God's people who were reduced from 32,000 to 300! This is the story of Gideon and his encounter with the Midianites. Gideon had 32,000 and the Midianites had 135,000. God told Gideon he had too many men.

What did Gideon learn from God?

Gideon must have wanted to argue with God because he was outnumbered four and one half to one. God told Gideon to tell all of those who were fearful to go home. 22,000 went home! God cannot use fearful men to lead because fear is contagious. Now Gideon has 10,000 men against 135,000 Midianites. The odds are thirteen and one half to one. God says, "You've still got too many men. Let's give them the water test to see if they are really alert and eager to serve." Gideon lost 9700 men this time. Now Gideon has 300 alert men. The odds are now 450 to 1! God says that's about right—go get 'em! God gave the 300 men the victory. There was no way they could claim that they had done it by their power and might, but they gave God the credit for the victory.

Servant-Driven Involvement Ministries

It's a great dream to strive to have every member using his gifts to the glory of God. It's a great dream to have every member using his gifts to build up the body of Christ. Unfortunately, this does not happen automatically and there has to be a lot of prayer, work, blood, sweat and tears before we are successful. While the implementation of this dream involves every leader and church member, the group who has the greatest responsibility for making this dream come true is the involvement ministry. The people in this ministry must be fellow servants who are in the trenches working with the people. Coordinating this effort should be a servant-driven Involvement Minister. Since I was the first Involvement Minister in Churches of Christ some twenty years ago, many people have asked me, "What does an involvement minister do?" Let's look at his role.

WHAT DOES AN INVOLVEMENT MINISTER DO?

1. His specific task is to involve every member in ministry so that each person uses his gift for the glory of God and in building up the local church.
2. He needs to assemble a great team of leaders to develop the involvement ministry. This is not a one-man show as a large group of people will have to be recruited and trained for this ministry.
3. He needs a great secretary because there are so many details connected with this type of ministry.
4. He needs to be an eternal optimist, encourager, and motivator. One of Satan's chief weapons is discouragement and procrastination. Each day people will be telling you of things which they cannot do which need to be done. The involvement minister needs to remember that our God is the great "I AM" not "I CAN'T."

65

> ## Our God is known as the great "I AM," not the great "I CAN'T."

5. He needs to be a loose coordinator and communicator with ministries. This is a very difficult role and the one where most involvement ministries have the greatest difficulty. There are several reasons for this. People today hate red tape. There is a strong tendency to make the involvement process too complicated and give the appearance to people of a lot of red tape. This may not even be the case, but if it is just *perceived*, then it causes a lot of trouble. This is especially true in the money, budget and approval areas. There needs to be enough organization to keep everyone working together in the direction of a common goal which keeps everyone motivated, responsible and accountable — but beyond this, it should be as simple as possible. The involvement minister is not a domineering boss in this area. He is a fellow servant driven to do all he can do for the glory of God.

How important are simple organizational guidelines?

   Sometimes there is difficulty in this area with elders, deacons and the involvement minister. All of these groups need to work together with a servant spirit to do what needs to be done.

6. The involvement minister serves as office coordinator for all of the ministries. This is another delicate and critical task. He must see that all events are on the church calendar, rooms are scheduled, conflicts are prevented, and each event is adequately publicized and communicated. He needs to strive to space events during the year so that everything does not happen at once. Since the involvement minister is dealing with people who have tremendous interest in their own, individual areas, it is easy to see how difficult this scheduling responsibility can be. He needs to also see that adequate secretarial support is provided for the events without overloading the secretaries.

7. The involvement minister needs to build a team to involve the present members in ministry. In a later chapter, we will be sharing some dozen different ways to do this.

8. He is also responsible for getting new members involved. This will also be included in a later chapter. New members are usually receptive when they first become members so involvement awareness and training for them should be implemented as quickly as possible after they become members. This would include getting adequate information from them, getting them a name tag, and making sure they have found classes and groups which meet their needs.

> # Team building is a key to leadership.

9. The involvement minister with his ministry is responsible for starting new ministries after they have been approved by the elders. He will usually be working with new leadership as they meet with the elders to get new ministries approved. After the ministries are approved, he will help recruit leadership and develop the new ministries.

How should new ministries be started?

10. The involvement minister needs to be constantly getting feedback from the congregation and the community. He must know these needs before ministries can be formulated and assembled to meet these needs.

11. He will set up an evaluation and communication process for the different ministries. He might use a communication form, other staff ministers or the elders' spiritual cluster plan to do this, but this is a necessity. Communication and accountability are important elements of this process.

12. He will work closely with the elders on the reselection of deacons on an annual basis.

13. He is an advisor and consultant for all ministry leaders.

14. He helps struggling ministries. On any given week some ministries will be doing great, some will be making slow progress, and some will really be struggling. Therefore, he must keep up with the ministries so he can help them as early as possible. It works much like a prevention program for couples to prevent divorce. If we can identify the problems early and work on them as soon as possible, we can usually prevent a divorce.

This same principle works with struggling ministries if we can help them as early as possible.

15. He sees that a New Members' Dinner is offered for every new member along with other programs which help them get acquainted. He knows if each new member makes five friends at the local church, he will probably never fall by the wayside.

16. He is usually responsible for ministry training, deacon training, staff and elders retreats. There is the daily informal training which he offers, but there is also the formal training in this category which is important.

17. He is a resource person for deacons, ministry leaders and church leadership. He must be well read and he must keep up. He recommends books, tapes, seminars, programs and workshops which will be beneficial.

18. He is responsible for all membership records and is called the Minister of Membership instead of Involvement Minister in some congregations. He is constantly making an analysis of membership to find out why people are becoming members, what their background is, and where they are coming from.

19. He usually coordinates the budget, planning, implementation and budget presentation. He carefully monitors events, programs, growth and giving.

20. He helps build fellowships and relationships among ministry leaders and church leaders. The entire program will break down without harmonious relationships.

21. He is always evaluating the ministry system and looking for ways it can be improved.

22. He establishes a communications network for brochures and materials to come to the involvement ministry. He cannot get people involved unless he has adequate information from the ministries. He is also usually in charge of publicity and promotion, and he cannot do an adequate job at this without accurate information.

> People who are spiritually down
> do not offer consistent leadership.

23. He does everything he can to keep the spiritual barometer up for deacons, ministry leaders, staff, elders and workers. This is not a secular leadership position but a spiritual one. People who are spiritually down do not offer consistent leadership. The continual development of spiritual, servant leadership is essential.

24. He works in the background a lot and is a constant promoter and encourager of elders, fellow ministers, deacons, ministry leaders and other workers. He does not let Satan play on his ego because he has committed himself to being first and foremost a servant.

25. He helps to develop a Master Planning Model along with purpose and vision statements. Input from as many members as possible is important in this process.

26. The Involvement Minister uses adult classes to train people to implement overall goals. It's a marvelous way to mold the congregation to implement the overall church goals.

How can adult classes be used to implement overall goals?

27. He uses short series in adult classes to involve and teach people about the needs and dreams of the church, a study of spiritual gifts, identifying my gift, and ways God can use me to his glory.

28. He makes sure six-week training for all new members is scheduled throughout the year. Many churches conclude training with each new member eating in the pulpit minister's home.

29. He coordinates special events. This is especially a good way to involve a lot of new people in a large project.

30. He may coordinate an annual church growth and involvement seminar to train other congregations as well as offer training opportunities for your own people.

31. He may develop a video training program for ministry leaders.

> ## Orientation packets for new members are extremely helpful.

What would you put in a new member packet?

32. He develops orientation packets for each new member.

33. He carefully tracks new members and other members to see

that they do not "fall through the cracks" in the involvement process.

34. He has a computer list of each person involved in each individual ministry as well as members who are wanting to be involved in particular ministries.

35. He has host people at all services to make new members feel welcome.

36. He has a telephone ministry to call all new members.

37. He sees that biographical sketches are obtained on every member. If there is room, it is a great idea to publish a family picture and pertinent information in the church bulletin. Some churches publish an annual pictorial directory of new members and this is very helpful.

38. He makes sure that refreshments, someone to lead a devotional and name tags are available for New Member Orientation.

39. He makes sure each new member receives an invitation to eat in homes with other members.

40. He makes sure every ministry leader knows about people who want to get involved in his ministry.

> ## Servant leaders pray individually by name for each new member.

41. He prays individually by name in private for each new member that God has provided. He prays that they will find "a place to call home" where they can use their God-given gifts.

THE INVOLVEMENT MINISTRY

The involvement ministry is one of the most important ministries in the local church. It is impossible for the involvement minister or any one man to do the 41 things previously listed. It's a major undertaking and the involvement minister assembles a team to get the plan off the paper and into action. The small church will need an involvement leadership team of four to six people. This ministry team should include men and women. The large church may have ten to twenty people on this leadership involvement team which also includes men and women. They have people responsible for these 41 areas previously described. They will probably need to meet with the Involvement Minister on a weekly or monthly basis. Illustration 6 is an example of how this work is carried out by using a work assignment sheet to keep track of those assigned to cover each area which needs to be covered. It is important to remember that "everybody's business is nobody's business" so there must be individual people responsible for each task.

> ## The involvement ministry team should include men and women.

HOW WE CAN HELP ONE ANOTHER

There needs to be a close working relationship between the Involvement Ministry and other ministry leaders. The sample sheet shown in Illustration 7 shows how each group needs to work with each other.

It's usually a good idea for the Involvement Minister to have an individual interview with each deacon on an annual basis. He will learn things in a meeting such as this that he usually will not learn anywhere else. Illustration 8 is a sample deacon interview sheet.

What should be discussed in the deacon interview?

Teacher recruiting has become a very difficult task in many congregations today. The Involvement Ministry can sometimes come to the rescue with an appointed task force which can be very successful. An example of this is the Supervisors Enlisting Additional Teachers recruiting task force shown in illustration 9.

The Involvement Ministry knows that not everyone is going to say yes when they ask people to get involved. They are working in the trenches with people who may never have been involved in a church before. They are trying to take these special servants from where they are to where God wants them to be.

They realize there are four different kinds of people in every congregation. There is the NO NO group. They torpedo every

INVOLVEMENT MINISTRY

Date _____

1. New Members' Dinner
2. Host people at all services
3. Telephone ministry
4. Computer work
5. Photography
6. Biographical sketches (writing for bulletin)
7. Refreshments
8. Getting packet material from ministries
9. Packing packets
10. Orientation from packets
11. Devotional at New Members meeting
12. Name tags
13. Home visits
14. Visitation contact
15. Welcome Home contact
16. Roots Class contact
17. Involvement Ministry fellowship
18. Involving new people in Involvement Ministry
19. Ministry Communication Form to elders
20. Starting new ministries
21. Help with new ministries or struggling ministries
22. Deacon follow-up — make sure all the contacts are made with people who want to get involved
23. Follow up of new members who didn't get involved after deacon contacts
24. Deacon and chairman training

25. Church Growth and Involvement Seminar
26. Involvement of membership other than new members
27. Membership records
28. Pictorial Directory
29. Involvement budget
30. Church Budget presentation
31. Prayer emphasis
32. Community Outreach emphasis
33. Extended orientation — School of Ministry
34. Community involvement
35. Analysis of new members — why coming, where from, talents, background
36. Evaluation of strengths and weaknesses in the ministry system. Study all Ministry Communication Forms.
37. Development of printed materials and brochures for Involvement Ministry
38. Audio and video presentations for Involvement Ministry
39. Involvement Ministry Library and Training
40. Contact with Singles Ministry
41. Contact with Youth Ministry
42. Involvement Newsletter
43. Exposure of elders and ministers to new members
44. Tour of building for new members
45. Assign every new member to Bible class. Contact with Bible School people to see if they are attending.
46. Get new members to lead prayers in third assembly.

Illustration 6

HOW CAN WE HELP ONE ANOTHER?

1. What We Can Do as a Member of the Involvement Ministry

    A. Excite new members about opportunities at Richland Hills.

    B. Tell them about Welcome Home, Wednesday Night Dinners and visitation from the standpoint of making friends.

    C. Explain to each new member the function of your ministry.

    D. Give new members printed information about your ministry.

    E. Recruit new people for you.

    F. Start new ministries as needed.

    G. Help coordinate ministries to avoid duplication and cross-direction.

    H. Increase weekly contribution (involved new people give much more).

    I. Share ways you can expand your ministry and involve more people.

2. What You Can Do as a Ministry Leader

    A. Provide correct printed information for new member packets.

    B. Host your booth and bring food for New Members' Dinner each six months.

    C. Get your people to Church Growth and Involvement Seminars for training.

    D. Make a follow-up contact with new members who express interest in your ministry as soon as possible (call, visit, have a meeting, Wednesday night, meal).

    E. Involve women in your ministry to help take care of details.

    F. Provide high level of positive leadership to your ministry.

    G. Provide information from your ministry for budget presentation.

    H. Provide information for congregational awareness of your ministry.

    I. Send in monthly Ministry Communication Forms and let us know of additions and deletions to your ministry.

    J. Call on us if we can help.

Illustration 7

DEACON INTERVIEW SHEET

Name _____ Ministry _____

The number of years in this ministry. _____

The year you became a member of Central. _____

Success in your ministry and what you most enjoy. _____

Frustrations in your ministry and major problems you are having. _____

Suggestions of how to improve your ministry. What can we do to help? _____

Who are the major people involved in your ministry? _____

What are your major goals? _____

Can we find a place for these new people in your ministry? _____

What do we need for them to do? _____

How can you best contact them? _____

How much time do you need? _____

When can you get this information back to the church office? _____

What suggestions do you have for next year's theme? _____

Do you want to serve as a deacon in this ministry next year? _____

What men do you suggest to serve as deacons and in what areas? _____

Illustration 8

SUPERVISORS ENLISTING ADDITIONAL TEACHERS

The SEAT recruiting program is of critical importance at this time to the Central Family. God has rescued us and blessed us beyond measure — but we must have teachers for these precious children. Our goal is to have each SEAT filled with a child in our Bible school program. John 6:45 says "they will all be taught by God." I deeply appreciate God calling your supervisors together for such a time as this. The task to recruit is difficult, but our God has promised to "fulfill His plans" for your department (Jer. 29:11). I'll be praying for you, doing all I can, and I hope the following outline will be helpful to you as "God's Recruiter."

1. Pray before each contact or call.
2. Believe God can help you.
3. Contact all present teachers to see if there is a possibility of their teaching until September. See if mates would like to join them.
4. Explain that the "Journeys" material is loaded with teachers' helps and is much easier to teach than what we have been using. We can also provide training and let the teachers know what we hope to accomplish as we take our students on a journey through the entire Bible during the next few years. We can let them see materials to be used for the next three years. Invite possible future teachers to these training sessions.
5. Contact all former teachers and see if they will teach.
6. Contact all parents and see if they will serve as subs in the program.
7. Initiate a program where you invite four parents a week to observe your class. This will let them know what we are teaching their children, show ways they can reinforce this teaching at home, establish closer relationships, provide possibilities for getting them on a substitute list, and possibly be future full-time teachers.
8. Contact graduating seniors to see if they are interested in teaching.
9. Let all present and past teachers know that they are invited to a special Teachers' Appreciation Night for them on May 13.
10. Be sure each teacher is on an adult class roll and is invited to their fellowships. We can tape our Sunday morning adult classes for them or have a makeup class on Wednesday nights or Sunday nights.
11. Explain to the younger parents that we now have Children's Bible Hour on Sunday morning and Sunday night.
12. Remember in discouraging times: "Your labor in the Lord is not in vain" (1 Cor. 15:58).

Illustration 9

> There are four different kinds of people
> in every congregation.

How would you develop a recruiting plan to work with the four different groups in a local church?

dream and are against everything. They say a quick NO when you first ask them to get involved. The YO YO group is another group. They run hot and cold. One day they say yes and the next day they say no. They are hard to work with because after they are recruited, they may still be undependable. The third group is the BLOW BLOW group. They talk big, but they don't work big. They are like the son in Matthew 21 who said, "Lord, I'll work in your vineyard," but never got around to it. The fourth group is the GO GO group. These are the GO people of the Great Commission who are always looking for a way for God to use them. This group is a special joy for the Involvement Ministry. It is the goal of the Involvement Ministry to lead members in the congregation to this fourth level of spiritual maturity. The members who reach this level of maturity are deeply appreciated and they are honored with a Volunteer Appreciation Proclamation on a special Sunday. (See sample in illustration 10.)

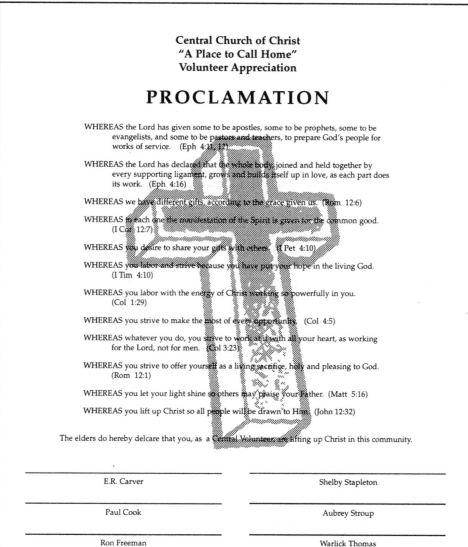

Central Church of Christ
"A Place to Call Home"
Volunteer Appreciation

PROCLAMATION

WHEREAS the Lord has given some to be apostles, some to be prophets, some to be evangelists, and some to be pastors and teachers, to prepare God's people for works of service. (Eph 4:11,12)

WHEREAS the Lord has declared that the whole body, joined and held together by every supporting ligament, grows and builds itself up in love, as each part does its work. (Eph 4:16)

WHEREAS we have different gifts, according to the grace given us. (Rom 12:6)

WHEREAS to each one the manifestation of the Spirit is given for the common good. (I Cor 12:7)

WHEREAS you desire to share your gifts with others. (I Pet 4:10)

WHEREAS you labor and strive because you have put your hope in the living God. (I Tim 4:10)

WHEREAS you labor with the energy of Christ working so powerfully in you. (Col 1:29)

WHEREAS you strive to make the most of every opportunity. (Col 4:5)

WHEREAS whatever you do, you strive to work at it with all your heart, as working for the Lord, not for men. (Col 3:23)

WHEREAS you strive to offer yourself as a living sacrifice, holy and pleasing to God. (Rom 12:1)

WHEREAS you let your light shine so others may praise your Father. (Matt 5:16)

WHEREAS you lift up Christ so all people will be drawn to Him. (John 12:32)

The elders do hereby delcare that you, as a Central Volunteer, are lifting up Christ in this community.

E.R. Carver	Shelby Stapleton
Paul Cook	Aubrey Stroup
Ron Freeman	Warlick Thomas
Dub Henderson	Jack Vincent
Bill Johnson	Leon Wood

Illustration 10

The Servant's Organization

A leadership game plan is important.

What needs to be done to implement this ministry organizational plan?

This is a critical chapter because we are now ready to put the plan for involving every member into action. This cannot be done very successfully unless the members accept and understand the organizational part. Many people in churches today dislike anything which even remotely speaks of organization. All they see is hierarchy and red tape when this is mentioned. Therefore, this part of the process not only needs to be understood and accepted; it should create a new exciting dream within the congregation. That is expecting a lot, but this type of organizational plan has done this in thousands of congregations. But, before we look at the organizational plan, we need to review what must be done before this is presented for acceptance to the congregation.

1. Pray — leadership should spend much time in prayer appropriating God's wisdom for this plan.
2. Leadership commitment — Leadership should be totally committed to this plan.
3. Congregation should be aware of leadership problems which we have discussed earlier.
   a. Workload of the elders and ministers.
   b. Wasted talents of members.
   c. Lack of numerical growth.
   d. Programs seemingly more important than people.
   e. Frustration.
   f. Lack of communication.
4. The congregation needs to know that all of these problems will be addressed with this new plan.

5. Leadership needs to ask and members need to meditate as to whether we have men and women with the following characteristics.
   a. People-centered.
   b. Compassionate
   c. Approachable
   d. Sure of the direction of the church
   e. Team-oriented
   f. Accountable to God for use of time
   g. Servant-minded in leadership style
   h. Not petty

What kind of ministry leaders are we looking for?

6. The congregation needs to understand that they will be trained and helped as they implement this new organizational plan. They should also understand how each member is vital to the fulfillment of this plan.

7. Objectives need to be established.
   a. Surveys need to be made of the church and the community to find out major needs.
   b. Philosophy and purpose statements need to be formulated.

> A step-by-step plan is needed
> to accomplish the objectives.

8. Program — a step-by-step plan needs to be determined of ways to accomplish the objectives.
   a. Elders should have another prayer and decision time about what we will henceforth call the Ministry System. They should determine the potential number of ministries with which to begin. This will depend upon church and community needs as well as available servant leadership to take care of these needs.
   b. Elders need to meet with the current deacons to explain the ministry system. This is usually a very tense time for elders, but I have never known these not to be very good meetings. Elders are afraid that deacons will not like the reselection of deacons process as well as other aspects of the new plan.

While there are a few deacons who may want to hold an "office" for life — most are overwhelming supporters of this new plan. It allows them to resign without people thinking they are having an affair. It allows them to change ministries and many of them have been saddled for many years with the same ministry which they no longer enjoy. It puts a new dignity and quality of leadership in the deacon's life. It gives them much more freedom and responsibility in their individual ministries.

    c. The congregation needs to select new deacons to serve in specific areas for one year.

    d. Training and orientation need to be provided for deacons and ministry leaders.

The annual renewal of deacons in the ministry system is important.

How do we educate and involve the congregation in this process?

9. Involving the congregation — the entire congregation should be closely involved in this process.

    a. There should be a series of lessons from the pulpit and in our adult Bible classes to teach the biblical part of this.

    b. After the series is taught in our classes, we should have the people sign up for ministries in our adult Bible classes.

    c. A ministry fair on Sunday morning or Sunday night can also be very effective. This lets the congregation meet the new deacons at tables or booths, talk to them, see items concerning their ministry which are visually displayed, creates an atmosphere of excitement and usually gets many more people to sign up to be involved in ministry.

    d. Ministries will need to be developing leadership teams of men and women.

    e. Talents are better utilized if each person in a ministry serves in a specific area of his ministry.

    f. It is better if no person serves as a ministry leader in more than one area. This is especially difficult at first, but we must allow room for many people to develop and get involved. We also need to prevent ministry burnout.

g. One of the ministries is an involvement ministry to provide personnel for the ministries.

h. Monthly evaluations made by the ministries are very helpful.

i. Elders need to make time for the ministries to meet with them. Nothing encourages an individual ministry more than for elders to invite them to an elders meeting, get on their knees to pray for them, listen to them and encourage them.

How can elders encourage ministry leaders?

j. Coordinating guidelines should be established.

k. Ministries should formulate their programs and budgets under elders' guidelines.

l. Communication brochures should be prepared for the congregation.

m. Leadership should serve as motivators, equippers, encouragers and delegators.

n. The spiritual leadership of a servant who desires to meet needs should be stressed.

10. Schedule — a schedule or chart should be set up concerning when to implement each part of this plan.

> ## The ministry system organizational chart has had a major impact for good on thousands of congregations.

THE SERVANT'S ORGANIZATIONAL DIAGRAM

Now that we have reviewed and looked at the basic elements of the ministry system, we need to look at the organizational diagram in illustration 11.

The first thing people notice is how unusual this chart is and they are intrigued with it. Many people could care less about any organizational chart, but this chart has had a major impact for good on thousands of congregations! It is certainly not *the* way to organize a congregation, but it is *a* way which has let thousands of servants use their gifts to God's glory. Let's look at how it all began.

Bill New, who later became an elder at the Richland Hills Church of Christ, was flying on a mission trip to South Africa. He was frustrated with the red tape and the bottlenecks at the church. He dreamed of someday being a servant elder to lead a congregation of servants with a servant model. He spent years studying the Bible to discover an organizational model which would accomplish all of these things. While in the airplane, Bill sketched out the first crude drawing of an organizational diagram for the ministry system. It was horizontal rather than vertical and this greatly shocked people and that first drawing only had seven ministries. It did not address the role of ministers and was just a sketch on a napkin — but that sketch became like the "shot which was heard round the world."

During this same time period of the 1970s I was working as the education director at the Broadway Church of Christ in Lubbock, Texas. The elders had asked me to develop a plan to involve a lot more people in the congregation and they placed me as chairman of the Committee on Committees. Therefore, I was doing a serious study about involvement and ways to organizationally help the situation. Bill and the elders at Richland Hills called me and shared their dream. I was shown the first crude sketches. I would be going to Richland Hills as an education director, but the real dream was to develop this new concept.

What do you like and dislike about the organizational chart?

> # A sketch on a napkin in an airplane flying over Africa gave me a revolutionary organizational chart.

When I came to Richland Hills, the congregation had not seen the sketch or heard of the concept. Therefore, we had to begin from scratch. Let's look at the chart. It is a horizontal chart which teaches some strong biblical concepts. Elders are to be out front leading the congregation as shepherds lead sheep. They lead by model and example. They are out front to lead because of specific goals and directions they have for the congregation. They know

The Key is the Ministries System

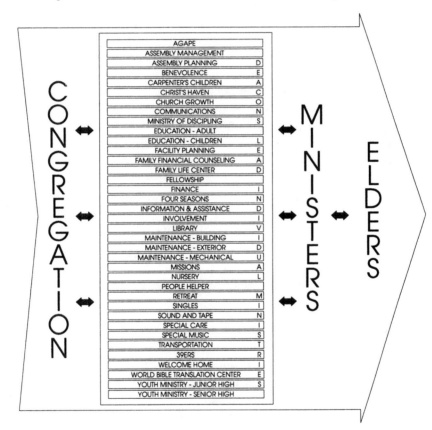

Illustration 11

What is the elders' role in this chart?

what these goals are and want to lead this great volunteer army of servants. The elders are not behind asking, "Where are you going?" They are out front leading. The elders are not some upper echelon hierarchy as everyone is on the same level playing field. They do not lord it over the flock or drive the flock. They do not say, "Look at us as master and you as slave." The chart teaches that we are all fellow servants of Jesus Christ. Our ultimate goal is heaven. The elders want to feed and shepherd the precious flock God has given them so heaven's destination can be reached. The chart also provides individual ministries with deacons to lead. Elders would delegate incredible responsibility to qualified deacons. This would cause a great positive change in the church. The original plan tried to strike down the concept that deacons were a junior board of elders who came together in a joint meeting each month. Many of these meetings were negative; those attending were not interested in a lot of the items discussed; it was hard to get this large group to make a decision; most of the deacons did not have individual responsibilities and were not fulfilling servant tasks for individual ministries for which they were desperately needed.

> There are no one-man shows
> in the ministry system.

The chart was just a beginning — but it became an incredible catalyst for change to take place in the church. My task was to develop this rudimentary, life-changing concept and strive to involve every member in ministry. The timing was perfect because in the next few years thousands of articles were written about the need to involve laymen.

Let's look at the chart as it has developed today for what we call the ministry system. Elders are still out front leading sheep the same way shepherds do. They constantly say, "Let's go forward!" That term was especially generated by a 90-year-old elder who would come to the first part of every elders meeting but could not hear a word. He would always put his fist in the air and yell, "Let's go forward!" Then he would leave. But I will never forget his leadership and the difference it made in our meetings. Elders lead as servants and models. They believe the greatest among you should be your servant. They are interested in the needs of the flock and shepherding the flock. They have purpose statements, goals and objectives for which everyone from the "least to the greatest" in the congregation has had input. Elders want to lead the congregation in the direction of these established objectives. They function as a team of servants, bound together in love with mutual support for each other. There are no one-man-shows.

The elders do not serve as ministry leaders for individual ministries. This is done by deacons who serve for one year at a time. The immediate task for each deacon is to get a team of men and women to work with him as ministry leaders. A good model to usually follow in the local church is the education ministry. The education program usually has to have key coordinators or supervisors to make the program function at maximum efficiency. Therefore, most churches already have part of this organization set up. You would have a supervisor for nursery, one for preschool, one for juniors, one for primary, one for youth and one for adults. You might also have someone for Children's Bible Hour, Vacation Bible School, Teacher Recruiting, Teacher's Workroom, audiovisual materials and bulletin boards. If you already have these people, the new deacon would get these people to serve with him on the leadership team for the education ministry. It would include both men and women. If the church does not already have an education leadership, then the new deacon would have to develop one. Each person on the ministry needs to have an individual responsibility as well as their tasks of working together on the ministry. Each ministry needs to develop a team similar to the way we have described the education ministry. If the ministry is for youth, it

What is the deacons' role in the ministry system?

> Our chart is not the only way to organize a congregation, but it is a way to move forward with a powerful servant model.

would include an individual to be responsible for retreats, another for Sunday morning classes, another for huddles or outside of church activities, someone for leadership development, someone for parent meetings and communication, someone for mission trips, etc. When the meeting takes place, each person gives a report on their individual area of responsibility.

> # The Jerusalem church had seven deacons in just one ministry!

How would you delegate jobs in your ministry so that each person has an individual responsibility?

In the beginning most churches will only have one deacon for each ministry. But the goal should be to have as many men as are needed who meet the qualifications. Some ministries are much larger than others and need more deacons. I sometimes point out that the Jerusalem church had seven deacons in just one ministry to take care of the widows and their food problems. We grew to nearly 300 deacons at Richland Hills to take care of 70 ministries! I will later supply you with a list of what is expected of deacons and what is provided for deacons.

Deacons are nominated by the congregation on an annual basis by the congregation. The most important people to make the nominations are the ones vitally involved in the individual ministries because they know the people who are best doing the job. Elders should not expect a lot of nominations to be turned in because people may not know a lot of qualified people at times. However, they should expect quality nominations to be turned in from the people presently working in the ministries. It is important to let every member of the congregation have the opportunity to turn in nominations so they will not feel they are left out of the process. The entire congregation must have ownership of this process. After the nominations are turned in, elders and ministers pray over the nominations, spend many hours looking at all the nominations and come up with a game plan based upon the nominations and qualifications of the people. The elders then visit each potential deacon who has been nominated. They also have the deacon's wife and older children present when they visit the home. They tell them that the congregation and elders have chosen them to serve in this specific area. They explain what their responsibilities would be and what would be expected of them. They also tell them what will be provided for them. They ask them to pray about this and give them an answer a week later.

If the deacon says yes, the name is placed before the congregation. If anyone in the congregation has any complaint about this person, they are asked to talk individually to the deacon. If this does not take care of the problem, they are asked to talk to an elder. If everything proceeds as planned, a special service charges the deacons on Sunday morning, all the deacons repeat a pledge to the congregation to serve as servants and celebration takes place.

As soon as the service is over, elders and ministers serve a meal to the deacons and their wives. This once again keeps the servant model of leadership before the deacons as they see elders and ministers wearing the aprons and cleaning up the messes. As soon as the meal is completed, there is a three or four hour training session for the deacons and their wives. The day the deacons are installed is the best time to do this as you usually have 100% present for the installation and training. Deacons need to understand the ministry system, their role, how to assemble a team, how the recruiting process works, and how to prepare their programs and budget. They are challenged to assemble a leadership team and prepare programs and budgets for the next year.

What should take place in the deacon-training session?

A reporting process and accountability are also discussed at this meeting. In some congregations, deacons are asked to turn in a Ministry Communication Form each month. (See illustration 12.)

> # Every deacon's family is visited in the home by the elders each year.

A far better reporting process is where each elder is assigned a certain number of ministries and he meets with these ministries once a month. Husbands and wives both need to be present and it

Ministry Communications Form

(This form is intended for communication purposes only and is not for approval or disapproval of activities carried on by your ministry. If more space is needed, use the back of this form. Thank you for taking the time to fill in this form.)

Ministry _____ Date _____

Prepared by _____

1. Brief summary of your ministry's involvement and activity for this past month.

_____

_____

2. Brief summary of your plans for the coming month. Please indicate date and times of special activities if already determined.

_____

_____

3. What can the elders do to help you better fulfill your ministry?

_____

_____

4. What can the staff ministers do to help you better fulfill your ministry?

_____

_____

5. List any new members since your last report.

_____

_____

6. List any members who have chosen not to serve on your ministry since your last report.

_____

_____

7. Other comments:

_____

_____

Illustration 12

usually works much better in the elders' homes. It gives the women a chance to participate, and they add so much to the meetings.

Let me share with you a new reporting concept that we recently started at Central Church of Christ. This has incredible potential to develop spiritual leadership as well as addressing the reporting part of the ministry system by the deacons which has been a weaker point. When Paul spoke about spiritual qualities, he talked about the "fruit of the spirit" in Galatians 5:22-23. If we are going to develop greater spirituality in our leadership, we must strive to model these qualities. We had nine elders and decided to divide the ministries into nine different groups based upon the fruits of the spirit. It got a tremendous response from the deacons and their wives. It has been the answer to prayer since it was always so hard to get the Ministry Communication Forms returned. Elders do not dominate these monthly meetings, but they primarily listen to reports, find out problems and needs, and talk about what we can do to improve. These monthly meetings create a spiritual bond and a relational bond between the elders and deacons. It makes the elders so much better informed because of this communication process. The elders send a report of the meeting to the involvement minister so this ministry can be informed and strive to address problems or needs. It has greatly helped the communication process in our elders meetings. It is virtually impossible to bring up anything concerning ministry which at least one of our elders do not know about.

> What are some of the ways leadership can best model the "fruit of the Spirit"?

> ## Spiritual clusters based upon the "fruit of the Spirit" provide a great plan for the ministry system.

This spiritual clusters concept has been so successful that we have divided our adult classes where each one of them has an elder. We publish the elder's name along with the teacher's name for each class, and this has really helped with both communication and shepherding. Since we have around fifteen adult classes, some of the elders are shepherds for more than one class.

We also have some 40 small groups called Family Life Groups. They meet in homes one Sunday night each month. We put these groups in our spiritual clusters plan so that each elder only has four or five groups. Our next giant step would be to divide the entire congregation of almost 2,000 members into nine spiritual clusters with a shepherd for each cluster. We could use the deacons and ministry leaders in an undershepherding plan to work with our elders. It would also give each member a tremendous sense of identity to know they were part of the love cluster, patience cluster, joy cluster, etc. A copy of our spiritual cluster plan is included in illustrations13 and 14.

> ## Spiritual clusters can be an answer to prayer.

What should we expect from deacons and what should we provide for them?

It probably would be helpful here if we share a complete copy of our brochure for the nomination of deacons which we give to every member (see Appendix B). This has a special message from the elders, what we expect from deacons, what we provide for deacons, qualifications for deacons, description of ministries for which they are to be nominated, a biblical plan to involve every member, special additional notes to members, and an organizational chart.

As we look at the Ministry System organizational chart again (illustration 11), there are two areas we have not addressed — the ministers and the congregation. Because of the training and expertise of ministers in their specialty areas, they will offer tremendous leadership in their areas. The youth minister should lead the youth ministry, the education director the education ministry, the family minister the family ministry, the involvement minister the involvement ministry, and the pulpit minister the worship ministry. However, this does not mean that they do not need a tremendous amount of leadership and help from deacons and ministry leaders. They should all work on a team together and bring out the best in each servant. Just as elders sometimes have difficulty letting go of certain areas, ministers can have the same problem. Therefore, the ministry should grow in trust and appreciation for each other. This team of additional leadership servants working with minister ser-

SPIRITUAL CLUSTER
ORGANIZATIONAL BONDING

Organized by 9 Characteristics of Fruit of the Spirit (Gal. 5:22-23) + Hope

MINISTRIES

Elder
LOVE

1. Baptismal Assistance
2. Bldg. Directories
3. Family Care
4. Community Care
5. Ushers
6. Greeters

Elder
KINDNESS

1. Bldg. Maintenance
2. Ground Maintenance
3. Bible Hour
4. Children - Theatrics
5. Dorcas & Timothy
6. Education, Children
7. Nursery & Child Care

Elder
SELF-CONTROL

1. Education, Adult
2. Library
3. Music Ministry
4. Missions
5. Attendance Reports
6. Fellowship Dinners

Elder
JOY

1. Scouts
2. Jail & Prison
3. Mother's Day Out
4. Children's Home
5. Transportation
6. Parking & Traffic

Elder
GOODNESS

1. Education, Youth
2. Huddles
3. Finance
4. Camps & Retreats
5. Personal Finance
6. Contribution
7. Meals on Wheels

Elder
PATIENCE

1. Involvement
2. New Members
3. Women's Ministry
4. Wedding Ministry
5. Church Growth
6. Youth

Elder
PEACE

1. Adult Recreation
2. Young Couples
3. Support Groups
4. Parenting Support Groups
5. Counseling-Volunteer
6. Grief Recovery

Elder
FAITHFULNESS

1. Hall Monitors
2. Lighting & Sound
3. Lord's Table Service
4. Tape
5. Information & Assistance
6. Media
7. Lord's Supper Preparation
8. Community Outreach

Elder
GENTLENESS

1. Calling & Caring
2. Communication
3. Visitation
4. Hospital Visitation
5. Church Directories
6. Office Volunteers
7. Visitation/Shut-ins
8. Welcome Home
9. Prayer

Elder
HOPE

1. Family Life Groups
2. Singles
3. Sunshiners
4. Publicity/Promotion
5. Divorce Recovery
6. College
7. Special Events

Illustration 13

BRIEF MEETING SUMMARY

Date _____   Cluster Name _____

Cluster Shepherd _____

Ministries or Groups Present

Ministries or Groups Not Represented

Ministry Leaders Present

Ministry Leaders Absent

Major Topics Discussed

Communication to give to Elders & Ministers

Communication to present to congregation

Shepherding Needs

Ministry Needs

Events needing to be cleared and added to church calendar (use back if needed)

BASIC ORGANIZATIONAL GUIDELINES

1. Keep everything as simple as possible.

2. Elders will emphasize shepherding, communication, and encouragement, as well as delegate responsibilities to ministry leaders.

3. Elders will be shepherding and communication coordinators of ten different clusters based on the Fruit of the Spirit. These clusters include Adult Classes, Family Life Groups, and Ministries.

4. Ministers will provide what expertise and training they have for appropriate ministries.

5. Elders will have contact with their groups at least once a month.

6. Ministry Leaders will be nominated to serve for one year.

7. Primary job of Ministry Leaders is to involve people in their ministry and for each person to use their gifts to meet the needs of the church and community.

8. Our goal is to involve every member of this church using his gifts to the glory of God.

9. Leadership training and retreats will be provided for these ministry leaders.

10. Leadership will provide direction for the congregation so that all ministries work to fulfill the overall goals of the congregation.

11. We must "love people into conformity" of what God wants this church to be.

12. Communication will be provided with the monthly meetings, as well as having different Ministry Leaders meet with our elders.

13. Prayer and spiritual leadership will be stressed.

14. Elders meetings will center around shepherding, communication about what's happening in clusters, and ways the church can be all God wants it to be.

15. We must develop a "comfort zone" which produces "team servants."

Illustration 14

92

vants should greatly maximize the manpower needed in a local church. The wise minister will let his ministry leaders make many of the proposals to the elders as he builds a leadership team that the elders really appreciate. This leadership team of volunteers can also be a tremendous support system as they communicate with their fellow volunteers. Ministers are important communication people as they communicate to the congregation what is happening in ministries. They also make sure that scheduled events are put on the church calendar, adequate promotion is given to each event, and adequate secretarial support is available. Ministers are also essential trainers of the congregation and ministry leaders in their areas of expertise. They are also encouragers to ministries in striving to get each member to use his gifts to the glory of God.

What do ministers do in the ministry system?

> # Followership is as important as leadership.

We can't all be leaders so followership is tremendously important. The major role of each deacon is not to do the work in his ministry, but to involve members of the congregation to do it. The whole system breaks down unless the congregation is made up of servant workers who will get involved as they are given the opportunity. When the involvement ministry has a member who wants to become involved in ministry, this information is given to the proper ministry along with a biographical sketch. These ministry leaders have three weeks to get the new prospects involved in the ministry and to get a report back to the involvement ministry. A copy of this biographical sketch form follows in illustration 15.

Now let's look at a new organizational chart of the ministry system in illustration 16 which demonstrates how it has grown.

There are several new categories addressed on this diagram. There is a category of other ministries which does not include deacons. These may be led by ministry leaders who do not meet the qualifications of deacons. There is another category of Women's Ministries which are made up entirely of women. Central has some

FAMILY BIOGRAPHICAL SKETCH

Date: _____   Family Unit Number: _____

Name: _____   Marital Status: _____

Address: _____   City, ST, Zip: _____

Home Phone: _____   Previous Church Home: _____

OCCUPATION

	Position	Employer	Phone
Man			
Woman			

SPECIAL INTERESTS

Man _____

Woman _____

RECORDS

First Name	Birthdate	Baptized by	Date	Congregation
Man				
Woman				
Child				
Child				
Child				

PREVIOUS CHURCH INVOLVEMENT

Man _____

Woman _____

EDUCATION (Tell where, what degrees, etc.)

Man _____

Woman _____

Child _____

Child _____

Child _____

Adult Bible Class: _____

Which assembly do you normally attend? 8:30 _____   11:00 _____

****

Man 1. _____   Woman 1. _____

2. _____   2. _____

3. _____   3. _____

Illustration 15

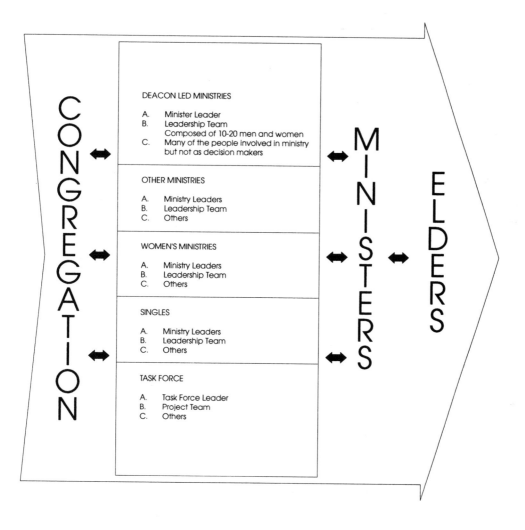

DEACON LED MINISTRIES

A. Minister Leader
B. Leadership Team
   Composed of 10-20 men and women
C. Many of the people involved in ministry but not as decision makers

OTHER MINISTRIES

A. Ministry Leaders
B. Leadership Team
C. Others

WOMEN'S MINISTRIES

A. Ministry Leaders
B. Leadership Team
C. Others

SINGLES

A. Ministry Leaders
B. Leadership Team
C. Others

TASK FORCE

A. Task Force Leader
B. Project Team
C. Others

Illustration 16

fifty different ministries just in this category! Some of the naturals include food for funerals, fellowship meals, letters to missionaries, wedding and shower ministry, women's classes, etc. Another major section is singles. Singles do not like to be led by married deacons. Therefore, it is usually better to let them develop their own leadership who are singles. The task force section is important because there are always special projects and studies which are needed. When this comes up, the elders assign a special task to fulfill the short-term responsibility.

One of the difficult questions to address is to explain the difference between deacons and ministry leaders. There is no good answer to this. At Central, you will notice on the new diagram that there are four things which make deacons unique from ministry leaders.

During these last 25 years, we have learned many valuable lessons from the Ministry System. Here are some of the major ones.

What is the difference between deacons and ministry leaders?

1. It is a fantastic way to produce leadership, build a broad base of leadership and provide support to keep a church growing and meeting needs.
2. It is an excellent way to get many new people in leadership on a regular basis. This is an absolute essential for longevity in church growth.
3. It is hard for some elders to let go. This is especially true in the areas of finance and missions.
4. It is sometimes hard for ministers to let go and delegate to other people.
5. It is hard for deacons to delegate out to other ministry leaders and members. It is sometimes hard for them to assemble a team and to work with them in the decision making process.
6. Unless you have a servant-driven church, power struggles can develop between deacons, ministers and elders.
7. Women are a major reason for the success of the ministry system. They are tremendous servants and usually make up

> Women are a major reason for the success of the ministry system.

about 60% of the Sunday morning attendance. When a ministry is not adequately functioning, one of my first questions is, "How many ministry leaders do you have on your team who are women?" Unless you have a lot of women involved, you will probably end up far short of what could be accomplished with their leadership and help.

Does the ministry system give women a greater opportunity to use their spiritual gifts?

8. Accountability is tremendously important. Ministry Communication Forms, the Spiritual Cluster Plan, Wednesday night elders meetings with individual ministries and the annual selection of deacons all address the accountability issues.

9. The involvement of people by an adequate involvement ministry is essential.

10. Training and retreats are tremendously important.

11. It is very important for ministers to have people skills. They need to understand their roles.

12. Getting as many people as possible involved in giving input for the ministry budget is very important.

13. Freedom, trust, accountability and responsibility are all necessities in the Ministry System. Balance is crucial.

14. This is a people system. Do not have too much red tape and keep things as simple as possible. Don't organize things too tightly. People are more important than money, forms or things.

Does the system provide a balance between freedom and accountability?

15. The pulpit minister is tremendously important as a motivator of the congregation, encourager of ministry leaders and promoter of ministry projects.

16. This system raises the role of deacons to unbelievable heights. They are given great responsibility. It is no easy task to involve many people and make sure their individual ministry is operating at maximum capacity.

17. It raises the role of elders to new spiritual heights. They develop future leadership in ways far beyond what they have ever dreamed. The church grows and they have a great dream again for the local congregation.

18. First and foremost, the Ministry System is a Servant System. It will be seriously handicapped unless each leader believes "He that is greatest, let him be your servant."

6 Recruiting, Equipping, and Motivating Servants

"I can do everything through him who gives me strength"
(Phil. 4:13).

What are some biblical examples of people who were tough to recruit?

Recruiting has always been difficult. Jeremiah thought he was too young to get involved. Jonah was afraid and tried to run away. Moses said he wasn't a good speaker and thought he was not the right person for the job. Saul didn't want the job and ran and hid himself. Gideon had an inferiority complex, bad family background and thought he didn't know how to do the job. Jesus spent the entire night in prayer before he recruited his disciples. As you can see, recruiting in Bible times was difficult even with these great men of God. But recruiting was successfully done.

The first three chapters of the book of Jonah say a lot about recruitment:

Jonah chapter 1—Jonah on his back sleeping.
Jonah chapter 2—Jonah on his knees praying.
Jonah chapter 3—Jonah on his feet teaching.

> ## Jesus spent the entire night in prayer before he recruited his disciples.

Recruiting is still difficult today. There continues to be an increase in the number of working women, with more than 70% working today. This gives the average woman much less time to do volunteer work at church. Men are also working longer hours with less holidays, and many men have second jobs. Today's people are highly mobile with 20% of the adults moving every year. This makes it much more difficult to build long range teams of volunteers. We are also highly mobile from week to week. Being out of town on weekends has become a way of life. Schools have more and more weekend holidays and parents take advantage of this to be out of town for a long weekend. Many people are already hopelessly overcommitted, and their families are falling apart. Marital and parenting problems have proliferated. There are many single parents, blended families and never married. There is much affluence in today's world, and this makes it possible for many people to travel or get involved in recreational activities. These activities are now scheduled on Wednesday nights and all day Sunday. Television and sensational national events like the Olympics and Super Bowl continue to get a larger audience involving more of our time. I'm not saying these things are wrong, but it does hurt the recruiting and involving process. Today's choices for families are not so much a choice between good and bad as it is between good and better. Many people today want to do something that is meaningful, exciting and fulfilling. Others want to get paid for any kind of extra work. The baby boomer generation has not been as loyal and committed to the church as previous generations. Of course, there are many exceptions to all the things we have mentioned, but these trends in today's world have made recruiting much more difficult.

Mobility makes recruiting more difficult.

There are some major categories which describe why people say no when they are asked to serve:

1. *Afraid of getting stuck.* They are afraid they will never be able to get out of the job once they have said yes. There is no doubt that some people have been abused in this area.

2. *Burnout.* These people are tired, frustrated and want out. They need a rest or change. Every individual is different. Some cannot even remotely comprehend what burnout is. Others have experienced it several times firsthand, and they know the need for a break, change or rotation. These people are usually overcommitted in several areas.

Why do people say no when they are asked to serve?

99

3. *Experienced failure.* These people have experienced failure with previous assignments, they cried out for help, and no one responded. They do not feel they are capable of doing the task and they do not want to get in this situation again.

4. *Don't want this job.* This is just not a job in which they have much interest. They might serve somewhere else, but not in this area.

5. *They don't know how.* If you wanted a lady to teach music to fifth grade girls and she did not know anything about teaching music, there would be frustration and failure.

6. *They may have health problems.*

7. *They may be overcommitted in other areas.*

8. *Too vague.* The task they have been asked to do may be too vague, and they may not understand the assignment.

9. *Voluntary organization.* The ministry system and involvement ministry is composed primarily of volunteers. These are dedicated people, but they may make some mistakes. Follow through may not be as prompt as needed. Something might be said in a light way or a curt way that may offend the person being recruited.

Why do people say yes when they are asked to serve?

There are also some major reasons why people say yes.

1. *Altruism.* They believe that what they have been asked to do is very important and will help others.

2. *Help the church.* They are committed to Jesus Christ and they believe their involvement will help his church.

3. *Help them grow spiritually.* They believe this will draw them closer to the Lord.

4. *Have discovered their gift.* They have gone through training and have discovered their spiritual gifts.

5. *Want to use their gifts.* They want to use the gifts God has given them for his glory.

People like to work on ministry projects with their friends.

---

6. *Work with friends.* They like to work on ministry projects with their close friends.

7. *Like to make new friends.* Many new people and some older members do not have many friends. They see this as an opportunity to work together and make friends.

8. *Good chance of success.* They feel they can do the task which they have been asked to do.

9. *Clear idea of what to do.* They have been given a clear description of their job assignment and believe they can do it.

10. *Sense of support and respect.* This gives them a feeling of being part of the team and supporting the ministry of the local church.

11. *Guilt.* Although not a good reason, some people are driven by guilt to do more and more for the church.

12. *Servant spirit.* The church has gone through a metamorphosis and has committed to being a servant-driven church. People are caught up in this overall spirit to be involved and use their gifts for the Lord.

An adequate recruiting program is essential.

There are eleven good ways to recruit the membership on an annual basis.

1. *Deacon recommendation forms.* During the annual selection of deacons, there is a heightened interest and awareness in ministry. The brochure contains a thumbnail sketch of each ministry, and the congregation is nominating qualified individuals to serve in these areas. There are usually some sermons and Bible classes about the importance of this. The recommendation form has a place for members to sign up to get involved. This always produces a lot of volunteers for ministry if it is handled correctly.

2. *Budget presentation.* At the annual budget presentation which usually comes in December or January, it is a good idea to show a slide or video presentation of the budget to the congregation. Emphasis should be upon the way God is using these various ministries for the glory of God. People should catch the overall dream and purpose of the congregation and see how God can use

How can we recruit people on an annual basis?

101

> A pledge of time and talent is even more important than a financial pledge.

them to fulfill this dream. There are two pledge cards usually handed out to the members after the budget presentation. One of these cards is a financial pledge, but the other card is a pledge of time and talent. These cards are even more important than the financial cards because they involve the people in a ministry. Studies show that those people who are involved usually increase their giving in a fairly dramatic way. In a later chapter, we will discuss budgets, budget presentations and budget cards for both increased giving and increased involvement.

3. *Ministry Fair.* This can be held on Sunday morning during Bible class, at the end of a service or on Sunday night. The specific purpose is to share what's happening in ministries and recruit additional personnel. Each ministry sets up a table or booth that demonstrates what they are doing. Video and slide presentations can be shown at each ministry area. Brochures, books and pamphlets can also be used. Each person in the congregation is asked to visit each booth. It is usually a good idea to have sandwiches or finger foods available at one table. Members come by and look at the materials at each booth. Each booth is manned by ministry leaders who answer additional questions. There are also involvement cards at each table for people to complete if they are interested in getting involved. The Ministry Fair informs a congregation about what is going on in each ministry, motivates your ministry leaders, gets people excited about ministry and recruits additional people. Although it takes a lot of work to have a ministry fair, it is an enjoyable and successful way to educate and recruit.

4. *Special Bible Class emphasis on recruiting.* A four-week series in all the Sunday morning Bible classes can be very successful. A good title for this class is "What's My Place?" The class needs to talk about the importance of spiritual gifts, where they come from, how they are to be used, how the gifts work together and how they are diverse. It is a good idea to give a gifts inventory

to the class. I like the one put out by Guidance Assistance Programs out of Winfield, Illinois, because it is much shorter than the others and can be completed in ten minutes. It is not as good an evaluation as the longer ones, but it is good for the Sunday morning class where you have a shorter time span for teaching. The study also needs to cover what really motivates me to serve, what the ministries of this congregation are, and how I can get involved. People can complete involvement cards in the class setting.

Another good way to involve people through a special Bible class emphasis is to have all the adult classes meet together on Sunday morning and have the ministry leaders share exciting ways God is using their ministries. Cards can be passed out and people can be told how they can get involved. This is usually a very successful way to recruit. Elders and ministers could also make some positive remarks at this gathering so that the congregation knows all are working together in this great effort.

> What are some things you can teach in your adult classes which will help recruiting?

Use your Bible classes for recruiting.

5. *Special sermons*. Special sermons can be very effective for recruiting. They are especially effective if they point out a major need in the church or community and make a passionate pitch for people to get involved. I saw this used very effectively when a sermon on pornography was presented and some twenty people responded at the invitation. An appeal was made for people to get involved in getting rid of pornographic materials in the 7-Eleven stores in the Fort Worth area. Many people responded and the campaign was very successful.

6. *Attendance cards*. If you use attendance cards on a regular basis, they can be very effective recruiting tools. Announcements need to be made which point out opportunity and need. This gives many different people a chance to respond.

7. *Individual recruiting*. People who are excited about the ministry in which they are involved are great recruiters as their excitement is contagious. They know what is needed for their ministry and they know what they enjoy. Therefore, they can answer

most questions needed for recruiting. This especially becomes a strong approach if they are friends with the people they are recruiting. This can be a problem if it is unorganized and people from different ministries are all pouncing on the same people.

How can you get new members involved?

8. *New members classes and orientation.* New members are some of the very most responsive people to the involvement process. The initial orientation needs to get proper records from new members, get them involved in a Bible class and small group, and give an overall description of what is happening and how they might get involved. They need to be invited to a six-week new members training course where they can learn in detail about the ministries and how they can get involved and use their gifts.

9. *Family Life Groups.* These are small groups designed for every member. They usually meet at least once a month on Sunday nights in homes. If group leaders are trained to recruit, they can be very effective in these small group meetings.

> # The adult Bible class can be a miniature congregation for the involvement of members.

10. *Bible Class Involvement.* The adult Bible class can be a miniature congregation for the involvement of members. Teachers can teach in ways to mold members in the direction of priorities which have been established. They can also try to involve as many members as possible in the adult class. This would include several teachers and substitutes, snacks and coffee makers, class chairpersons, greeters, visitation teams, calling teams, fellowship leaders, etc.

11. *Family Involvement and Growth Services (FIGS).* This is a highly successful program for communication and recruiting. A survey is first made through all the Sunday morning adult classes. In the survey, people are asked:

    a. Why are you coming to Central?

    b. Make a list of your needs as well as church and community needs.

    c. Ministries in which you would like to get involved.

> ## The FIGS program calls everyone in the congregation for input.

A good way to approach this is to invite people alphabetically to come to a meeting at 6:00 p.m. concurrent with the Sunday night service. This usually provides for children in Bible classes and nursery use. Some 100 different members are invited each week from the membership list and usually about half attend. This meeting can take place on three Sunday nights a month but be dismissed on the night of Family Life Groups. People not only receive a card inviting them to the meeting, but the involvement ministry also tries to call each person and give them a special invitation. This not only greatly improves attendance, but it also provides much information from those who do not attend. This information should be carefully recorded and gotten to the appropriate ministry. Within a few weeks, you will have called everyone in the congregation and this will provide valuable information to you.

What do you do at a FIGS meeting?

Results of the survey should be shared at the meetings. Possible new plans and dreams can be shared. Response and input would be requested from those present. Needs can be addressed and people then have the opportunity to dialogue. These "town hall" type meetings can be very successful, and it gives every member an opportunity to express themselves and provide valuable input to leadership. It also gives each person an additional chance to sign up to be involved in other ministries.

The Waterview Church of Christ in Richardson, Texas, does an excellent job of recruiting for Ministry. Illustration 17 shows a New Member Assimilation Plan and illustration 18 shows in a flow chart arrangement how both new members and current members get involved.

The Preston Road Church of Christ has also developed an excellent involvement plan. Appendix C shows how a task force did surveys, brainstormed and developed a very successful involvement program. It should be very useful for those who are looking for a tool such as this.

HOW DO I BECOME INVOLVED?

First, be sure you know that you do not need to get permission to serve the Lord! Literally hundreds of things are done by members all the time just as individual acts of kindness or generosity. This chart is intended to be a graphic guide to what avenues are available to members in order to participate fully in the ministries at Waterview.

NEW MEMBER

When you became a member:
New Member Information
 *Directories
 *Budget Information
 *Items of interest

Talk with any member of involvement, any elder or any minister, or call church office **if you are having any difficulty.**

Elders Welcome Circle
(It's fun, honest!)

Welcome Ministry Luncheon
 *Meet other members

Adult Bible Class
LOA group, etc.

2 Orientation Sessions
 *New Member Packet
 *Building Tour
 *Review of Ministry System

Involvement Form
(In Packets)

CURRENT MEMBER

Involvement Form
Available in church office

Deacon/or Ministry Leader Contact
(You don't have to wait for a call, feel free to contact them for information)

Brand New Idea
for a Ministry or Project
Talk with any member of involvement, any elder or any minister

Illustration 18

NEW MEMBER ASSIMILATION PLAN

FIRST SUNDAY OR ASAP
 Picture
 New Member Packet
 Information Sheet

FIRST MONTH
 Visit with Elders
 Visit by Involvement
 Visit by Members
 Visit by an Elder
 Assignment to Group
 "Check Up" Phone Call

SECOND MONTH
 Orientation Session
 Membership in Bible Class
 Participating in Group
 Completed Involvement Form
 Making Friends/Feeling Good about Membership
 "Check Up" Phone Call

THIRD MONTH
 Contacted by Ministry Leader
 Attendance Patterns
 Level of Involvement as Desired
 "Check Up" Phone Call

SIXTH MONTH
 "Check Up" Phone Call
 Attendance Patterns

NINTH MONTH
 "Check Up" Phone Call
 Attendance Patterns

Illustration 17

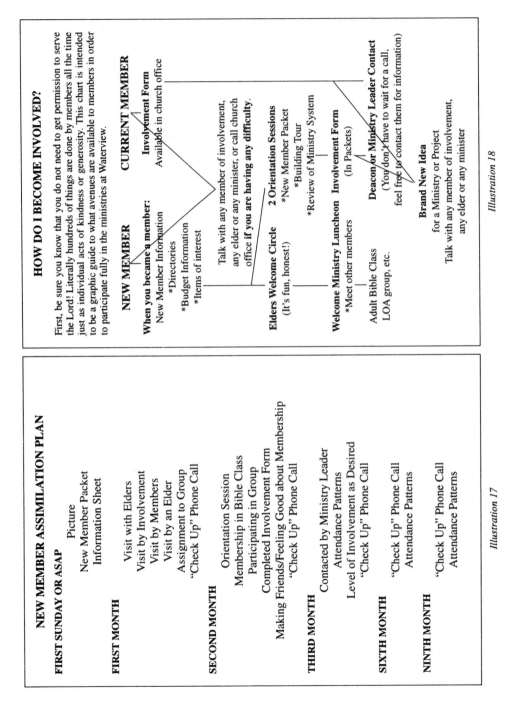

TRIBUTE TO WOMEN SERVANTS

Recruiting, equipping, training and motivating servants would be highly unsuccessful if it were not for thousands of women servants. These servants receive little recognition in our churches, but they are our unsung heroes. We can learn great lessons about servanthood from them. I find about two-thirds of the day-to-day work in the ministry system is done by women. In our public prayers in the assemblies, we pray for our elders, deacons, ministers and missionaries, but seldom do we pray for our women. We sometimes spend more time telling them what they cannot do in the church rather than thanking them for what they have done.

> Two-thirds of the day-to-day work in the ministry system is done by women.

God knew the importance of women, and he stresses this importance in the Bible. Five women are listed in the genealogy of Jesus. In Luke 8 Joanna and Suzanna contributed to the financial support of the ministry of Jesus. Anna had the gift of prophecy in Luke 2. Joel foretold that both sons and daughters would prophesy in Joel 2, and this prophecy is repeated in Acts 2. Paul encouraged women to exercise the gift of prophecy in 1 Corinthians 11. Peter's mother-in-law served in Luke 4. Priscilla used the gift of teaching in Acts 18. Dorcas is cited as a servant in Acts 9. Single women also used their gifts as Philip had four virgin daughters who prophesied in Acts 21. Lydia had a prayer ministry in Acts 16. Women were in the Upper Room in Acts 1 praying with the apostles before Pentecost. In Romans 16, Phoebe was commended by Paul for her work as a servant or deaconess. Eight other women are commended by Paul in Romans 16. These are but a few of the biblical references of the importance of women as they relate to the ministry system.

What are some biblical examples of the importance of women?

I have found that it is primarily the women in the ministry system who cook the meals, get their homes ready for meetings, send the notes and letters, make the phone calls and are the follow-through people. There ought to be at least one service on an annual basis where we have all the women stand and the men sing to them: "We love you with the love of the Lord."

> ## Women are "angels among us."

What do you think of WINGS?

Not only can women be key people in the ministry system program as they work with deacons and ministry leaders, they can have a tremendous women's ministry program of their own. The Women's Ministry at Central Church of Christ has nearly fifty ministries. It is called Women in God's Service (WINGS). Men call them "Angels Among Us." They have produced a bound booklet which has become a model for Women's Ministries for scores of congregations. The first pages list the officers of the women's ministries with their title, name and phone number. This is followed by a brief index of the various ministries. Their ministries are grouped under six major categories: (1) Fellowship, (2) Education, (3) Family Matters, (4) Visitation, (5) Community Outreach, and (6) Spiritual Development with the pages color coded to represent each category. A sample showing the cover page and a couple of sample pages describing ministries is shown at illustration 19. It is our prayer that this will raise up a great volunteer army of women working for the Master with the gifts God has given them. It is my prayer that God will fulfill the prophecy of Joel for women in the 21st century, and that this will propel the church to new heights in service and growth as we better meet the needs of the people in the church and in the community.

SPIRITUAL GIFTS TOOLS AND SURVEYS

In the process of recruiting, equipping and training, spiritual gifts tools and surveys are very helpful. There are many different surveys available today. Some are much longer and more detailed than others. Some are more specific. Some go with entire courses of study. I have found that most of them are very helpful. The shorter ones are more successful in Sunday morning large classes and the longer ones are more useful with specialized training classes where more time is available and people are highly

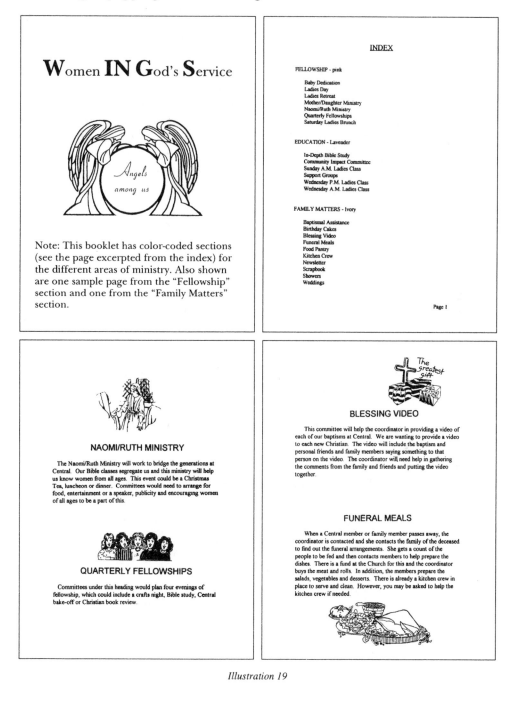

Women IN God's Service

Angels

among us

Note: This booklet has color-coded sections (see the page excerpted from the index) for the different areas of ministry. Also shown are one sample page from the "Fellowship" section and one from the "Family Matters" section.

INDEX

FELLOWSHIP - pink

Baby Dedication
Ladies Day
Ladies Retreat
Mother/Daughter Ministry
Naomi/Ruth Ministry
Quarterly Fellowships
Saturday Ladies Brunch

EDUCATION - Lavender

In-Depth Bible Study
Community Impact Committee
Sunday A.M. Ladies Class
Support Groups
Wednesday P.M. Ladies Class
Wednesday A.M. Ladies Class

FAMILY MATTERS - Ivory

Baptismal Assistance
Birthday Cakes
Blessing Video
Funeral Meals
Food Pantry
Kitchen Crew
Newsletter
Scrapbook
Showers
Weddings

Page 1

NAOMI/RUTH MINISTRY

The Naomi/Ruth Ministry will work to bridge the generations at Central. Our Bible classes segregate us and this ministry will help us know women from all ages. This event could be a Christmas Tea, luncheon or dinner. Committees would need to arrange for food, entertainment or a speaker, publicity and encouraging women of all ages to be a part of this.

QUARTERLY FELLOWSHIPS

Committees under this heading would plan four evenings of fellowship, which could include a crafts night, Bible study, Central bake-off or Christian book review.

BLESSING VIDEO

This committee will help the coordinator in providing a video of each of our baptisms at Central. We are wanting to provide a video to each new Christian. The video will include the baptism and personal friends and family members saying something to that person on the video. The coordinator will need help in gathering the comments from the family and friends and putting the video together.

FUNERAL MEALS

When a Central member or family member passes away, the coordinator is contacted and she contacts the family of the deceased to find out the funeral arrangements. She gets a count of the people to be fed and then contacts members to help prepare the dishes. There is a fund at the Church for this and the coordinator buys the meat and rolls. In addition, the members prepare the salads, vegetables and desserts. There is already a kitchen crew in place to serve and clean. However, you may be asked to help the kitchen crew if needed.

Illustration 19

motivated to discover their spiritual gifts. It is exciting to work with a highly motivated group as they discover God's gifts to them. It is equally frustrating at times to work with some in the church who have very little interest in this.

We will include or mention several different spiritual gifts inventories or surveys because they meet so many different needs for today's church. In the 1970s I wrote a Talent Interest Profile (TIP). It was specifically designed for the Richland Hills Church and measured interests rather than spiritual gifts. Answers were weighted according to your number one choice. Results were tabulated by the Involvement Ministry, other ministries were notified to interview these people, and we had surprisingly good results. Although this was a very crude beginning, God was blessing us and we knew we were pursuing something which needed to be developed. The complete TIP profile is found in Appendix D.

> # Tools which help us discover our gifts and get involved are valuable.

Which survey do you like the best?

Tools continued to be developed, refined, improved and people tested. The current Spiritual Gifts Survey at Richland Hills Church of Christ is one of the best in the nation. The complete survey is in Appendix E.

Some of the other good spiritual gifts surveys include:

1. The Wagner-Modified Houts Questionnaire developed by the Charles E. Fuller Institute. It is thorough, has 17 pages, and can be ordered from P. O. Box 91990, Pasadena, CA 91109-1990.

2. The Spiritual Gift Assessment and Spiritual Gift Reference Assessment prepared by the Willow Creek Church in Chicago. This is tremendous material and is part of their program called Network (The Right People. . .In the Right Places. . .for the Right Reasons). This material can be ordered by asking for it from Network, produced by Willow Creek Community Church, Zondervan Publishing House, Grand Rapids, Michigan 49530.

3. The Team Ministry Spiritual Gifts Inventory Questionnaire is very complete and useful. I've given it to more than 1,000 people throughout the years. It can be ordered from Church Growth Institute, P. O. Box 4404, Lynchburg, Virginia 24502.

4. The Saddleback Community Church in Orange County, California where Rick Warren is Senior Minister has developed the most thorough survey of anyone. Their goal is to turn members into ministers and their survey discovery program is called SHAPE. This comprehensive program covers far more than spiritual gifts. It helps discover where each member is in five different areas:

S piritual gifts

H eart

A bilities

P ersonality

E xperiences

What do you think of the SHAPE program?

This material can be ordered from: Saddleback Seminars, 23456 Madero, Suite 100, Mission Viejo, California 92691.

5. The Spiritual Gifts Inventory produced by Guidance Assistance Programs. Although this is the briefest and least detailed of all, it can be used successfully. It is the only one of the surveys which I would recommend to give to every member in the Sunday morning adult Bible class program. The reason I recommend this is because it is brief and most adults can take it in about ten minutes. There is also ample material for what the gifts are and feedback methods on your gifts that it makes a good one-session Sunday morning lesson. It can be ordered from Guidance Assistance Programs, P. O. Box 105, Winfield, Illinois 60190. A complete Spiritual Gifts Survey by Guidance Assistance Programs is found in illustration 20.

This chapter cannot be completed without talking about the importance of motivation. This is the missing ingredient in many programs. Churches will do the things we have discussed concerning recruiting, equipping and training — but they still have a lot of members who are not involved. Motivation was rarely addressed during the early years, but it is of major importance in the involvement process. We must go beyond the external and find out what motivates people to get involved.

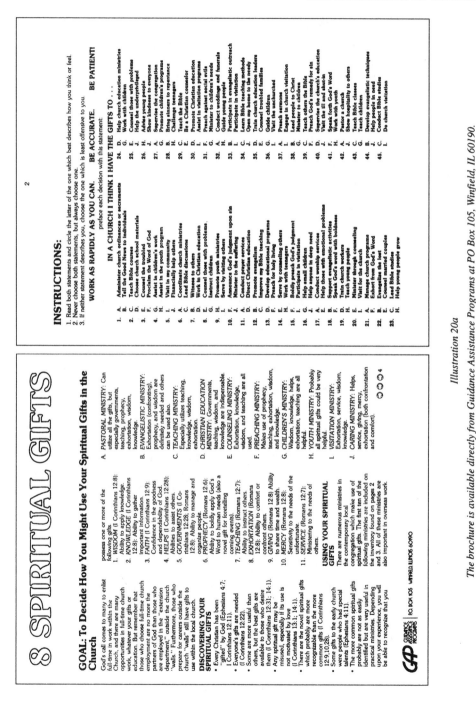

Illustration 20a

The brochure is available directly from Guidance Assistance Programs at PO Box 105, Winfield, IL 60190.

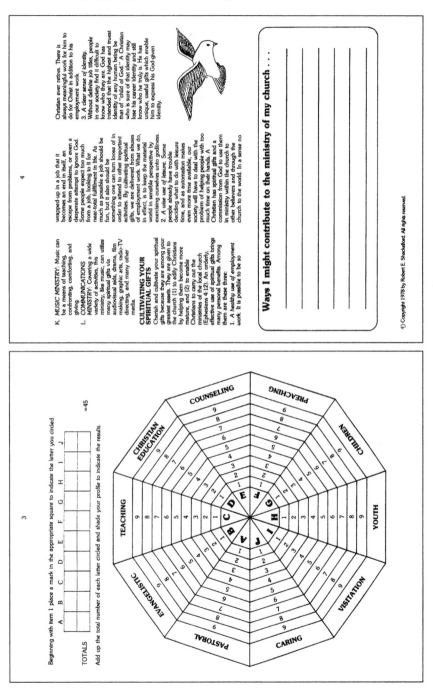

Illustration 20b

This material is copyrighted and used by permission.

> We not only have to have members discover their spiritual gifts, but we also have to find out what motivates them to serve.

There are nine very important principles which can help motivate people.

1. *By creating a need through personal exposure to reality.* People need to see a valid need, and they need to be exposed to this on a firsthand basis. If an elderly person calls needing a ride to church, and a member visits with them to see this firsthand need, they are more likely to help. If the church building roof has a terrible leak, people will probably respond to do something about it. If you visit someone who is struggling over the recent death of a loved one, you will probably be very supportive of a Grief Recovery Ministry to help them.

How can leadership feed and develop responsibility?

2. *By feeding and developing responsibility.* People are motivated when they are given significant, important jobs. They do not want to do unimportant tasks, and they do not want to become involved unless they are given the responsibility to complete the task. Sometimes, it is hard for some churches to delegate out real tasks and allow the people to develop to where they can take care of these tasks without someone looking over their shoulder every second. This lack of trust kills motivation.

3. *By providing encouragement and recognition.* Nothing motivates any more than encouragement. People desperately need this in today's world. This is a major role of elders, ministers, deacons and ministry leaders. Recognition can be provided in church bulletins, assembly programs, cards, letters, announcements, volunteer appreciation Sundays, servant of the month and bulletin boards. Video tapes and slide presentations can be made in the auditorium to both encourage and provide recognition. At Richland Hills, we published a booklet on an annual basis which showed every member who was involved as well as what he was doing. It was a mammoth task, but it really encouraged people as all wanted to be included in the Hall of Servants publication. Many churches use pictures and bulletin boards to recognize special activities and

recognize servants of the month. Letters or thank you notes are always appreciated. Special all-church appreciation dinners or individual appreciation meals in homes are important. Inviting ministries to meet with the elders for encouragement and prayer are also very beneficial.

4. *By showing an individual how.* Many people are not motivated to get involved because they do not know how to carry out what they have been asked to do. Training and equipping classes can help in this area. They will also work with individual mentors who can train them. No one would lead singing if they did not know how. When we know how to do something, we are much more apt to be motivated to use our gifts to the glory of God.

5. *By personal enthusiasm and example.* People are much more apt to get involved if they are approached by excited, enthusiastic people. They do not want to work long in a ministry where people feel like it is a total burden. It's hard to recruit people if you tell them how bad everything is. People are also motivated to get involved when the people who ask them have been setting a marvelous servant example. They would rather see a sermon than hear one in many instances.

> The closer you are to people
> who are trying to recruit you,
> the more apt you are to get involved.

6. *By intensifying interpersonal relationships.* The closer you are to people who are trying to recruit you, the more apt you are to get involved. That's the reason that relational recruiting is as important as spiritual gifts recruiting. Many people have trouble understanding this, but people like to work on ministry projects with their friends.

Why is relational recruiting as important as spiritual gifts recruiting?

7. *By dissolving emotional blocks.* This is a difficult one to describe, but it is very important. Some people will not get involved because of an emotional block — and they will not get involved until we dissolve this emotional block. It might be that someone is upset with an elder, minister or deacon. They may be

having a tremendous problem in their life or in their marriage. They may be having great difficulty coping with a major problem in life. Before we get these people involved, we will have to get close enough to them to find out what the real problem is and find ways to dissolve the emotional block. John Savage does a tremendous job in his seminars and workshops teaching us to really hear what people are saying and find ways to dissolve these emotional blocks. His material and seminars are called "Skills for Calling and Caring Ministries: Learning the Language of Healing." This material can be obtained by writing LEAD Consultants, P. O. Box 311, Pittsford, New York 14534.

Nothing motivates like love.

---

8. *By unconditional love.* Nothing motivates like love. You may be trying to recruit some people who have failed in the past and they are filled with guilt. Let them know how much you love them and how much God loves them. One of the values of the annual selection of deacons is that it lets them know how much the congregation and the elders love them. Spiritual Valentine cards can let members know how much they are loved. Love recruits and binds us together. It develops a team of servants bound together in love to do what is best for his church.

Have you used spiritual Valentine cards?

9. *By believing that God can make him into a significant person.* Low self-esteem is a major problem in today's world. This must be overcome before people will get involved. When people truly believe that God can use them to accomplish great things for him, it makes a major difference. I've seen people just going through the motions and not accomplishing much. But, when they were filled with his Spirit and believed that Jesus could use them in a significant way — their entire life changed. We need to believe that God can take us where we are and lead us to where he wants us to be. He is in the business of making nobodies into somebodies!

There is an interesting Bible school lesson to reinforce these nine motivational principles. You look at the eleven verses from

SCRIPTURE SEARCH FOR MOTIVATIONAL PRINCIPLES

Nine Motivational Principles

1. By creating a need through personal exposure to reality.
2. By feeding and developing responsibility.
3. By providing encouragement and recognition.
4. By showing an individual how.
5. By personal enthusiasm and example.
6. By intensifying interpersonal relations.
7. By dissolving emotional blocks.
8. By unconditional love.
9. By believing that God can make him a significant person.

Philippians 1:1-11 (NASB)

1. Paul and Timothy, bond-servants of Christ Jesus, to all the saints in Christ Jesus who are in Philippi, including the overseers and deacons.
2. Grace to you and peace from God our Father and the Lord Jesus Christ.
3. I thank my God in all my remembrance of you.
4. always offering prayer with joy in my every prayer for you all,
5. in view of your participation in the gospel from the first day until now.
6. For I am confident of this very thing, that He who began a good work in you will perfect it until the day of Christ Jesus.
7. For it is only right for me to feel this way about you all, because I have you in my heart, since both in my imprisonment and in the defense and confirmation of the gospel, you all are partakers of grace with me.
8. For God is my witness, how I long for you all with the affection of Christ Jesus.
9. And this I pray, that your love may abound still more and more in real knowledge and all discernment.
10. so that you may approve the things that are excellent, in order to be sincere and blameless until the day of Christ:
11. having been filled with the fruit of righteousness which comes through Jesus Christ, to the glory and praise of God.

Make Marginal Notes

Illustration 21

117

What Motivates Me to Serve?

I. Understanding God's Purpose for the Church.
  A. God wants his people to be the instrument He uses to show the Good News with all the world (Matt. 28:16-20).
  B. It is relatively easy to see how God manages the machinery of the universe and the great movements of history to fulfill His intentions, but it isn't easy to see how He fulfills His will in the individual human life.

II. Meeting God's Conditions
  A. Mind-Reversal
    1. We need to come to a point in life when we choose to let God be the center of our life.
    2. Luke 1:3
    3. Matthew 6:33
    4. The basic issue is: Who shall be in charge of my life?
  B. Mind-Renewal
    1. The basic issue is: What do I need to do to fulfill my destiny? This is the process of searching for the right values, choosing those values and disciplining the life accordingly.
    2. Romans 12:2
    3. Philippians 3:14

III. Our gifts from God are to be used for Him.
  A. Our mental process, sensory equipment, emotions, energy, talent, time opportunities, and experiences of others are to be dedicated to God and used wisely. These things motivate us to serve.
    1. Using my head.
      a. Thinking things through clarifying values, considering alternatives and consequences, setting goals, making plans.
      b. Proverbs 9:6
      c. Proverbs 14:15
      d. Philippians 4:8
    2. Listening to my heart.
      a. Consulting my inner feelings, heeding my intuition
      b. Isaiah 30:21
      c. Ecclesiastes 1:9
    3. Yielding to circumstances.
      a. Letting life unfold, accepting events as they happen, going with life by resigning myself to it as it comes.
      b. Ephesians 1:11
      c. Romans 8:28
    4. Seizing opportunities.
      a. Taking advantage of all timely and attractive prospects, ambitiously looking for chances to capitalize upon the situation.
      b. Matthew 25:14-30
      c. Ephesians 5:15-16
    5. Getting sound advice.
      a. Capitalizing upon the wisdom and experience of others who are experts and admired.
      b. Proverbs 19:20
    6. Serving others.
      a. Looking for ways to help people, considering myself a voluntary servant of all, making an effort to be concerned about their needs.
      b. Philippians 2:3-8
      c. Galatians 5:13-14
      d. Romans 12:10
    7. Putting out the fleece.
      a. Expecting God to reveal His directions by special events, circumstances or messages. Sensitive to God's leading.
      b. Judges 6:36-40
    8. Living spontaneously.
      a. Living in the present moment as much as possible, turning to that which comes easily and genuinely. Do it now with no red tape.
      b. Ecclesiastes 2:24
      c. Matthew 6:34
    9. Striving for my dreams.
      a. Pursuing my personal cherished desires and goals for this church. Doing the things I have long wanted to do.
      b. Psalm 37:4
      c. Deuteronomy 14:26
    10. Acting responsibly.
      a. Assuming primary responsibilities for meeting my own needs. Making my own decisions, facing the consequences of my actions, blaming no one else for my mistakes, accepting responsibility for my actions.
      b. Romans 14:12
      c. 1 Corinthians 3:12-15
  B. Discovery instrument to find what motivates me.

Illustration 22a

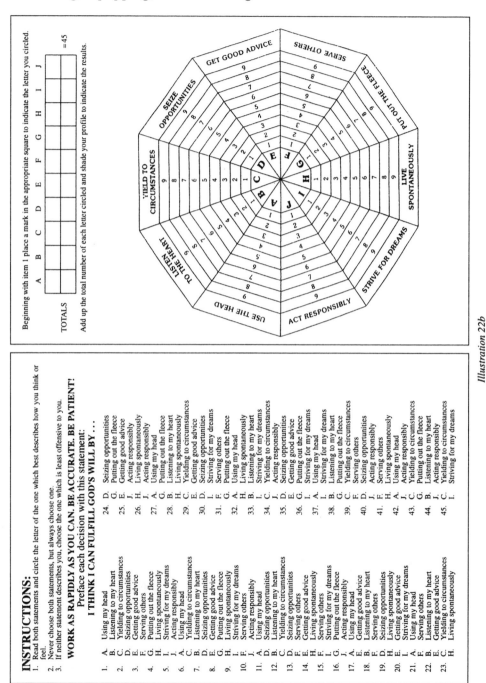

Beginning with item 1 place a mark in the appropriate square to indicate the letter you circled.

A	B	C	D	E	F	G	H	I	J

TOTALS | | | | | | | | | | = 45

Add up the total number of each letter circled and shade your profile to indicate the results.

Illustration 22b

INSTRUCTIONS:

1. Read both statements and circle the letter of the one which best describes how you think or feel.
2. Never choose both statements, but always choose one.
3. If neither statement describes you, choose the one which is least offensive to you.

WORK AS RAPIDLY AS YOU CAN. BE ACCURATE. BE PATIENT!

Preface each decision with this statement:
I THINK I CAN FULFILL GOD'S WILL BY . . .

1. A. Using my head
    B. Listening to my heart
2. C. Yielding to circumstances
    D. Seizing opportunities
3. E. Getting good advice
    F. Serving others
4. G. Putting out the fleece
    H. Living spontaneously
5. I. Striving for my dreams
    J. Acting responsibly
6. A. Using my head
    C. Yielding to circumstances
7. B. Listening to my heart
    D. Seizing opportunities
8. E. Getting good advice
    G. Putting out the fleece
9. H. Living spontaneously
    I. Striving for my dreams
10. F. Serving others
    J. Acting responsibly
11. A. Using my head
    D. Seizing opportunities
12. B. Listening to my heart
    C. Yielding to circumstances
13. E. Getting good advice
    F. Serving others
14. G. Putting out the fleece
    H. Living spontaneously
15. I. Striving for my dreams
    G. Putting out the fleece
16. A. Acting responsibly
    H. Using my head
17. B. Listening to my heart
    G. Getting good advice
18. A. Serving others
    B. Listening to my heart
19. D. Seizing opportunities
    H. Living spontaneously
20. E. Getting good advice
    A. Using my head
21. F. Serving others
    H. Striving for my dreams
22. B. Listening to my heart
    E. Getting good advice
23. C. Yielding to circumstances
    H. Living spontaneously

24. D. Seizing opportunities
    E. Getting good advice
25. J. Acting responsibly
    H. Living spontaneously
26. A. Using my head
    G. Putting out the fleece
27. B. Listening to my heart
    H. Living spontaneously
28. C. Yielding to circumstances
    E. Getting good advice
29. D. Seizing opportunities
    I. Striving for my dreams
30. F. Serving others
    G. Putting out the fleece
31. A. Using my head
    H. Living spontaneously
32. J. Acting responsibly
    B. Listening to my heart
33. I. Striving for my dreams
    C. Yielding to circumstances
34. J. Acting responsibly
    D. Seizing opportunities
35. E. Getting good advice
    F. Serving others
36. G. Putting out the fleece
    I. Striving for my dreams
37. A. Using my head
    I. Striving for my dreams
38. B. Listening to my heart
    G. Putting out the fleece
39. C. Yielding to circumstances
    F. Serving others
40. D. Seizing opportunities
    J. Acting responsibly
41. F. Serving others
    H. Living spontaneously
42. A. Using my head
    C. Yielding to circumstances
43. J. Acting responsibly
    G. Putting out the fleece
44. B. Listening to my heart
    J. Acting responsibly
45. C. Yielding to circumstances
    I. Striving for my dreams

119

> **God is in the business of making nobodies into somebodies!**

Can you find nine motivational principles in Phil. 1:1-11?

Philippians 1:1-11 and ask which motivational principles apply to each verse. This lesson is in illustration 21.

Another lesson entitled "What Motivates Me to Serve?" is great for study. It is much like a spiritual gifts survey except that it deals with what motivates us. Each of the motivational points are discussed along with Scripture study. Then, people complete the survey to find out what motivates them. This is a tremendous soul searching study which will really help people understand more than they ever have about the importance of motivation in ministry. This material is produced by Guidance Assistance Programs, P. O. Box 105, Winfield, Illinois 60190. A copy of the material is found in illustration 22.

We've covered a lot of material in this chapter about recruiting, equipping, training and motivating. It might be helpful to consider now a simple flowchart (illustration 23) that we used in the early days of the involvement ministry at Richland Hills.

Notice at the third step going down the chart, we go in one of two directions. People may be ready to make a ministry preference and may even complete an abbreviated gift survey. If that is the case, the flow continues downward, the ministry in which they are interested is contacted, the ministry contacts them to see how interested they are and then strives to get them involved.

If they need more time, which most people do, they go to the track at the right. Here they go through a personal interview and more detailed gifts or motivational surveys may be given to them. They may choose a new ministry preference and move back to the left column or they may lose interest and go in a holding block where the question mark is. We will regularly be doing things to try to get them interested in ministry. We may also have some who are so interested after the personal interview that they quickly flow to the interest in ministry diamond so they can quickly get involved before they lose interest.

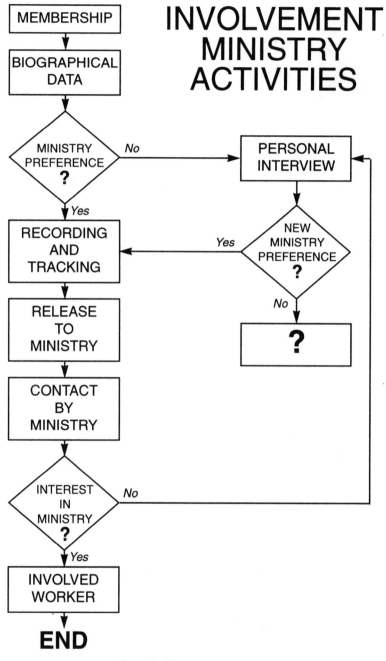

Illustration 23

121

7 The Servant's Renewals and Game Plans

This chapter is about leadership, implementation and follow-through. Many churches have great dreams and wonderful purpose statements, but the plan is never put into practice. This is a difficult chapter to write, but I will attempt to cover what is a missing link in so many churches. We will look at the behind-the-scenes roles of ministers, elders, deacons and ministry leaders to build a winning team where all work together. When this spiritual synergism of leadership takes place, God provides great victories. We will conclude the chapter by pulling all of these servant forces together as we look at programs and budgets for each new year.

> Renewals help put dreams
> and plans into practice.

What are some major topics to be covered on a retreat?

If the local church has a multimember staff, all of this should begin with a staff retreat. This ministers retreat is very important and should include the following topics. Custodians and secretaries should be brought in for the portion of the retreat which relates specifically to their areas.

1. *Devotional thought* such as Jeremiah 29:11: "'For I know the plans I have for you,' declares the LORD, 'plans to prosper you and not to harm you, plans to give you hope and a future.'"

2. *Prayer time* — one minute prayers by each staff person for wisdom and power.

3. *Affirmation time.* This is always greatly needed and causes tremendous bonding. Call out a person's name and each person should share what he appreciates about them. There is usually not a

dry eye after you do this. For larger groups, written affirmations can be conveyed.

4. *Personal.*

a. *Share where you are spiritually* and how you best develop spiritually. If we accomplish all of our overall goals, and a minister is not developing spiritually, we have a great problem.

b. *Share your God-given gifts with each other.*

c. *Share your areas of responsibility.* Job descriptions can be included in this because we must know who is responsible for each area of work.

d. *Personal need.* Each person should share their greatest needs at this time.

e. *Training needs.* Each person should share what training needs they have so plans can be put in motion to meet these needs. Each minister should share which training he would like to have for the coming year.

f. *Family needs.* Each person should share what family needs they have. Wives may need friends, help may be needed with children or schedules, etc. If a staff member is struggling in a family area, it causes great stress. Each member of the staff needs to know how important each person's family is and why we work together to help one another in this vital area.

5. *Staff.* The previous list dealt with individual needs while this one addresses the entire staff working together.

a. *Spiritual development.* This looks at how the entire staff can have maximum spiritual development as they serve together. Many suggestions should be discussed in this important area.

b. *What each person does.* This is especially important as it relates to each individual staff member and his role on the staff.

> Is it sometimes hard for you to share some of this information?

Everyone should work together on the team.

123

c. *How we work together as a team.* We do not need to duplicate efforts and we do not need to tear each other down. Communication, teamwork, loyalty and spiritual bonding are so important in this area. We also need to discuss such things as meetings and forms of communication and training to enhance this area.

d. *Communication.* What are the best ways to communicate as a staff?

e. *Leadership development.* What do we do to take a staff from where we are to where God wants us to be? What kind of formal and informal training is needed? What kind of mentoring is needed? How do we develop responsibility and accountability? How do we work smarter and better as a team together?

f. *Schedules.* How do we provide team coverage of everything that is happening in ministries as well as other church activities. This would also include the coordination of days off, vacations, out of town activities, office hours, secretarial availability, use of building and many other activities.

g. *Staff needs.* This would include secretarial help, computers, software, equipment, supplies, etc.

What are the best ways to communicate as a staff?

A Service Center is a better name for the church office.

---

6. *Church Office "Service Center."*

a. *Secretaries need to be included in this session.* We like to call our church office a service center because this is exactly what it is. This is the center of all church activities because this is also the communication center. There is a fine line to walk between keeping office equipment excluded from the membership and provided for the membership. Many members feel they have helped pay for all equipment and therefore ought to be able to use it at any time. Many secretaries feel this would not be allowed at any other job in town. They are also tired of having things disappear from their desks or other things broken. It is not an easy problem with which to deal, and if the wrong spirit enters into the picture, great problems can arise. The best answer to this problem is hardworking, servant secretaries who constantly project the attitude: "What can we do for you?" This open attitude solves most problems when servants are involved. Occasionally, the office manager will have to solve the problem.

"What can we do for you?" are six great servant words.

---

   b. *What each secretary does.* This is very important in the serving and implementing process. Each secretary needs a list of her job assignments, her routine tasks and other special activities. This needs to be reviewed on a regular basis so that proper balance can be maintained.

   c. *Times and communication.* This includes the times people will arrive and leave, who is part-time and who is full-time, and the best way to communicate.

   d. *Training.* What training is needed for the secretaries?

   e. *Motivation and morale.* People should openly discuss what improves morale the most. Special activities on Secretary's Day, special things done by elders and ministers, flexibility in scheduling, encouragement and annual salary increases all help in this area.

   f. *Office needs.* What do the secretaries need in the way of equipment, break rooms, etc.?

7. *Elders.*

   a. *Spiritual development.* Since we know that a church will never go beyond the spiritual life of its leaders, how can we best help each elder develop to his spiritual capacity

How can each person develop to his spiritual capacity?

realizing that most of these men are volunteers and Satan will try to get to them in this category.

b. *Talent*. Discuss what each elder does best.

c. *Communication*. Share the best ways for elders and staff to communicate and work together.

d. *Implementing change*. Since change must come, discuss the best ways staff and elders can work together to implement change.

> ## Retreats can be great tools for implementing changes.

e. *Training*. What training needs to be provided for the elders?

f. *Image*. How do we best keep a strong spiritual image of our elders before the congregation?

g. *Shepherd's role*. How can our elders best shepherd and how can we help them with this mammoth task?

h. *Elders renewal*. Get with the elders to plan an elders renewal.

8. *Ministry leaders, deacons and the ministry system.*

a. *Spiritual development*. How do we best help each of these people develop spiritually?

b. Discuss the best functioning ministries.

c. Discuss the least functioning ministries.

d. Share the strengths of the ministry system.

e. Share the present weaknesses of the ministry system.

f. Discuss the selection of new ministry leaders.

g. What training needs to be provided for our deacons and ministry leaders?

h. Plan a time calendar for annual selection, training, etc.

i. Discuss ways to delegate and maximize each staff member's role in the ministry system.

9. *Adult education.*

a. Discuss present strengths.

b. Discuss present weaknesses.

c. What have we done the last two years in the way of program and curriculum?

d. What curriculum is needed for the coming year? How do we use the adult class to mold the congregation toward the overall goals of the church?

e. What training is needed for teachers?

f. What training is needed for class leaders?

g. What new classes are needed?

h. Discuss the Wednesday night program.

i. Discuss the Sunday night program.

10. *Children's education.*

a. Strengths.

b. Weaknesses.

c. What are the major things we have done the last two years with program and curriculum?

d. What curriculum is needed?

e. What training is needed for teachers?

f. What training is needed for supervisors and other support cast?

g. What new classes are needed?

11. *Youth program.*

a. Strengths.

b. Weaknesses.

c. Needs.

12. *Community outreach.*

a. Strengths.

b. Weaknesses.

c. What have we done that was successful?

d. What else can we do?

13. *Singles and college.*

a. Strengths.

b. Weaknesses.

c. Successes.

d. What else can we do?

14. *Assemblies.*

a. Strengths.

b. Weaknesses.

    c. Major successes last few years.

    d. Series and themes where all study the same material.

    e. Singing.

    f. Sermons.

    g. Communion.

    h. Ushering.

    i. Children's Bible Hour and nursery.

    j. Multimedia material needed.

    k. Wednesday nights.

> ## Everyone should have input in the budget.

15. *Budget.*

    a. How the ministry leaders can prepare their budget and get input from each member of their ministry.

    b. How to get the congregation involved in the budget and provide support.

    c. Date for final approval as well as meetings to obtain final approval.

    d. Best way to communicate the budget to leadership as well as each member.

    e. Discuss best way to present budget to the congregation.

    f. Budget enhancement or the best way to increase giving.

16. *Possible major events* for the coming year to implement our dreams.

17. *Goals.*

    a. What does the congregation think of when they think of this church?

    b. What do we want to accomplish?

    c. What leadership involvement is needed?

    d. What congregational involvement is needed?

    e. Discuss theme and a few major goals.

18. *Publicity and promotion.*

    a. Who are we? Statement of goals and objectives.

    b. What do we want to communicate to the community?

    c. What do we want to communicate to the congregation?

    d. Discuss ways to communicate to the congregation and to the community.

19. *Prepare a calendar projection* of the major themes and events for the coming year.

MINISTERS PERSONAL TRAINING WORKSHOP

Ministers must also deal in these renewals with their personal concepts in four different areas.

1. Contracting: what do we expect from each other?
2. Team building: how to work together as a spiritual family.

How can ministers better function together?

> ## The ability of ministers to work together as a team greatly enhances the work of the local church.

3. Dealing with conflict: how to work it out when things get hot.
4. Goal setting: just what and how much can we do together?

Ministers must identify relationship problems. The following steps have a succinct way of revealing problems.

1. If you could be anywhere in the world, where would you be?
2. If you won an all-expense-paid, one-month vacation to the Holy Lands, who on the staff would you take with you?
3. Who on the staff have you had difficulty feeling positively toward during the past year? Why?
4. Who on the staff have you found it particularly easy to relate to during the past year? Why?
5. Has the influence of the person you have had difficulty in feeling positively toward, and the person that you have found it easy to relate to affected your other relationships? Why? How?

Staffs need to make personal commitments to each other. The following example is a good one.

1. Concerning our task as a staff, I promise to:
2. Concerning my relationship to the staff, I promise to:
3. Concerning my personal and professional development, I promise to:

4. As a Christian brother and fellow staff member, I promise to:

> # Weekly staff meetings are important.

What causes staffs to spiritually bond together?

Weekly staff meetings are also important in the communication and implementation process. These meetings should include ministers, secretaries and the chief custodian. It should include both part-time and full-time people. Wednesday morning is usually a good time to have these meetings. People have until 5:00 p.m. Monday to turn in what they want on the agenda. There needs to be a staff coordinator to prepare the agenda and see that everything is communicated, covered and implemented each week. There should always be a devotional and prayer time. Every person should have the opportunity for input on each agenda item. Plans should be developed which will be presented to the elders by the staff. This is a time to communicate, build spiritual bonding and build a team approach so that all areas of work are covered. Events scheduled and multimedia materials or other items needed for the classes are always covered. Without these weekly meetings, many things slip through the cracks and are never implemented.

ELDERS AND MINISTERS RETREATS

I have conducted more than 350 elders and ministers retreats, and I do not believe there is anything which produces more positive change than these retreats or renewals. Elders are busy volunteers who are always having to put out "brush fires." They primarily deal with immediate problems on a week to week basis. They hear many more negative remarks than positive remarks. Therefore, it is essential for these men to spend time away together to get the big picture and formulate God's plans which need to be implemented in the local church. As we have seen, the paid staff needs to first have their retreat and do their homework. They need to do all the preliminary work they can to help make this retreat a tremendous success. They need to have researched all the basic topics which will be discussed. They should have a game plan to present to the elders which needs a high level of elders' involvement and wisdom.

The elders and ministers retreat can be very similar in format to the staff retreat. It will hopefully not be as long or have as much open-ended brainstorming if the staff has done its job. However, it will allow time for maximum input and needed change by each elder. There once again needs to be a devotional to begin with, a theme verse, a time of prayer for God's power and wisdom, a spirit of expectancy and a time of affirmation. Elders probably need affirmation as much as staff does. It is usually hard for any of them to take five minutes of verbal affirmation without the tears flowing freely. During the affirmation period, I've seen many hugs, past problems in relationships healed, and the courage to launch out and move forward. I've seen a tremendous bonding take place between staff and elders.

There can be a general element to the renewal, but it needs to have a special agenda to fulfill the goals which need to be accomplished. Much of the outline can be the same as the staff retreat. After the affirmation time, quality time needs to be spent on spiritual development. The short outline can look something like this:

1. What causes you to grow the most spiritually?
2. What are your greatest needs?
3. Pray for one another.

> There is no way for spiritual dwarfs
> to lead a congregation.

There is no way for spiritual dwarfs to lead a congregation. Satan will constantly be striving to prevent leadership from growing spiritually. If he can do this, he can stop a church.

There needs to be a time where each elder can share his dreams for the church. A study of the book *To Dream Again* by Robert Dale and some of his more recent books can be especially helpful at this point. Other things which need to be discussed at the renewal include:

What are your dreams for your congregation?

1. Purpose or vision statement.
2. Major goals for the coming year. Are these goals in agreement with our purpose statement?
3. Development of a successful game plan. Staff should have already worked on a game plan to present. Elders should make needed changes in this game plan and provide wisdom for implementation.
4. Ways to implement the game plan.
5. Staff responsibilities and changes.
6. Ways to build winning teams.
7. Ways to be better shepherds.
8. Major ministries and programs of the local church.
9. Growth steps needed.
10. Family needs.
11. Programs and budget ideas for the next year.
12. Review of input from the congregation and other leaders.
13. Formulation of a game plan for the next year.
14. Responsibilities divided up for implementation. Much of the implementation usually is the task of the paid staff. Therefore, the eldership must give approval and backing for the game plan.
15. Prayer on knees for God's help with this great effort.

How do we best implement the game plan after the retreat?

There is now the tremendous responsibility of implementing this game plan. There now needs to be a renewal for deacons, ministry leaders, ministers and elders to enhance this process. Before we deal with this, I want to stress the importance of follow-up reports to be given at the elders and ministers retreat. We cannot just make a lot of plans and not do adequate follow-up. Elders and ministers get excited when they see results. Illustration 24 is an actual follow-up report given at Richland Hills which greatly encouraged staff and elders. It also shows the tremendous value of renewals to further the cause of Christ in the local congregation.

ELDERS, MINISTERS AND DEACONS TRAINING AND RETREATS

Deacons and ministry leaders have key roles to play in the formulation and implementation of the church's annual game plan. Nothing probably helps this more than the annual selection of dea-

WHAT'S HAPPENED SINCE LAST ELDERS-MINISTERS RETREAT

1. Phenomenal Growth Last *6 Months*

	Jan. – Feb.	Sept. – Oct.
Sunday Morning	1563	1950 + 387 people (25%)
Bible School	1269	1513 + 244 people (19%)
Sunday Night	799	1152 + 353 people (44%)
Wednesday Night	763	1141 + 378 people (50%)

2. Outreach

A. Have been 83 baptisms so far this year - 68 since the retreat. Previous high in the history of the church was 51 in 1965.

B. Eldred Echols has done a marvelous job teaching in Bill New's class on Sunday morning as well as teaching two classes each Wednesday evening.

C. Adult Michigan campaign was completed.

D. Freeway sign was installed.

3. Involvement

A. Ray has moved about half-time into involvement and office coordination as well as half-time with education.

B. Hope to have a new Minister of Education beginning January 1.

C. Involvement Ministry has been restructured with ten people on inner ministry, monthly coordinators, and fifteen couples per month. Flow charts, interview books, and new packets are being provided. Training of host couples is being conducted.

4. Expanding Facilities

A. Feasibility study with Bill Null is being conducted.

5. Family Life Center

A. Bobby Fairman is new liaison of Family Life Center and we have a person to supervise children's activities. We have a printed set of new guidelines for use of the FLC.

B. We did not make a trip to Springfield, Missouri, but heard Dr. Money explain the program in Irving.

6. Service Center

A. Have installed cubicles to take care of office space problems. This gave us space for seven secretaries where we originally had three. We provided a snack area for secretaries as they are not allowed to leave during the noon hour. We have also converted a cry room and closet into offices.

B. Everything is functioning beautifully except we need to develop a work and communication area when the offices are locked during services. We also need to improve our office situation in the areas of computers, phones, and dictating equipment.

Illustration 24

cons. This needs to be done in late summer or early fall so that their first important task is the formulation of the ministry program and budget for the coming year. There is tremendous enthusiasm when deacons are visited by the elders, installed before the congregation, and then have elders "lay hands on them," the congregation sing words of appreciation to them, and ministers, elders and wives feed them a special noon meal right after the Sunday morning service during which they were installed. They have been challenged to "Rise Up, O Men of God!," and they have been given a card with the words of the song printed on it so that they are now card-carrying deacons. After the meal, the deacons and their wives attend a three to four hour training session.

Rise up, O men of God!
Have done with lesser things;
Give heart and mind and soul and
    strength.
To serve the King of kings.

Rise up, O men of God!
The church for you doth wait,
Her strength unequal to her task;
Rise up, and make her great!

Lift high the cross of Christ!
Tread where His feet have trod.
As brothers of the Son of Man
Rise up, O men of God!

_____

Deacon's Signature

Central Church of Christ

Deacon training is important

During the training session, the roles and responsibilities of the deacons and their wives are explained. They are inspired and encouraged to develop spiritually and to develop each person in their ministry. The Ministry System is explained to them along with the best ways to enhance their ministry. Their first major challenge is to get with other members of their ministry and plan next

134

year's program and budget. The acrostic lesson for deacons is used at many of these training sessions:

Dedicated to this church with its people, programs and dreams.

Educated in your area of service with continual training to learn how to better serve in your specific area.

Animated and excited about serving in your ministry in a way that is contagious to other people.

Consecrated to God and pleasing Him.

Obligated to fulfill a vital role of service for one year.

Noted example in front of the church by you and your family.

Served in previous ways, and this is one of the reasons you have been nominated to serve. You want to serve and you want to involve people in your ministry to serve.

What do you think of the acrostic DEACONS training plan?

"Whoever wants to become great among you must be your servant" (Matt. 20:26).

Some actual sheets used for training are included in illustrations 25 and 26. Illustration 27 is a form for ministry leaders to complete when planning their budgets.

All of this material is now passed along to the Finance Ministry and Involvement Minister. It will be assembled and given to the elders for approval or rejection in each area. The Involvement Minister and his team are especially interested in ways to present the budget and ways to involve as many as possible in the assembling process as well as the approval process. We must remember that the budget is only a proposed budget when it is presented to the congregation. Ultimate approval is in the hands of the congregation as we cannot spend money we do not have.

> ## Giving goes up when everyone has input in the budget process.

The Involvement Minister and his team assemble all of this material, write a budget script, and prepare written budget materials for the congregation. It is usually better for the pulpit minister and key leaders to narrate the script. A multimedia presentation

1997 JOURNEY TO THE HEART OF GOD

OVERALL PURPOSE STATEMENT

The Central Church has an incredible past. God has used people of great vision to lift up Christ in this community. We want to lift the Cross so high that it will say to the thousands in this church and community that there is . . .

. . . a LIGHT that never goes out,

. . . a HEART that never grows cold,

. . . a MESSAGE that never grows old,

. . . an EAR that is never closed.

We believe that God has providentially called us together. Providence is the hand of God in the glove of history. Who knows but that all of us have been called together at Central for "such a time as this" (Esther 4:14). Journey to the HEART of God

    H eaven Bound

    E ncourage the Family

    A dore God

    R evive the Church

    T ouch the Community

SCRIPTURES

Jesus replied: "'Love the Lord your God with all your heart and with all your soul and with all your mind.' This is the first and greatest commandment. And the second is like it: 'Love your neighbor as yourself'" (Matt. 22:37-39).

"The seventy returned with joy and said, 'Lord, even the demons submit to us in your name.' The Lord replied: 'Do not rejoice that the spirits submit to you, but rejoice that your names are written in heaven'" (Luke 10:17 & 19).

OVERALL GOALS

1. Develop spiritual leadership to fulfill the needs of this church and community.

2. Help each member mature spiritually and use his gifts for the glory of God.

3. Reach the community and world with the Gospel of Jesus Christ.

4. Lead the people in your ministry to the very heart of God.

Name of Ministry: _____

Name of Cluster: _____

Cluster Shepherd: _____

Major Goals

1.

2.

3.

4.

Purpose Statement

Illustration 26

Let's Dream and Plan!
Strategy for Local Congregations

1. Write a sentence of less than ten words which describes your ministry.

2. What one word best describes your ministry?

3. What are two or three Bible verses which you would give as reasons for your ministry?

4. What kind of leadership team people are you trying to assemble?

5. What would be some of their specific assignments?

6. What are some good ways to involve new people in your ministry?

7. How do elders, deacons, and ministers best communicate?

8. How do you best communicate with the congregation?

9. What are your ministry's major goals for this year?

10. What is the best way to prepare and present the budget?

Illustration 25

136

featuring video or slides is usually highly effective. This is usually done at the beginning of the new year. It is important that the membership is excited about the dreams and plans for the coming year. Get as many pledges as possible on the Sunday the material is presented visually to the congregation, but allow an entire month for the pledges to be turned in to the elders. The pledge cards for the Time and Talent part should be turned in to the involvement ministry.

It is always important to first challenge your leadership of elders, deacons, ministry leaders, teachers and ministers to give more as an example for the coming year. This total can be announced to the entire congregation to both challenge the congregation and to let them know of leadership's commitment. A simple but effective way to do this is to ask the leadership to increase their giving by 2%.

What are the major things you want to communicate in your church budget?

Involvement is a key to giving.

I have been asked by hundreds of congregations throughout the years to help them with their budgets, giving and presentations. To answer some of these requests, I am going to include a Budget Involvement Program with schedule, a sample budget script, and numerous examples of themes and budget cards and material to be given out to the membership. All of this material is found in Appendix F. Appendix G includes many budgets with envelopes, budget outlines and pledge cards for money as well as involvement. The themes for each year of these sample budgets were as follows:

1994—THE YEAR OF THE FAMILY
1993—LIFTING UP CHRIST
1990—A LOVING HEART SEES THE NEED
1987—THE STORY OF A FAMILY
1985—THE STORY OF A FAMILY'S FAITH
1984—LET'S GO FORWARD
1983—THE STORY OF A FAMILY'S DREAM
1982—LET'S LOOK CROSSWARD! LET'S GO ONWARD!
1977—MONEY BACK GUARANTEE

MINISTRY _____

NAME OF PERSON COMPLETING THIS FORM _____

8. To help with our cash flow, please check month and amounts when major expenditures will be made from your budget:

Month	Dollar Amount	Activity or Program
January		
February		
March		
April		
May		
June		
July		
August		
September		
October		
November		
December		

MINISTRY _____

NAME OF PERSON COMPLETING THIS FORM _____

7. List your Budget Proposals for 1996:

Category	1995 Expend. (thru June)	1995 Budget	1996 Budget
1.			
2.			
3.			
4.			
5.			
6.			
7.			
8.			
9.			
10.			
11.			
12.			
13.			
14.			
15.			
16.			
17.			
18.			
19.			
20.			
21.			
22.			
23.			
24.			
TOTAL			

MINISTRY _____

NAME OF PERSON COMPLETING THIS FORM _____

1997 MINISTRY BUDGET PROPOSAL

1. What are the major goals and programs of your ministry for 1997?

2. What are some facts and activities from your ministry you would like to see us use in the budget presentation to the congregation?

3. How many people are involved in your ministry? _____

4. List the names of people in your ministry who are authorized to make or okay expenditures.

5. Write us an article about your ministry that we can use for the assembly program or bulletin.

6. What are some major things your ministry has done or will do to implement our 1996 theme "Journey to the Heart of God"? What have you personally done?

*Please get your financial materials to the church office or Finance Ministry by November 1.

Illustration 27 (width compressed for sake of space)

138

Let me also share some new thoughts for budgets and fund raising for the 21st century. The more personal we can make the presentation, the more successful we will be. That's one reason that a program involving elders, deacons and ministers to visit every home in the congregation within a two-week period of time can be so successful. This shows leadership example and commitment. Leave a prayer card or "prayer tent" in each home that includes the major goals and events for the coming year. Ask for the members to pray for this daily in their homes. Samples of prayer tents as well as thoughts on fund raising for the 21st century are included in Appendix H.

What can leaders do to make a significant difference in congregational giving?

> # All of the money in the world is useless unless we implement our goals and dreams.

All of the money in the world is useless unless we implement the goals and dreams for the coming year. Credibility and trust is at stake here and we must strive to implement. This will do more than anything else to keep our giving up throughout the year. Otherwise, we may start out with a "big splash," lose credibility, and see the giving decline throughout the year. This can also happen if the congregation has not been included in the planning process, and they are not really excited about the goals for the coming year. A brief sample sheet of the importance of implementation plans is included in Appendix H. Also included is a song which reflects the year's theme and serves as a constant reminder to the congregation of the theme and goals the church is striving to implement.

The Involvement Budget needs to include money for the budget presentation and printed materials, money for training and implementation throughout the year, money for packets and name tags, money for brochures and publicity and promotion, money for retreats, and money for special events.

When a group of servants are informed, included in the planning and have a dream, giving greatly increases in the local church. The "Ten Commandments for Giving" card (illustration 28) was included in Central's 1997 budget materials.

10 COMMANDMENTS FOR GIVING

1. Thou shalt thank God for every gift and blessing He has supplied to you.
2. Thou shalt not let debt and other priorities keep you from giving back to God what He has loaned you.
3. Thou shalt not mock God's name by refusing to give back to Him as He has blessed you.
4. Thou shalt be present and give to God on His Holy Day.
5. Thou shalt be a blessing to Christian parents who have taught you to give.
6. Thou shalt not kill the opportunity of people to minister by withholding your funds from the church contribution.
7. Thou shalt not use your money for unimportant or evil uses.
8. Thou shalt not rob God by failing to give back to Him what He has loaned to you. Thou shalt not expect something for nothing.
9. Thou shalt not engage in a "pity party" attitude as a Christian, but you shall receive God's blessings in faith and disburse it with love and wisdom.
10. Thou shalt not covet your neighbor's wealth and things, but you should be content with what God has provided you.

CENTRAL CHURCH OF CHRIST 1997

I will read and pray each week for:

_____ Our **Vision** (Where we're going.) **"An exciting place to call home."**

_____ Our **Mission** (What we do.) **"Attract all people to a relationship with Jesus."**

_____ Our **Values** (Who we are.) We **BELIEVE**:

1. The Bible is the inspired word of God and is our final authority in all matters.
2. Each member is to use their gifts for the glory of God.
3. Every soul is of immeasurable value to God.
4. We are to accept one another just as God has accepted us.
5. We are stewards of all God has given us.
6. God wants all believers to be one in Christ.
7. The "Great Commandment" defines our primary love.
8. The "Great Commission" is our charge from Jesus.
9. We are to have the "attitude of Christ."
10. God answers prayer.
11. We are saved by the grace of God.
12. The Trinity consists of the Father, Son and Holy Spirit.

_____ The **10 Commandments of Giving** (on other side)

_____ I pledge to give _____ weekly to the Central Church of Christ for 1997.

*Please place this material in your Bible or with your prayer materials and pray each week.

Illustration 28

Spring Elders/Deacons/Ministers Retreat

Richland Hills Church of Christ
March, 1990

1. This past year (1989) where has your spiritual life been on a scale of 1 (low) to 10 (high)?

2. In your perspective, has the personality of the Richland Hills church changed in the past two years? If so, how?

3. In reflecting on the previous question:
   — share what has been your most significant reward at Richland Hills the past year.

   — share what has been your most significant frustration at Richland Hills this past year.

4. Have the elders contributed to this frustration? If so, how?

5. Has the ministerial staff contributed to this frustration? If so, how?

6. Have I played a part in contributing to this frustration? If so, how?

7. Has the current financial status of the Richland Hills church contributed to this frustration? If so, how?

8. As a group, determine what you perceive to be the three most significant frustrations of the Richland Hills church. Use the back of this sheet to answer this question.

   PLEASE KEEP THIS SHEET AND BRING WITH YOU ON SATURDAY.

Illustration 29

> Renewals can be life-changing and powerful.

Deacons and ministry leaders need to have regular meetings with the people involved in their ministry as they strive to develop it. They also need to attend monthly spiritual cluster meetings in the elders' homes. They also need additional renewals and training throughout the year. The renewals and training should include some of the following categories:

1. Devotional and time of prayer.
2. Affirmation time.
3. Time of meditation.
4. Spiritual building activities.
5. Relational building activities.
6. Team building materials.
7. A look at where we've been, where we are and where we are going.
8. Leadership training.
9. Sharing of how we are doing implementing our dreams and goals.
10. Ways to recruit, motivate and involve.
11. Get feedback from this group about the launching of some new dream. I saw this happen once whereby a congregation decided to sell their old facility, buy land and build a new facility and raise millions of dollars to make this dream become a reality! Renewals can be very life changing and powerful!
12. Dealing with specific problems to the ministry system and putting out "fires." It takes a lot of courage to address this area, but it is greatly needed on some occasions. I saw the following agenda used for a retreat address some major problems, get all the group together, and turn the entire congregation to become a united team which produced unbelievable results. It was not an easy retreat, but it was very successful. It began with all of us on our knees praying for the first hour. Then, we discussed the material in illustration 29 which had been given to the deacons before the retreat so they could fill it out.

A Servant's Plan to Involve Every Member

Many church leaders have a great interest in a plan to involve every member. They understand the concepts which have been taught in this book, but they still need a step-by-step plan to implement this dream. This chapter is an attempt to answer this vital need.

> ## God wants his church to grow.

God wants his church to grow. He has given each member of his body different gifts, talents and abilities. These gifts have been given so the church can grow spiritually and numerically. However, the modern church has been compared to a football game: 22 people on the field tired out and hundreds of people in the stands as spectators. God gave each person gifts with which to minister. This must happen if we are to be the 21st century church for which God gave his Son. Every person using his gifts to minister sounds like an impossible dream, but let's look at a game plan to begin to make this happen in a local church.

1. Get the leadership on their knees praying for wisdom to lead the local church to be all God wants it to be. This praying servant model will set the example for the rest of the church to follow.

2. Get input from the congregation concerning their dreams and needs. People will not get involved if they do not have opportunity for input and ownership. Two-way communication is imperative in today's church.

3. Have a staff leadership retreat or renewal. Then have an elders and ministers retreat. Discuss how each leader can grow spiritually. If God builds a 10,000 member church, and some of the

leadership declines spiritually, this is a major cause for concern. Develop a plan for a winning spiritual team. Analyze all the input from the congregation and develop themes and goals. An annual theme is especially helpful. Develop a purpose statement and measure everything you do in light of this purpose statement.

We believe that God has providentially called us together. Providence is the hand of God in the glove of history. Who knows but that all of us have been called together at Central for "such a time as this" (Esther 4:14).

> ## People will get involved if they know *who* we are, *whose* we are and *where* we are going.

The leadership retreat also produced a theme for Central. Central is "a place to call Home." Four major goals were set for Central.

What do you think of these four major goals and the overall theme?

H onor God.
O utreach to Community.
M ature the Church.
E ncourage the family.

We currently have a real identity problem in the church. But we have found people are ready to get involved if they know who we are, whose we are and where we are going.

4. This theme and purpose statement was shared with the congregation, and it was enthusiastically received. Then Carlie Burdette, one of our members, wrote the theme song entitled "Central . . A Place to Call Home" which we shared in chapter two. The song was published and glued in our songbooks.

5. "Forty Days of Prayer" needs to be launched whereby each family prays daily for the work of the church and for God to provide the best ministry leaders forty days later when they are installed. The information for this campaign is included in illustration 30.

This "Forty Days of Prayer" guide does wonderful things for families. Many families tell us it is the first time the entire family has gotten together to pray and meditate on God's word on a regular basis. The material for each day is very brief, but that's part of the reason for its success. We usually have several children baptized by dads throughout this period of time because the forty days of prayer have brought them spiritually closer together.

How would 40 Days of Prayer help your family?

The main reason for the forty days of prayer is to experience God's power and wisdom as we select new ministry leaders in the annual selection of deacons process. God answers prayer in incredible ways, and He produces prayerful, servant leaders. Many have asked for a deacons selection schedule as follows:

The annual selection of deacons works.

DEACON SELECTION SCHEDULE

Oct. 6	40 Days of Prayer ready for congregation (Starts Oct. 9, concludes Nov. 17)
Oct. 13	Deacon brochure ready
Oct. 13-20	Deacons nominated by congregation. (Nomination forms primarily come through boxes in adult classes. However, some are placed in boxes at the information booths outside the auditorium and some are received in the mail.)
Oct. 23-Nov. 6	Elders pray and contact deacons
Nov. 10	Deacons' names before congregation
Nov. 17	Deacons installed Sunday morning Deacon meal hosted by elders and ministers Sun. noon. (Also deacon training. Wives included. Other ministry leaders and Bible school supervisors also included.)

6. A structure must be developed to utilize people to fulfill the needs and dreams of the congregation. The congregation should have the opportunity to nominate many different deacons and ministry leaders on an annual basis for the various ministries. This ownership is a key factor in the involvement of members as they

40 Days of Prayer

Central Church of Christ . . . *a place to call home.*

Matthew 4 teaches us that Jesus fasted 40 days and nights before He began His Galilean Ministry. We want to call on you to be faithful in prayer (Romans 12:12).

Day 1, October 9

Today we begin our 40 days of prayer. Pray for world peace and our national, state and local government leaders. Pray for our community to be receptive to our "Turn Your Heart Toward Home" film series.

I urge, then,. . . that. . . prayers. . . be made for everyone — for kings and all those in authority. . . 1 Tim. 2:1-4.

Day 2, October 10

Pray for your own spiritual development.
Devote yourselves to prayer Col. 4:2.

Day 3, October 11

Pray for the spiritual development of your family.
These commandments. . . are to be upon your hearts. Impress them on your children. Talk about them when you sit at home. . . Deut. 6:6-7.

Day 4, October 12

Pray for a clear vision of His dreams for our own church family.
"I know the plans I have for you," declares the LORD, ". . .plans to give you hope and a future. . ." Jer. 29:11.

Day 5, October 13

Pray for our shepherds and their wives.
I will give you shepherds after my own heart Jer. 3:15.

Day 6, October 14

Pray for our young people, Youth Program, and Huddle Groups.
Don't let anyone look down on you because you are young, but set an example. . . 1 Tim. 4:12.

Day 7, October 15

Pray for ministry leaders and their mates.
Whoever wants to become the greatest among you must be your servant. . .just as the Son of Man did not come to be served, but to serve. . . Matt. 20:26-27.

Day 8, October 16

Pray for our Women's Ministry and our secretaries.
I commend to you our sister Phoebe, a servant Rom. 16:1.

Day 9, October 17

Pray for our mission efforts.
Go and make disciples of all nations Matt. 28:19.

Day 10, October 18

Pray for our Counseling Ministry to mend lives and bring people to Jesus.
You guide me with your counsel Psalm 73:24.

Day 11, October 19

Pray that we will seek opportunities to encourage others in our church family.
. . .encourage one another and build each other up 1 Thess. 5:11.

Day 12, October 20

Pray for our Family Life Groups.
Be devoted to one another in brotherly love Rom. 12:10.

Day 13, October 21

Pray for our Public Relations Ministry as they communicate what this church is all about.
. . .pray for us that the message of the Lord may spread rapidly and be honored 2 Thess. 3:1.

Day 14, October 22

Pray for our Community Care Ministry.
. . .I was hungry and you gave me something to eat Matt. 25:35.

Day 15, October 23

Pray for our preachers and their wives.
Devote yourself. . .to preaching and to teaching 1 Tim. 4:13.

Day 16, October 24

Pray for our Child Care and Children's Home Ministries.
Religion that God our Father accepts as pure and faultless is this: to look after orphans and widows in their distress. . . James 1:27.

Day 17, October 25

Pray for our Clothing Ministry.
I was a stranger and you invited me, I needed clothes and you clothed me Matt. 25:35-36.

Day 18, October 26

Pray for our Family Care and Personal Financial Counseling Ministries as they help our members.
. . .do good. . .especially. . .to the family of believers Gal. 6:10.

Illustration 30a

Day 19, October 27

Pray for our worship assemblies.

. . .let us consider how we may spur one another on toward love and good deeds Heb. 10:24.

Day 20, October 28

Pray for our Jail Ministry.

I was in prison and you came to visit me Matt. 25:36.

Day 21, October 29

Pray for our Fellowship Ministry.

They. . .ate together with glad and sincere hearts Acts 2:46.

Day 22, October 30

Pray for our greeters and ushers.

Greet one another with a kiss of love 1 Pet. 5:14.

Day 23, October 31

Pray for Camp Blue Haven.

And Jesus grew in wisdom and stature, and in favor with God and men Luke 2:52.

Day 24, November 1

Pray for those in our hospitals as well as our shut-ins.

I was sick and you looked after me Matt. 25:36.

Day 25, November 2

Pray for our Involvement and Welcome Home Ministries.

Each one should use whatever gift he has received to serve others 1 Pet. 4:10.

Day 26, November 3

Pray for our singing and Special Music Ministries.

Sing and make music in your heart to the Lord Eph. 5:19.

Day 27, November 4

Pray for our Transportation Ministry.

So the servants went out into the streets and gathered all the people they could find Matt. 22:10.

Day 28, November 5

Pray for our Nursery, Bible Hour, and Children's Education Ministries.

Whoever welcomes one of these little children in my name welcomes me Mark 9:37.

Day 29, November 6

Pray for our Maintenance Ministries.

I rejoiced with those who said to me, "Let us go to the house of the LORD" Psalm 122:1.

Day 30, November 7

Pray for our Preschool and Mothers Day Out Program.

Let the little children come to me Matt. 19:14.

Day 31, November 8

Pray for all of us to be more fervent in prayer.

Lord, teach us to pray Luke 11:1.

Day 32, November 9

Pray for our debt, giving, and Finance Ministry.

Each man should give what he has decided in his heart to give, not reluctantly or under compulsion, for God loves a cheerful giver 2 Cor. 9:7.

Day 33, November 10

Pray for our Bible School Teachers and our Adult Education Ministry.

They shall be all taught of God John 6:45, KJV.

Day 34, November 11

Pray for our Sunshiners.

Do not rebuke an older man harshly, but exhort him as if he were you father. . . .Treat older women as mothers 1 Tim. 5:1.

Day 35, November 12

Pray for our Communications Ministry.

Faith comes from hearing the message Rom. 10:17.

Day 36, November 13

Pray for our parents.

Children, obey your parents in the Lord, for this is right Eph. 6:1.

Day 37, November 14

Pray for World Bible School and college students.

Go into the world and preach the good news to all creation Mark 16:15.

Day 38, November 15

Pray for our visitation, welcome friend, community outreach efforts.

Every day they continued to meet together. . .and the Lord added to their number daily those who were being saved Acts 2:46-47.

Day 39, November 16

Pray for our singles, widows and widowers.

Come to me, all you who are weary and burdened, and I will give you rest Matt. 11:28.

Day 40, November 17

Pray for our Ministry Leaders as they are installed today.

If anyone serves, he should do it with the strength God provides, so that in all things God may be praised 1 Pet. 4:11.

Illustration 30b

choose people they personally know to lead them in the various ministries. New leadership needs to be added on an annual basis or a congregation will stagnate. Church growth experts tell us that a congregation needs to have one-third of its leadership to be new every three years. At first reading this seems like an impossible task. They define leadership as elders, ministers, deacons and teachers. The annual selection of deacons and ministry leaders makes this impossible task possible.

One of the often forgotten benefits of the annual selection of deacons and ministry leaders is the powerful shepherding role of the elders in this process. Within a two-week period of time, the elders visit every deacon prospect in their homes. They meet with their wives and older children. They share with them their desire for them to serve along with the congregation's desire. They share what their responsibilities would be and pray with them. They ask the prospects to pray about this as a family and give them an answer a week later. This is a tremendous workload on the elders for a two-week period of time, but if it is done right, it produces incredible spiritual results. I call it "Leadership Shepherding" and it is a powerful tool. We usually think of shepherding as going after the "lost sheep," but this "Leadership Shepherding" can help spiritually develop your leadership core, get them even more enthused and develop a tremendous loyalty and appreciation for the shepherds. Don't shortcut this step or sell it short. It is a powerful positive step in the development of a plan to involve every member.

How do you feel about "Leadership Shepherding"?

> ## Elders must allow deacons and ministry leaders the freedom to develop their ministries.

7. Elders must allow deacons and ministry leaders the freedom to develop their ministries. Responsible ministry leaders must be trained, and they need to be held accountable for their important ministry assignments. Training begins the very day the ministry leaders are installed. They need to also be assigned to an elder's spiritual cluster where they will meet with their spiritual cluster

shepherd once a month. Deacons and wives should both attend these meetings as the woman is so vital in the ministry system. These spiritual cluster meetings will provide spiritual training, help for those needing help, communication, and will help foster greater accountability. Ministers should also be involved in these cluster meetings to provide leadership in their areas of expertise.

> ## This is a coordinated effort of the church staff and the adult classes.

8. Church staffs and secretaries can help coordinate these various ministry activities in the areas of communication, publicity and promotion, and scheduling of events. All of these things can best be done through the church office.

9. Adult classes need to mold the congregation toward the overall goals and objectives. Central used the following plan:

   a. Four week positive study of the book of Philippians showed, "I can do all things through Jesus Christ." Central really needed this positive study because they had devastating financial problems and membership had declined for years.

   b. A six week study on the "Power of Prayer" while our "40 Days of Prayer" was happening in our homes.

   c. A four week series on "What's My Place?" We studied why God gave us spiritual gifts, why they are important, how they work together in a positive way with all their diversity, what is my gift, how do gifts build the church, and what motivates me to serve.

   d. A giant "Family Reunion Day" complete with meal in our adult classes followed. Many people came back home to Central on this day and were excited about what was happening. The meal within the classroom is especially good because it causes relationships to be developed with class members. It does not have to be a full-fledged meal — a brunch can be very successful.

e. After we completed our "What's My Place?" study and had our "Family Reunion Day," we gave each person a chance to get involved. We gave each person in our adult classes a form to complete during the class period if they were interested in getting involved. We had an incredible response.

> Every deacon or ministry leader needs to form a leadership team of men and women.

10. Ministry leaders and deacons have been installed and they have begun to build leadership teams in their ministries. They now contact the large number of people who have signed up in our adult classes to get involved in their ministries. This is a very important step. It is a catastrophe if we go through all of this teaching, set up a leadership plan to get people involved, sign people up in class, and then do not contact them. It is imperative that deacons and ministry leaders contact these people as soon as possible.

Each ministry needs to form a leadership team of four to six people in the small church or ten to twelve people in the larger church who are the decision-makers in this ministry. They can help the deacon contact people who have signed up for this ministry. They coordinate the activities of many others in their ministry in the same way as Visitation Captains work with visitation teams or supervisors work with Bible School Teachers.

Have you developed a purpose statement for your ministry?

11. Ministry leaders need to prepare purpose statements for their ministries which enhance the overall purposes of the local church. They need to recruit and build leadership teams. They need to formulate their programs and budgets with suggestions of how best to present their budgets. Each person on the leadership team needs a specific area of responsibility within the ministry.

12. The annual budget can either involve a lot of people or be a discouragement to many people. Ministry leaders should have ownership of their budgets and they should present them to the elders or finance ministry. There are a number of good ways to involve a large number of people in the annual budget process.

> # The budget process can either involve or discourage many people.

a. Have ministry leaders get input from everyone who works in their ministry as it is being prepared.

b. Have all adult teachers teach a four-week series on giving in all the adult classes.

c. Prepare a 15 to 20 minute slide or video presentation to be shown to the congregation.

d. Have the congregation meet in homes in groups of twenty or less to discuss the budget. Group leaders need to be trained for this, but it is important for each person to have a chance to dialogue about ministry programs and budget. This is especially easy to implement if you have Family Life Groups meeting in homes once a month on Sunday nights.

e. Have each ministry leader set up a "Ministry Fair" booth on a Sunday morning. Following services while sandwiches are served, people can ask the ministry leaders firsthand about their budgets.

13. Cards should be printed along with the budget and financial pledge cards which allow people to volunteer to serve in additional ministries.

14. Now that the internal spiritual structure has been put together, we are ready to turn outside and reach people with the Gospel of Jesus Christ. We should now have the structure set up to both reach them and retain them.

After we set up the internal spiritual structure, how can this be used to reach people with the Gospel of Jesus Christ?

15. A giant "Friend's Day" where hundreds are involved inviting neighbors and friends to Bible School and church can be very successful.

16. Special "appreciation nights" for Community Teachers and Police and Firemen can be a great success. Special events presented at Easter, Christmas and Thanksgiving can draw incredible crowds who become responsive to the gospel.

17. Saturday morning breakfasts can involve another group of people to reach the community.

18. Noon meals for visitors prepared by different Bible classes on a rotating basis are also winners for the visitors.

19. Even Family Life Groups meeting in homes can become evangelistic by showing the four-lesson video produced by Terry Rush called *High Hope for the Human Heart.*

> # New people can be the easiest of all to get involved.

20. New people can be the easiest of all to get involved. They should go through an orientation as soon as possible and be given a packet of material about the local church. Cassette tapes and video tapes can be given to new members to get important communication to them. They need to get involved in an adult Bible class and a small group. It is also helpful for every new member to go through a six-week new members class which culminates with their eating in the home of the minister and his wife. Other people will prepare the food for this special occasion. Virtually all of these people will sign up to get involved after attending the six-weeks new members class.

21. Another chapter of this book discusses numerous ways to involve the present membership on a year-around basis. We should not forget about their importance, and we should give them opportunities to get involved throughout the year. One of the best ways to do this is a program called Family Involvement Growth Services (FIGS). In this program leadership meets with a group each Sunday night to receive their input, find out their needs, listen to them, communicate, explain what we are trying to do, and give them an opportunity to get involved in additional areas.

What do you think of this step-by-step plan to involve every member?

Hundreds of congregations have followed a similar program as they strive to involve every member. Some have had dramatic results. All have achieved some measure of success. Much of the future of the church depends upon the success of the local church in involving its members to meet the needs of the local church and meet the needs of the community. May God bless you as you strive to use the spiritual gifts God has given to each member.

Servants Use Special Events to Let God Grow Churches

Special events are one of the greatest ways for God to grow churches in today's world. One church in Kentucky formulates most of its growth strategy and planning around the special event of Easter. Whatever the Easter attendance is, they make plans to have that same number present on an average basis three years later. The Southeast Christian Church in Louisville, Kentucky has been very successful with this plan and is now running over 10,000 in attendance. Likewise, I have found special events to be of major importance in regard to church growth.

Special events not only foster church growth, they offer excellent opportunities to get many people involved using their gifts. You can get many people involved in a once-a-year special event who would never get involved in a year-round ministry.

As great as special events are, let me share two statements of caution about special events.

> **Special events foster church growth and provide an excellent way to get many people involved.**

1. Do not attempt major special events until you have the personnel in your ministry system set up. As you are planning special events, you are first looking at personnel available through your present ministry system to implement the plan. You will have a meeting with them and make sure they can implement their part of the plan. You will need such people as ushers and greeters, parking lot attendants, publicity and promotion people, etc. Many people have tried to have great special events without this system in place,

Do you agree with these words of caution about special events?

153

and it is nearly impossible to implement the plan. If it is implemented, it is very easy to have "burnout" among a small number of people.

In addition to your regular ministry people, you will probably need to get many other people involved because of additional and specific job requirements for the special event. This allows many new people to get involved along with people who have a specific interest in this particular event.

2. Do not allow special events to "burn out" your people. Special events are "extra work" on each person involved. It is a special event which is not part of the regular, routine program. It is a tremendous amount of work in a short period of time. People need to be united and behind the event.

There are several special events which have been successful for both church growth and the involvement of many people. For many years, we have done an annual Community Teachers Dinner for all the public and private school teachers in the community. You can imagine what a major undertaking this is because there are thousands of teachers in the community. Permission for contacting the teachers must be obtained, invitations must be printed and given to the teachers, a program must be planned, food must be prepared and served, and plans for a warm response for a huge crowd must be made.

A Community Teachers Appreciation Dinner can be powerful.

Is it possible for you to have a community teacher appreciation dinner in your community?

We have had tremendous success with the Community Teachers Appreciation Night. It is an unbelievable amount of work which needs to be shared by many people, but it is a tremendous success with the teachers. The crowd for the special event usually numbers over 1000. It is best to have it during the month of May or during the Teachers Appreciation Week set aside by the schools. Get it on the school schedule as part of this activity. Hundreds of dollars of postage are saved if you can put the invitations in the teachers' boxes at their local schools. This takes a lot of volunteers to deliver the invitations to all the schools, but they are well received. It is a great morale booster to the teachers, and they are overwhelmed that a church is doing this for all of them. Of course, many of the teachers cannot come on the special night, but they call or write notes of "thank you." It is really a can't lose situation with them whether they get to come or not because they are overwhelmed by the invitations. Obviously, each invitation needs to have an RSVP so you can have a dinner prepared for each person.

The program includes a dinner, children's chorus, drama and skits presented by children from the church, special singing groups, a very brief message by the pulpit minister, or a guest speaker or video presentations, and a parchment thank you gift presented to each teacher. Teachers treasure these small appreciation gifts, and you see them later on walls in their homes or even in their schoolrooms. Three of the popular small gifts we gave to teachers were "The Teacher's 23rd Psalm," "Molders of Dreams" and "Three Letters from Teddy" which are shown in illustration 31.

One of the most important things for the involvement of servants is the famous checklist which we use for all special events. We invite ministry people and other volunteers to come to this special meeting, and they leave as a united volunteer army to complete their tasks. This is tremendously important. A sample checklist is included in illustration 32.

Why is the famous checklist so important?

The dinner can be a serious roadblock since it is such a mammoth undertaking. In some cases, many ladies have cooked lasagna or spaghetti for this special event. In recent years, we have had restaurants from the community wanting to provide the food free for all the teachers and their immediate family members! Members of the church pay for their meals on this special night, but all teachers eat free.

> ## Students get unbelievable results when they personally give invitations to teachers.

Sample invitations are also included (illustration 33) as they are very important. They include an announcement card describing

The Central Church of Christ
Would Like to Thank You Teachers for Being...

MOLDERS OF DREAMS

Teachers,

You are the molders of their dreams —
The "gods" who build or crush their young beliefs of
 right and wrong.
You are the spark that sets aflame the poet's hand
Or lights the flame of some great singer's song!
You are the "god" of the young, the very young.
You are the guardian of a million dreams.
Your every smile or frown can heal or pierce a heart.
Yours are a hundred lives, a thousand lives.
Yours are the pride of loving them — and the sorrow,
 too.
Your patient work, your touch make you the "gods" of
 hope
Who fill their souls with dreams, to make those dreams
 come true.
Your life is a letter — You Molder of Dreams!

Handwritten note given by President Ronald Reagan
at the White House to Guy Doud, Teacher of the Year in 1986.

CENTRAL CHURCH OF CHRIST
"...a place to call home."

The Teacher's 23rd Psalm
by Ray Fulenwider

The school is my work place;
 I have many wants.
The school gives me abundant opportunities
 To teach students with many different needs.
 This gives me great joy!
I strive to teach my students what's right,
 Even though I live in a world
 That pulls them many different directions.
I am fearful that drugs, sex, guns, alcohol,
 Low morals, politics and broken homes,
 Will destroy what I'm trying to accomplish.
I prepare my lesson plans and objectives
 In the presence of many
 Who try to discourage teachers.
But, God provides me with daily strength.
 I am overwhelmed at His power!
I pray for my students regularly by name,
 Even though I cannot say a prayer at school.
I read my Bible every day,
 Even though I cannot teach it at school.
Surely goodness and mercy will follow my students
 All the days of my life:
And they will dwell in the house of the Lord forever,
 Because the teacher is allowed to be a "living Bible,"
 For students to read at school every day.

Central Church of Christ
"A Place to Call Home"
Amarillo, Texas

Illustration 31a

THREE LETTERS FROM TEDDY

Teddy's letter came today, and now that I've read it, I will place it in my cedar chest with the other things that are important to my life. I have not seen Teddy Stallard since he was a student in my 5th grade class, fifteen years ago.

Teddy was dirty, not just occasionally, but all of the time. He had a peculiar odor about him. By the end of the first week I knew he was hopelessly behind the others.

While I did not actually ridicule the boy, my attitude was obviously quite apparent to the class, for he quickly became the class "goat." He was a little boy no one cared about, and I made no effort in his behalf.

To justify myself, I went to his cumulative folder from time to time.

FIRST GRADE: Teddy shows promise by work and attitude. But has poor home situation.

SECOND GRADE: Teddy could do better. Mother terminally ill.

THIRD GRADE: Helpful, but too serious. Slow learner. Mother passed away end of the year.

FOURTH GRADE: Very slow, but well behaved. Father shows no interest.

Well, they passed him four times, but he will certainly repeat fifth grade! Do him good! I said to myself.

And then the last day before the holiday arrived. Teachers always get several gifts at Christmas. There was not a student who had not brought me one.

Teddy's wrapping was a brown paper bag, and he had colored Christmas trees and red balls over it. It was stuck together with masking tape.

The class was completely silent, and for the first time I felt embarrassed because they all stood watching me unwrap his gift. As I removed the last bit of masking tape, two items fell to my desk: a gaudy rhinestone bracelet with several stones missing and a small bottle of dime store cologne — half empty.

I could hear the snickers and whispers, and I wasn't sure I could look at Teddy. "Isn't this lovely?" I asked, placing the bracelet on my wrist for all of them to admire. There were a few hesitant ohs and ahs, but as I dabbed the cologne behind my ears, the little girls reluctantly lined up for a dab behind their ears.

When all of the students had left, Teddy walked toward me. "You smell just like Mom," he said softly. "Her bracelet looks real pretty on you, too. I'm glad you liked it."

He left quickly. I locked the door, sat down at my desk, and wept, resolving to make up to Teddy what I had deliberately deprived him of — a teacher who cared. I stayed every afternoon with Teddy from the end of the Christmas holidays until the last day of school.

Slowly, but surely, he caught up with the rest of the class. In fact, his averages were among the highest in the class. Although I knew he would be moving out of state when school was out, I was not worried for him.

I did not hear from Teddy until seven years later, when the first letter appeared in my mailbox.

Dear Miss Thompson,

I just wanted you to be the first to know I will be graduating second in my class next month.

Four years later, Teddy's second letter came.

Dear Miss Thompson,

I wanted you to be the first to know. I was just informed that I'll be graduating first in my class. The university has not been easy, but I liked it.

And now — today — Teddy's third letter.

Dear Miss Thompson,

I wanted you to be the first to know. As of today I am Theodore J. Stallard, M.D. How about that??!! I'm going to be married in July, the 27th to be exact. I wanted to ask if you could come and sit where Mom would sit if she were here. I'll have no family there, as Dad died last year.

I quickly wrote a letter of reply to Ted.

Dear Ted,

Congratulations! You made it, and you did it yourself! In spite of those like me and not because of us, this day has come for you.

God bless you. I'll be at the wedding with bells on.

CENTRAL CHURCH OF CHRIST
". . . a place to call home."

Illustration 31b

COMMUNITY TEACHERS' APPRECIATION DINNER (CHECKLIST)

Invitations

A. Printed

B. Inserted into envelopes

C. Note from Superintendent's office giving permission to take invitations to schools for the school offices.

D. Meet with volunteers delivering invitations after evening service April 23.

E. Invitations delivered to schools April 24-26.

F. Invitations from children taken to children's classes on April 30 and May 7 for the children to personally deliver to their teachers.

Meal

A. Individual to contact caterer.

B. Individual to oversee physical arrangements, example — number of serving tables (food tables & dessert tables), where they need to be placed, etc.

C. Volunteers to serve tea, coffee, etc. during meal.

D. Individual to be in charge of desserts. Responsibilities are as follows:

1. Sign up in Bible classes for desserts — April 30 and May 7

   a. Take sign-up sheets to Bible classes.

   b. Pick up or have sheets returned to the office.

   c. Desserts to be at church building by 4:00 Wed., May 10

2. Contact volunteers to cut and serve desserts.

3. See that left over desserts are taken home or placed in the refrigerator.

E. Decorations

F. Ticket sellers — Tickets available April 30 and May 7 at all Information Booths before and after services.

G. Ticket takers — People to take tickets and hand out plates.

H. Men to assist in removal of walls and setting up tables.

I. People to clean up (remove trash from tables, wipe down tables and clean kitchen).

J. Men to assist in putting walls back in place and removing tables.

Program

Illustration 32

Community Teachers' Appreciation Night
Wednesday, May 10

What: Special night honoring area public and private school teachers.
Come for all or part of the evening's activities.

Meal: A free meal will be served for you and your family in the
Family Fellowship Center from 6:30 pm to 7:15 pm.

Program: A musical appreciation program for you begins at 7:15 pm.

Where: Central Church of Christ
1401 S. Monroe
Amarillo, Texas 79101

Phone: 373-4389

Why: We want to thank you for teaching our children.
Appreciation parchments will be given to all teachers.

Central Church of Christ
"...the year of the family."

Dear Teacher,

Thank you for teaching me this year. We are having a special Community Teachers' Appreciation night to honor you on Wednesday, May 10. We will be providing a free meal for you and your family from 6:30–7:15 p.m. in the Family Fellowship Center. Then, we'll share a brief musical appreciation program with you.

With appreciation,

Your Student

P.S. I'll be looking for you at the meal.

Central Church of Christ
"...the year of the family."
1401 S. Monroe
373-4389

Yes ☐ I will be attending the Community Teachers' Appreciation Night on May 10.

Number Attending Dinner: _____

No ☐ I will not be able to attend the Community Teachers' Appreciation Night.

Teacher: _____

School: _____

We would appreciate your reply no later than May 8. Please complete and return this card, or you may call the church office, 373-4389.

Illustration 33

159

the event, an invitation card and a return reply card with the return address of the church preprinted on the reverse side.

Adults deliver the invitations to the schools to be placed in teachers' boxes, but there is an incredible second invitation which gets phenomenal results. The second set of invitations given out are for the children at church to give to their teachers at school. They tell them how much they appreciate having them for a teacher, give them the invitation in person, and tell them they will meet them at the appreciation dinner to sit with them. This gets unbelievable results and really touches the hearts of the teachers. When the big night arrives, there is a great appreciation night of celebration, and you usually receive excellent television and newspaper coverage.

Teachers are highly visible people in the community. They are also the molders of the community of the future. They really appreciate this special night and are very responsive. Central has done this for five consecutive years and the number of teachers in our membership has grown from 12 to over 100!

> ## Special events get free television and newspaper coverage.

How is the Police and Firefighters Appreciation night different from the Teachers Appreciation Night?

Another successful special event is the Police and Firefighters Appreciation Night. This reaches a totally different crowd who also need a "strong dose" of appreciation. They put their lives on the line for us. We follow much the same format for this as we do for the teachers. Some of the major differences are:

1. We usually have this one on Sunday night and we have the teachers appreciation activities on Wednesday night.
2. We deliver the invitations to the fire stations and police stations.
3. We meet in the auditorium instead of the fellowship area.
4. We like to have a Christian police officer and firefighter do the speaking. There are also some good videos available for this.
5. Our teenagers take food to the police officers and fire-

fighters who are on duty and cannot attend. This makes a tremendous impression on this group. Everyone else eats at the church building.

6. We give them special parchment gifts such as "Fire-fighter's Prayer," "An Officer's Prayer," or "A Police Officer's Prayer." These are included in illustration 34.

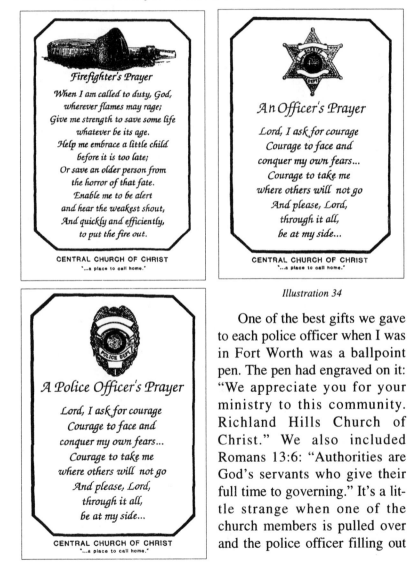

Firefighter's Prayer

When I am called to duty, God,
wherever flames may rage;
Give me strength to save some life
whatever be its age.
Help me embrace a little child
before it is too late;
Or save an older person from
the horror of that fate.
Enable me to be alert
and hear the weakest shout,
And quickly and efficiently,
to put the fire out.

CENTRAL CHURCH OF CHRIST
"...a place to call home."

An Officer's Prayer

Lord, I ask for courage
Courage to face and
conquer my own fears...
Courage to take me
where others will not go
And please, Lord,
through it all,
be at my side...

CENTRAL CHURCH OF CHRIST
"...a place to call home."

Illustration 34

A Police Officer's Prayer

Lord, I ask for courage
Courage to face and
conquer my own fears...
Courage to take me
where others will not go
And please, Lord,
through it all,
be at my side...

CENTRAL CHURCH OF CHRIST
"...a place to call home."

One of the best gifts we gave to each police officer when I was in Fort Worth was a ballpoint pen. The pen had engraved on it: "We appreciate you for your ministry to this community. Richland Hills Church of Christ." We also included Romans 13:6: "Authorities are God's servants who give their full time to governing." It's a little strange when one of the church members is pulled over and the police officer filling out

161

POLICE AND FIREFIGHTERS APPRECIATION NIGHT FEB. 28 (6:00-8:00 p.m.)

CHECKLIST

1. Invitations to police officers, firefighters, sheriff's department — Huddles & Firefighters & Police.

2. Stuff envelopes - Sunshiner Volunteers

3. Prayer support - Steve Cearley

4. Meal - Dale Wesley

5. Special event - John Butterfield

6. Film "Barrett" and sound - A.F. Pyeatt

7. Prayer Parchments - Pat and Sunshiner Volunteers

8. Parking & Traffic - Doug Hershey and Steve Wood

9. Newspaper & Radio - Benny Dement and Dick Marcear

10. Follow-up - Alex Fairly

Illustration 35

POLICE AND FIREFIGHTER APPRECIATION NIGHT

Sunday, February 28

WHAT: Special night honoring area Police and Firemen. Come for all or part of the evening's activities.

MEAL: A free meal will be served for you and your family in the Family Fellowship Center from 7:00-8:00 p.m.

PROGRAM: Inspirational film entitled "Barrett" will be shown. This film depicts the work and influence for good of a public servant.

WHERE: Central Church of Christ
1401 S. Monroe
Amarillo, Texas 79101

PHONE: 373-4389

WHY: We want to thank you for serving our community. Appreciation parchments of "A Firefighter's Prayer" and "A Police Officer's Prayer" will be given to all public servants.

- -

CENTRAL CHURCH OF CHRIST

...a place to call home.

I will be attending the Police and Firefighters Appreciation Night on Feb. 28.

Number Attending Dinner: _____

I will not be able to attend the Police and Firefighters Appreciation Night.

_____

NAME: _____

We would appreciate your reply no later than Feb. 25.
Please complete and return this card, or you may call the church office: 373-4389.

the ticket is using the ballpoint pen we gave him, but all of this really seemed to help the community as well as the church.

Included in illustration 35 are the invitation sheet and checklist to help you with your implementation.

> # The Funavil is an excellent Christian alternative to Halloween.

The Funavil is a great way to involve a different group and touch the lives of many children in the community. The Funavil is a Christian alternative to Halloween. It is conducted on the Sunday night which is closest to Halloween. It is tremendously successful for getting community children to attend. We had over 2000 attend in Fort Worth and up to 700 attend in Amarillo. It is a good project to involve young couples, youth, children and singles. Booths and games are set up for the children to enjoy from 6:00 to 7:30 p.m. on Sunday night. We have it concurrent with our Sunday night service with something special being presented to adults. Booths and games include such things as candy walk, black light chalk area, balloon decorating, beanbag toss, ring toss, dart throw, kiss the pig contest by the ministers, candy count, fishing for treasure, face painting, treasure chest, shoot out, football throw, big bouncer, cookie decorating, pumpkin painting, movie, basketball shooting, wishing well, golf, bowling, penny count, and sponge throw. It is usually easy to get people in the adult classes to furnish cookies and refreshments for the night's activities. A hospitality booth needs to be set up complete with brochures and information about the church and its programs. A brief devotional with some spirited singing can also be a winner. A rather scary room can be set up for the children to walk through that portrays a story in the Bible. An example might be Jonah in the belly of the whale or Jesus stilling the waters when the storm came up.

Walk through the Bible Seminars headquartered out of Atlanta, Georgia, can be a beneficial special event. We like to do this on three consecutive Sunday nights. The program is arranged so that

Is the Funavil idea a possibility for your congregation?

you learn the Old Testament in six hours! Classes can be designed for adults, youth, children and preschool. We had something like 900 attend on three Sunday nights with many community visitors. We also had a small alternative class in the chapel for those members who did not want to attend. Giving people an option is so important in today's world. The *Walk through the Bible* Seminar is a fun way to learn the Bible for all ages. A sample checklist is included in illustration 36 to show how to involve people.

> ## Giving people an option is so important in today's world.

Retirement Sunday can be a beneficial special event as you recognize each person who retired during the year. The church gives them a Retirement Appreciation Parchment with lists of church ministries in which they can now get involved. This can be a great day for retired people and give them new purpose in life as they now realize how significant their contribution can be to the church.

Would these special events be successful in your congregation?

We like to make major community presentations during our second service on Easter Sunday, Thanksgiving and mid-December. You can attract hundreds or even thousands of visitors using these three special events. We always have the traditional first service for those who want to attend it, and the outreach service at 11:00 a.m. We have had as many as 2000 for the second service alone on Easter Sunday. The service features special singing groups, our adult chorus, drama, video, slides and a brief message. Our Thanksgiving and December programs follow a similar format except they are tied to the theme the world is thinking about at that time of year. Our latest December program was a drama and musical version of the book entitled *The Little Crippled Lamb* written by Max Lucado. Carlie Burdette took the book and arranged an unbelievable musical presentation. The December program also includes much involvement by our Children's Chorus.

Family Reunion Day or Friend's Day is another great special event. I like to either have it on the time change Sunday in the fall

WALK THROUGH THE BIBLE '96

Seminar Director	Fred Rutherford
Attendance/Building	Frank Stepp & Leon Wood
Central	Kelly Utsinger, Jim Hollifield, Olen Wilson
Other Churches of Christ	Everett Blanton, Dick Marcear, Ray Fulenwider
Other Churches/Promise Keepers	Steve Trafton, Rusty & Cathy Burns, Everett Blanton, Wib Newton
Community	David Kilpatrick, Steve Wood, Jake Holster, Paula Bliss, Ben & Gail Powell, Emmett Poynor, Lisa Hancock
Publicity/Media	April Johansson, Benny Dement
Youth	Kyle Meador
Finance	Brian Toldan
Registration/Name Tags	Brice Kelley, Pat Dye
Prayer	James Vaughan
Support Services	Steve Wood/John Noyes
Facilities	Al Blount
Sound & Video	Don Case and Andy Tonne
Food/Refreshments	Celia Tidmore
Childcare	John Richardson
Children/Preschool	Becky Kelley, Harold Knight
Chapel Service	Jim Carver
Usher	George Terry, Jake Holster
Ministry Products	Dale Scott

Illustration 36

when people get an extra hour of sleep or not follow the government's time schedule in the spring so people can get an extra hour of sleep. This seems strange after all these years, but it will usually make a great difference in your attendance. People still resent losing that hour of sleep in the spring, and they will really rally around a program where you keep them on the old schedule where they get the extra rest and change your watches as the services conclude on Sunday morning. The 10-Step Plan for Family Reunion Day is included in illustration 37. I have also included "A PLACE TO CALL HOME" sheets which were completed by adults and children before Family Reunion Day. Hundreds of these personally completed sheets were taped to halls throughout the building. Visitors were tremendously impressed by these sheets and deeply interested in reading why hundreds of members thought Central was a place to call home.

Will the 10-Step plan for Family Reunion Day work in your congregation?

> ## People love an extra hour of sleep on time-change Sunday.

Don't fail to take advantage of Mother's Day and Father's Day. We always give some small item to the mothers and fathers on their respective days. One of the best things Dick Marcear ever did on Mother's Day was to take time right in the middle of the sermon to call his bedfast mother on a mobile phone to tell her how much he loved her. There was not a dry eye in the auditorium. Some of the materials we have had the children hand out to their mothers and fathers are included in illustration 38. It is a big winner to let the children do it. The little card was especially a winner with our fathers.

Other special days include Volunteer Appreciation Sunday, Parent's Day, Baby Dedication Sunday where all parents are encouraged to dedicate their children to God and work with the church to raise that precious child to become what God wants them to become. We also have Senior Sunday for our graduating seniors.

A new, very successful program is "The Blessing" for all of

CLASS INSTRUCTION FOR
FAMILY REUNION DAY

October 26

1. Personally contact every member on your class roll to encourage them to be present October 26.

2. Postcards are available for you to mail personally to your friends, family members and church members to encourage them to be present for our family reunion.

3. Encourage members to complete forms that state: "Central Church of Christ is a place to call home: because. . . (Complete in 25 words or less and place in boxes in foyer or at entrance by Fireplace Room.)

4. Check "Count on Me" on the attendance registration form if you are planning to come to the reunion. Encourage class members to make this commitment.

5. Class to provide a brunch (donuts, juice, etc.) in your class-room on Oct. 26 from 9:45 - 10:45 a.m. This is a great time for you to have fellowship with those who are visitors and people you have encouraged to come back to class. Auditorium class will meet for brunch with another adult class.

6. We will have regular Bible class from 9:45 - 10:45 including brunch and fellowship time. All adults and children will meet in their regular classes. Refreshments will also be served in our children's classes.

7. Worship service will be from 8:30 - 9:30 a.m. and 11:00 - 12:00 noon. Sermon will be on "A Place to Call Home" and theme will be shared with the congregation. New theme song will also be shared with the congregation.

8. Success of the Family Reunion Day depends upon every member of this spiritual family doing all we can.

9. Goal is 1800 souls for God's glory on Oct. 26.

10. Pray daily for a great Family Reunion.

"A PLACE TO CALL HOME"

(Complete in 25 words or less and place in boxes in foyer or at entrance by Fireplace Room.)

"Central Church of Christ is a place to call home" because. . .

_____

_____

_____

_____

_____

_____

"A PLACE TO CALL HOME"

(Complete in 25 words or less and place in boxes in foyer or at entrance by Fireplace Room.)

"Central Church of Christ is a place to call home" because. . .

_____

_____

_____

_____

_____

_____

Illustration 37

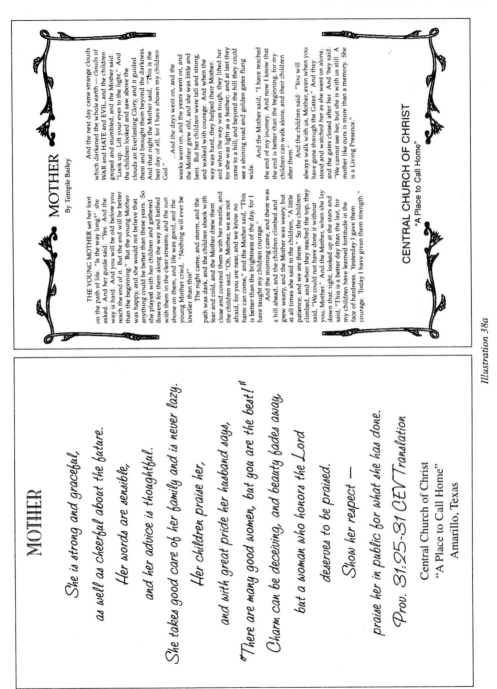

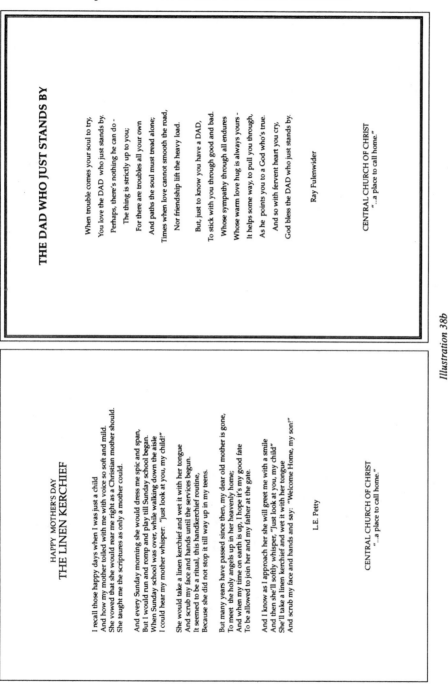

THE DAD WHO JUST STANDS BY

When trouble comes your soul to try,
You love the DAD who just stands by.
Perhaps, there's nothing he can do -
 The thing is strictly up to you;
 For there are troubles all your own
 And paths the soul must tread alone;
Times when love cannot smooth the road,
Nor friendship lift the heavy load.

But, just to know you have a DAD,
To stick with you through good and bad.
Whose sympathy through all endures
Whose warm love hug is always yours -
It helps some way, to pull you through,
As he points you to a God who's true.
And so with fervent heart you cry,
God bless the DAD who just stands by.

Ray Fulenwider

CENTRAL CHURCH OF CHRIST
"...a place to call home."

HAPPY MOTHER'S DAY
THE LINEN KERCHIEF

I recall those happy days when I was just a child
And how my mother toiled with me with voice so soft and mild.
She vowed that she would rear me right as a Christian mother should.
She taught me the the scriptures as only a mother could.

And every Sunday morning she would dress me spic and span,
But I would run and romp and play till Sunday school began.
When Sunday school was over, while walking down the aisle
I could hear my mother whisper: "Just look at you, my child!"

She would take a linen kerchief and wet it with her tongue
And scrub my face and hands until the services begun.
It seemed to be a ritual, this handkerchief routine,
Because she did not stop it till way up in my teens.

But many years have passed since then, my dear old mother is gone,
To meet the holy angels up in her heavenly home;
And when my time on earth is up, I hope it's my good fate
To be allowed to join her and my father at the gate.

And I know as I approach her she will greet me with a smile
And then she'll softly whisper, "Just look at you, my child"
She'll take a linen kerchief and wet it with her tongue
And scrub my face and hands and say: "Welcome Home, my son!"

L.E. Petty

CENTRAL CHURCH OF CHRIST
"...a place to call home."

Illustration 38b

Both of these had had artwork on them in the form handed out: a border ornamentation on the one for mothers (see also the previous page) and a screened background picture of a father on the poem for dads.

"Father's Day" June 20, 1993

"Fathers, do not exasperate your children; instead, bring them up in the training and the instruction of the Lord." (Eph. 6:4)

Central Church of Christ
"A Place to Call Home"

"Some fathers exasperate their children by being overly strict and controlling. They need to remember that rearing children is like holding a WET BAR OF SOAP — too firm a grasp and it shoots from your hand, too loose a grip and it slides away. A gentle but firm hold keeps you in control."
(*Disciplines of a Godly Man*)

Business size card (front and back) handed out by kids to their dads.

Illustration 38c

Fathers Are Wonderful People

Fathers are wonderful people
too little understood,
And we do not sing their praises
as often as we should. . .
For, somehow, Father seems to be
the man who pays the bills,
While Mother binds up little hurts
and nurses all our ills. . .
And Father struggles daily
to live up to "his image"
As protector and provider
and "hero of the scrimmage". . .
And perhaps that is the reason
we sometimes get the notion
That Fathers are not subject
to the thing we call emotion,
But if you look inside Dad's heart,
where no one else can see,
You'll find he's sentimental
and as "soft" as he can be. . .
But he's so busy every day
in the grueling race of life,
He leaves the sentimental stuff
to his partner and his wife. . .
But Fathers are just wonderful
in a million different ways,
And they merit loving compliments
and accolades of praise,
For the only reason Dad aspires
to fortune and success
Is to make the family proud of him
and to bring them happiness. . .
And like our Heavenly Father,
he's a guardian and a guide,
Someone that we can count on
to be always on our side.

author Helen Steiner Rice

Hendersonville Church of Christ
". . .a place to call home."

THE PARENTS' FAITH

WE believe — our children are a gift of God — the hope of tomorrow.

WE believe — that immeasurable possibilities lie slumbering in each son and daughter.

WE believe — that God has planned for their future, and that His love shall always surround them; and so

WE believe — that they shall grow up! — first crawling, then toddling, then standing, stretching skyward for a decade and a half — until they reach full stature — a man and a woman!

WE believe — that they can and will be molded and shaped between infancy and adulthood — as a tree is shaped by the gardener, and the clay vessel in the potter's hand, or the shoreline of the sea under the watery hand of the mighty waves; by home and church; by school and street, through sights and sounds and the touch of our hands on their hands and Christ's Spirit on their hearts! So,

WE believe — that they shall mature as only people can — through laughter and tears, through trial and error, by reward and punishment, through affection and discipline, until they stretch their wings and leave their nest to fly!

O, GOD — we believe in our children. Help us so to live that they may always believe in us — and so in Thee.

Edited and adapted from "Power Ideas
for a Happy Family" by Robert Schuller

Illustration 38d

> **"The Blessing" for incoming sixth graders to the youth program is a powerful way to change lives.**

our fifth graders as they are about to enter the youth program and become sixth graders. This group is given Bibles to be used in the youth program for the next seven years, challenged from the pulpit, and encouraged by the youth minister as they are leaving childhood to ascend to another spiritual level. All of the present youth group come forward at the close of the service, lay hands on them during the prayer, hug them, tell them how much they love them and how much they are needed. It is a tremendous spiritual, emotional climax to the service. The congregation has been encouraged to write hundreds of personal letters to these fifth graders. At the conclusion of the service, there is a special meal for the fifth graders and their parents. Here they sit at a table with their parents, read the congregational letters, and parents share their own letters and words of blessing to their child. It is an exciting event.

What do you think about "The Blessing"?

The most incredible special event was the "Fifty Day Spiritual Walk" which we had at Central in 1996. This material and program was motivated and inspired by the "Fifty Day Spiritual Adventure" seminars out of Wheaton, Illinois under the direction of David Mace. Please attend one of these seminars if at all possible as it will greatly bless you and your church.

We did our "50 Day Spiritual Walk" somewhat differently because we wanted a program to install new elders, reaffirm existing elders, and reinforce the theme of "Journey to the Heart of God." One of our members had paid several thousand dollars to purchase forty large colored pictures on poster board. These pictures were scattered throughout the building and designed to show us what a "Journey to the Heart of God" is. These pictures are beautiful and highly inspiring. These four foot pictures are an immediate conversation piece for nearly every visitor.

Let me share with you the results before we proceed any further. We had an immediate increase of 150 a Sunday in attendance, $3,000 a week in contributions and averaged a dozen responses at second service alone! These statistics all held for the full six weeks of the program. Let's look at some of the reasons for the success of the "50 Day Spiritual Walk":

1. Dick Marcear and I attended the "50 Day Spiritual Adventure" workshop in Tulsa, Oklahoma. This stimulated many new ideas.

2. We put together a plan on the long ride back from Tulsa.

3. We had a season of prayer to begin our next elders meeting. We talked about the need for additional elders, the need for reaffirmation, and a plan for doing all of this. Together, we reshaped a plan which would work.

4. The theme was "What Do You Do When You Don't Know What to Do?" There are eight biblical answers to this question. We pointed out to our present elders that each one of them was a living personal example of each one of the answers. The meeting with the elders was both scary and spiritually moving. We asked the elders if they would be willing to give their testimony both services on Sunday morning on the topic that specifically fitted them. After sobering prayer and discussion, they agreed to do this. What an incredible job they did! The response from the congregation was overwhelming! Sometimes there was an unbelievable shattering of applause of appreciation. They shared incredible ways they had coped when they did not know what to do. One had experienced the death of his only daughter, another had a daughter go through a divorce and she had a large number of children, another had his father die when he was a teenager, another had adopted and raised a family member after a tragic accident and another had just learned he had cancer. It was not easy to share these testimonies, but the congregation was touched and inspired to new heights.

> Testimonies by the leadership concerning how they cope in troubled times are powerful.

5. I wrote a devotional and prayer guide for each member to follow on a daily basis. We gave out nearly 5,000 of these! Each

Why was the "50 Day Spiritual Walk" successful?

day people would look at a biblical answer to the problem, read a Scripture which related to this, look at the heart of the teaching from *The Message*, list their prayer requests, keep up with prayers answered, share what brought them joy each day in the Joy Jogger space, and meditate on a statement in our "Faith Walk" called "Faith is. . ."

> ## People could not wait to do something that would bring joy to someone else.

Sundays were extra special days for people because there was an additional question which asked: What did you do that brought joy to someone else today? You talk about, encourage and admonish each other on the Lord's Day; people could not wait to get to church to do something that would bring joy to someone else. They also were built up as other people did things which brought them joy. People meditated upon and filled out these devotional guides for fifty days.

Do you think this is a good plan for the reaffirmation of elders?

6. There was an elder nomination plan on the front of the devotional books which kept this before the congregation.

7. Dick brought brief but highly inspiring messages each week. The people were prepared for the message because they had been studying the material in their daily devotional guides.

8. The elders gave their testimony each Sunday on their special topic. There was an incredible spirit of great expectations for each service because of the way people were being brought closer to God.

9. Hundreds of nominations were turned in to be considered for elders and three great spiritual servants were selected.

10. Pictures of the present elders were placed on a sheet, and people were asked to affirm or reject each one of them. Over 1,000 of these forms were turned in. They were not signed as we did not want anyone to be intimidated by this. The elders received a 98% reaffirmation! That is the highest one I have seen in recent times. The talk shows, press, radio and television along with some legiti-

mate scandals have caused a distrust of leadership like never before. The newest Gallup Poll lists the clergy as the group most trusted in the United States today, but it is only around 65%! One-third of the people do not trust the preachers and every other occupation is below this. The entire "50 Day Spiritual Walk" was quite a testimony by the Central Congregation to their love and appreciation for their servant shepherds!

The complete booklet of the "50 Day Spiritual Walk" is in Appendix I for your use.

> The clergy are the most trusted group
> in the U.S. today, and
> one-third of the people do not trust them!

10 The Servant's Spiritual Life and Worship

How important is prayer and Bible study for servant leaders?

Few things are as important to the servant leader as his spiritual life and worship. He knows that Satan will do everything he can to inhibit his spiritual life. Once Satan does this, he reduces a servant leader from a spiritual giant to a spiritual dwarf. I recommend that every servant leader keep a copy of the old classic book named *Spiritual Leadership* by Oswald Sanders. It is a tremendous book and should be read weekly by spiritual leaders. Don't let Satan destroy your prayer life. Keep a prayer journal, pray for his people and other prayer requests, and marvel at the power of prayer and how God answers prayer. Spend much time on your knees pouring your heart out to God.

Don't let Satan rob you of your Bible study time. He is afraid of that powerful book and knows what it will do to a servant leader. Take time for your "manna in the morning" quiet time or your "quail in the evening" quiet time. Remember to spend quality spiritual time with your family. Model the Christian life before them and train them to walk down God's path. Remember to feed the entire flock as shepherds and minister to their needs. This is also your "spiritual service." Be a mentor and train future spiritual leaders for the congregation.

Nothing challenges a servant leader in today's church any more than his worship and the worship services which leaders have in the local church. Worship is the most difficult area to change. It has been compared to a play. For every speaker on stage, there is a critic in the audience who disagrees with any changes made in worship! It deals with the following areas which can become very controversial if much change takes place:

1. Singing.
2. Preaching.
3. Reading of Scripture.

    4. Prayers.
    5. People's responses and "amens."
    6. Exhortation and encouragement.
    7. Announcements and assembly programs.
    8. Giving.
    9. Lord's Supper.
   10. Baptisms.

A thick book could be written just about tradition, controversy, what different people think and what the Bible specifically teaches and doesn't teach in these ten areas. This will stretch leaders to the full length of their patience.

This chapter is so important and can be so controversial, I've decided to use my WORSHIP acrostic lesson to teach seven vital lessons about worship.

W orthy
O utsiders
R esponses
S inging
H allelujah
I nsiders
P lanned

I hope servant leaders will remember this acrostic to deal with some of their major problems in the local church.

> ## Worship means demonstrating
> ## what God is worth to me.

WORTHY (John 21:15-18)

The basic biblical meaning of worship is: What is God worth to me? Do I honor, love and adore him with all of my heart, soul, mind, body and strength? Is he Lord of my life seven days a week and twenty-four hours a day? We come to church with great joy and anticipation to proclaim as they did in the book of Revelation: WORTHY IS THE LAMB WHO WAS SLAIN FOR ME! This sets the tone for everything we do on Sunday morning. Is he worth my all? I show in my praise and service to him how much I feel he is worth!

OUTSIDERS (1 Corinthians 14:24-25)

Many people used to say that worship was just to be designed for church members. But Paul in 1 Corinthians 14 talks about the value of worship services for nonbelievers. All of the new church growth paradigms stress the tremendous desire of today's younger generation to focus services also for the benefit of non-Christians. That is a dramatic change for most churches and can really stretch us.

We have two different types of worship services on Sunday morning at Central. The early 8:30 a.m. service is a traditional service for members. They, especially the older members, like to get up early on Sunday morning and attend a traditional service.

But the 11:00 a.m. service is a contemporary service and the vast majority of our nonmembers attend this service. Nonmembers are more prone to sleep in late on Sunday morning and come to a later service. They may not get up in time to go to Bible school so an 11:00 a.m. Children's Bible Hour for their children is essential. Most of them like a very spirited song service with hand clapping and even raising of hands by some each time a song is directed toward God. They like the newer upbeat songs. We have six men and women who sing with microphones which gives us an incredible song service with congregational singing. We found as much Scripture for six song leaders as we did for one song leader in the New Testament.

> ### We found as much Scripture for six song leaders as we did for one.

We have much more singing in the second service because outsiders love spirited singing. Many times they like to just listen and not participate. Therefore, solos and special singing groups really touch their lives.

How can we have a service where non-members will fall down, worship God, and exclaim, "God is really among you"?

178

The sermon second service is much shorter. It is the same sermon outline handed out for the first service, but the sermon in second service is around ten minutes while the sermon in first service is around 25 or 30 minutes. Many church members like an expository-type, detailed message with a lot of Scripture. Most nonmembers are more easily reached with real life stories or parables such as the ones Jesus taught.

Nonmembers are not usually very interested in long prayers or the Lord's Supper because it shuts them out. When I was in Lubbock at the Broadway Church of Christ, we televised our Sunday morning service. We found out that our audience consistently dropped by 50% during one part of the service — when we served the Lord's Supper!

What are nonmembers looking for in a worship assembly?

Nonmembers love friendliness and warmth.

Nonmembers love friendliness and warmth. At first, they are spiritual, but not too spiritual! They do not like for services to last for over an hour, they do not want to be separated from their children too long, and they want a quality program for their children. They usually do not come back on Sunday night to a traditional service, but they may come back on Wednesday nights for special classes in marital communication, parenting, spiritual weight loss, divorce recovery, grief recovery, etc.

Churches will not have much growth if they do not have seeker sensitive services where the outsider feels welcome. Many churches are having great success reaching the nonmember with seeker sensitive services on Saturday night. They are filled with very visual and colorful material for the adults, and their children are very important. They also respond to video presentations and overhead projections. They are not interested in songbooks, but they like to visually focus on a big screen where all the songs and everything else are projected. These outsiders are a little impatient and selfish. They like abundant parking nearby, a quality facility and a quality nursery program. They do not like things done in a boring, halfway manner.

179

We had a third service at Fort Worth that was especially designed for nonmember singles. We had tremendous success with this service and grew to over 900 singles!

> # Worship is a time for people to respond to the power of God and the word of God.

RESPONSES (Matthew 11:28-29; James 5:16)

Worship is a time for people to respond to the power of God and the word of God. Look deeply into the eyes of the people and see how they are responding. The nonmember especially shows his appreciation for different things by clapping while a few of the members are more prone to say "amen." People should be responding at the invitation. It has bothered me at times when we have few responses in many Restoration churches. The Bible tells us to "Confess our faults to one another and pray for one another!" We have trouble doing this. We can learn a lesson from the 5th Ward black church in Houston. About 1500 attend this church. I was preaching there one Sunday morning and around 30 people responded at the invitation. Now, it certainly wasn't because of my preaching. They have around 30 responses every service! The elders hand the people a microphone when they come forward to confess their sin. I will never forget one beautiful girl around 30 years of age who came forward. She spoke into the microphone and said, "I want to request the prayers of the church because I have been having an affair with another man." Then she pointed to a man in the audience and said, "I have been having an affair with that man right there and he ought to also come forward and confess sin." And he did!

There are several ways we can encourage responses. We can teach a strong grace message about God's love and forgiveness. We can have people respond by filling out a card in the audience and not come forward. About half of our responses at Central are this way and we follow up on these responses. You can have elders go to a room outside of the auditorium where people can respond. One

How can we best encourage people to respond?

180

of the most successful things we have done is for husband and wife teams along with counselors to receive responses. We sing three invitation songs in an informal way. People come forward and the husband and wife teams pray for them up front, and then they return to their seats. We do not keep any records of these informal responses, but they are very, very successful. As you have probably already gathered, we use the husband and wife teams at the second service and not at the first service. However, the actual fact is that very little is said about invitations in the Bible and there is no mention of an invitation song anywhere!

> There is no mention of an invitation song anywhere in the Bible.

SINGING (Ephesians 5:19)

Send me a tape of your song service, and I will tell who you will attract to your worship services and what your chances for growth are. In today's world it is the single greatest attraction to the visitor after he enters the auditorium and sits down. A recent survey in Dallas, Texas of our musical listening habits teach us a lot. The Middle School students primarily listened to Rock, the Senior High to Classic Rock, the 18-24 age group to Classic Rock, the 25-34 to Contemporary Christian, the 35-44 to Contemporary, the 45-54 to Contemporary, the 55-64 to AM news, and the 65 and up to AM news. Not one person under the age of 18 listed a single AM station as one of the three choices. Over half of the 55-64 group listed an AM station as their first choice, and 69% of the over-65 group listed an AM station as their first choice. Most of those over the age of 65 primarily listened to one station while those under the age of 35 listened to half a dozen different stations.

The people in the survey listened to 28 different stations. Christian and country had a strong showing. The survey showed how strongly today's younger generation is drawn to music compared to older generations. Our younger people have a tremendous hunger for music and many especially like contemporary Christian music. Music takes a back seat to news and information stations with most of the older generation.

> Send me a tape of your song service, and I will tell you what your chances for growth are.

No wonder we have so much disagreement with the song service. The survey points out we need different strokes for different folks. Many people think the older songs we sing out of our songbooks are a mandate from God as the only ones we can sing. The ironic thing is that the controversy over today's religious songs is usually not over the words. Most of the new songs are more biblical than the older songs. Many of the words to the new songs are straight out of the Bible and repeated over and over. The controversy is over the rhythm or tunes. The strange thing about this is that many of the popular tunes of the old songs came straight out of tunes sung in the bars hundreds of years ago! They were the modern popular songs of that age! The great song leader John Newton (1725-1807) thought it wise to put the gospel message in simple language and sing it to tunes more like the "pop songs" people were singing on the streets and in the pubs! His most famous song in this category was "Amazing Grace"! Some of the old-timers severely criticized John Newton and others for writing these modern songs! Today, they are old classics. I wonder if we can learn great lessons from the past today.

How will your congregation respond to this paragraph?

There are no tunes in the Bible for us to follow. There are some great words where we can teach and encourage one another as well as praise God with psalms, hymns and spiritual songs. Most of us would probably be aghast if we primarily sang chants as many in the early church did, because we certainly do not like rap. We would also have trouble teaching one another with singing groups as the early church did with antiphonal singing. One group would sing, "What can wash away my sins?" and the other group would respond by singing back, "Nothing but the blood of Jesus!" May God help us develop a level of spiritual maturity where we

182

can design worship services to bring ALL PEOPLE INTO A CLOSER RELATIONSHIP WITH GOD BY USING BEAUTIFUL SPIRITUAL SONGS IN A DYNAMIC WAY.

> We need different strokes for different folks.

HALLELUJAH (Psalm 122:1; 1 Corinthians 14:15-16)

Our worship services need to be celebrative hallelujah times together. Our God is not dead, he is alive! People hear so much negative news in today's world, they need to come to one place where they hear "good news" in an exciting and celebrative way. These times together should touch our hearts and our minds. There is nothing wrong with expressing strong feelings and emotions. If people want to say "amen" or clap, that's fine. If they do not want to, that's also fine. We need not forsake the assembling of ourselves together, but look forward to a service where we can praise God and encourage one another. Drama can be a very useful tool to make a point or teach a lesson. The *Dramatized Bible* can be very useful for several people reading the Scriptures.

INSIDERS (Romans 15:1; Matthew 20:26)

Insiders or present members need to have services which meet their needs and lead them to a closer relationship with God. They enjoy a traditional service and love great sermons. They are usually very good givers and provide much of the financial support for the total church program. The first service is just as good as the second service. Both services are designed to praise God and encourage one another. We have already covered most of this material under the title "outsiders" where we shared the differences needed for services for members and nonmembers. One of the most important things for the insider group to do is to allow the other group to have a contemporary service without being critical of it. This takes a lot of spiritual maturity and strong leadership, but this is very important for the future of the church. We need to challenge this group to build a church where their children and grandchildren will attend.

How do we develop the spiritual maturity where one group will allow a contemporary service without being critical of it?

183

PLANNED (1 Corinthians 14:40)

The difference between a good and bad service is usually determined by the flow, the togetherness and the planning. The entire service from start to finish needs to be planned and carefully coordinated. We only have one hour a week to lead these people to a closer encounter with Jesus Christ. Because of his training and expertise, the pulpit minister should lead the worship ministry. However, he needs plenty of help and input from the Worship Ministry leader, the music ministry coordinator, the communion coordinator, the worship scheduler, the head of ushers and greeters, and the sound technician.

> The difference between a good and bad service is usually determined by the flow, the togetherness and the planning.

The pulpit minister should plan his sermon outline, suggested songs, suggested Scriptures and assembly program as early in the week as possible. The Worship Ministry leader works with him to:

Would this kind of planning help most services?

1. Promote the worship ministry and the joy of worship in every way possible.
2. Listen to people's ideas and suggestions.
3. Set short-term and long-term goals for this ministry.
4. Develop a plan of the best way to implement needed change.
5. Equip members in this ministry area to do the work. This would include training communion helpers, prayer leaders, ushers and music groups or song leaders. He might not do these particular things in training, but he needs to make sure it gets done.
6. Provide leadership for the Music Ministry Coordinator, Communion Preparation Coordinator, Worship Scheduler and Sound Technician.
7. Work with key people to provide opportunities for many different people to serve in the worship ministry. Leading prayer and serving communion can especially involve a large number of different people.

> ## Leading prayer and serving communion can especially involve a large number.

8. Pray for the members by name who serve.
9. Keep the church mission statement before the members by using worship as a communication vehicle.
10. Attend training courses as needed to improve skills.

The Music Ministry Coordinator has the following responsibilities:

1. Keep a current list of song leaders and praise team groups.
2. Provide training as needed.
3. Provide schedule for singing groups or song leaders.
4. Provide songs by means of songbooks, transparencies, slides, video or photocopies.
5. Know strengths and weaknesses of each song leader and praise team group. Keep up with their out-of-town schedules.

The Worship Ministry Leader needs to:

1. Schedule individuals for announcements, opening and closing prayer, men waiting on the table, Scripture reading and people to count the contribution.
2. Prepare a schedule which he gives to the church secretary to be placed in the assembly program.
3. Call those scheduled in advance to remind them of their service.
4. Replace those individuals who are absent.
5. Train new volunteers as they become available.

The Communion Preparation Coordinator:

1. Oversees and makes sure communion is prepared for all services.
2. Recruits and organizes volunteers for communion preparation and set up.
3. Purchases items necessary for preparing the Lord's Table.
4. Trains new volunteers as they make themselves known.
5. Sees that communion is taken to shut-ins and to those who request it in hospitals.
6. Recruits a cleanup crew to take care of all cleanup.

Ushers:

1. Arrive at the building 45 minutes early to unlock doors, turn on lights, set temperature controls, turn on sound system.
2. Greet people as they arrive and hand out assembly programs, provide information and instruction to visitors, and make everyone feel welcome and appreciated.
3. When service is completed, turn off lights and lock doors.

> One deacon and usher arrives at our
> church building at 3:30 a.m. every Sunday
> to take care of his ministry.

The sound technician:

1. Knows how to run all parts of the sound system.
2. Gets remote mikes to preacher and music groups or song leader.
3. Makes a sound check of all remote microphones as well as stationary microphones.
4. Checks batteries.
5. Makes sure someone is scheduled to record all services.
6. Has all media presentations ready.

The Tape Ministry personnel:

1. Make sure all messages are taped and filed.
2. Duplicate all tapes needed to fulfill tape requests.
3. Collect money for tapes. Develop marketing plan for tapes in a series.
4. Prepare information for membership concerning what is available for people to purchase.

The Servant's Way to
Manage Conflict & Change

This might be the most important chapter in this book! Never have I seen so many church leaders and church members so frustrated in this area. Here is the summation of some of the calls I received in a one-week period of time.

1. We want to put the Ministry System in here, but some people don't want us to change anything. What do we do?
2. I'm an elder in this congregation and know of important changes which need to be made, but I don't know how.
3. I'm a minister. Can you help me relocate? Some of the people are very upset because of some of the changes I've suggested.
4. Our church just split as we were appointing additional elders.
5. I'm a deacon and the elders will not let me make any changes in our ministry.
6. We got a Plexiglas pulpit, and it nearly split the church.
7. We moved the communion table to the back of the auditorium for one week. I never saw so many people upset.
8. We sang during communion and two families walked out.
9. We ought to worship just like we did when I was growing up in the 1950s.
10. We have lost many younger families because they met with us and asked us to make some changes in our worship services. We told them no—not because what they asked was not biblically correct, but because it would upset some of our members. We are now a church primarily of older people and declining each week. What would you suggest?

Do you identify with these problems?

The servant leader knows that rapid change is taking place in the world, and he knows that this greatly affects the church. He will

> Rapid change is taking place in today's world, and this greatly affects the church.

not compromise biblical principles because of this, but he will make needed changes if they do not contradict the word of God. Let's look at some of the major changes in today's world.

1. *Mobility.* There is tremendous mobility in today's world with one family in five moving each year. Many people today have moved far away from their families and do not have much of an emotional support system. They do not have deep roots or many friends. This has contributed to the disintegration of the home.

2. *Rapid growth of non-Anglo ethnic groups.* While the growth of the white Anglo population is very small, there is a growth explosion among the blacks, Hispanics and other ethnic groups. These people have far different cultural backgrounds. Many churches have never dealt with this.

How are these changes affecting the church today?

3. *Aging population.* There are now more Americans over the age of 65 than there are teenagers. Many of these people retire in good health and can provide years of service in ministry to a church.

4. *Role of women.* Over two-thirds of our women now work. They are heads of corporations, governors, senators and are highly educated. Women's roles in the church will be a major issue for the future.

5. *Choices.* Not too many years ago all cars came in either black or black. Menus at restaurants were short and limited. There was little choice among a few television channels or radio stations. Have times ever changed!

6. *Shifts in segmentation.* There used to be three primary classes in America — lower, middle and upper. They would be symbolized as driving a Chevrolet, Oldsmobile or Cadillac. Each family segment was composed of a husband, wife and a large number of children. Today, there are more divorced and remarried than there are of what was once known as the typical family. People today are more apt to make decisions based more on demographics and psychographics than they are on geography. Demographics is

188

dividing people into groups by gender, age, education, income, marital status, ethnic origin and other characteristics. Psychographics seeks to segment society by life orientation or the choices people make. For example, some people are called survivors and others are high achievers. People will drive past many churches to go to a place where they feel comfortable and where their needs are met.

7. *Short-term commitments.* Modern America places great emphasis on self, independence and personal fulfillment. Combined with mobility and uncertainty, these trends make long-term commitments seem inappropriate. A person will work at a dozen different jobs within his lifetime, and make three major career changes if he is a typical American. Very few will live in a house long enough to pay off the mortgage. In fact, most do not have any hope of living in the house long enough to pay off the mortgage. They are less interested in joining clubs or churches, taking on assignments, signing contracts, or doing anything that will reduce their options for future decisions. Over 75% of the marriages which end in divorce do so in the first two years. Half the marriages end in divorce, and divorce is now socially acceptable. Sunday school teachers are much harder to recruit, sermons are shorter and usually are more successful if they "stand alone" rather than being in a series.

How can churches adjust to the short-term commitment mentality?

> Over 75% of the marriages which end in divorce do so in the first two years.

8. *Decline in work habits and purpose.* A generation ago, college students were most interested in developing a meaningful philosophy of life. Our primary interest today is "making money." There continues to be a greater interest in material success and a declining interest in serving others. Work ethics of the younger and older generation constantly clash. The person of the older generation saw his job as a way to make a positive impact on the world and had deep loyalty to it. The younger generation person knows

the job is probably temporary, has little loyalty and fulfills his commitment to make money and have the material lifestyle he desires. Of course, there are many exceptions to these trends, but this does represent the vast majority.

> ## Today's visitor is not very interested in doctrine and hates church squabbles.

9. *Isolated people with a worldview philosophy.* Today's person wants to be independent and take care of himself. He wants his marriage to stay intact, but he will leave a church which has narrow views concerning divorce and remarriage. He is not very interested in doctrine and hates church squabbles. He likes anything which works on closer relationships. He is not mission minded, but he gets upset if people anywhere in the world are being mistreated. He will generously give food for the hungry children in Africa seen on a television campaign, but not give a cent to a church evangelistic crusade in the same area.

How can churches best meet the needs of young families on Sunday?

10. *Home centered.* The '90s person has a great desire for the home and its relationships to be the center of his life. Time spent at home, even if it is just in front of the television, is increasing. Home delivery food services are rapidly growing. This person has little time to be with family at home and is zealously trying to protect home time. Many work six days a week and Sunday is the only family day available. The number of work hours is now on an increase each year. These people would rather be at home with their families on Sunday night than at the traditional Sunday night church service. In fact, some young families will leave churches which overly promote the Sunday night church service because they perceive this as the church being opposed to family values!

Potential visitors are more likely to be attracted by special events and direct mail efforts. Evangelism is carried out more effectively through existing webs of friendship.

The servant leader looks at these ten dramatic changes taking place in America, shakes his head, doesn't like a lot of things that are happening, but meditates about it. He doesn't stick his head in the sand and ignore it. He prays about it and decides to deal with it. He knows that these sweeping changes are altering the face of religion in the world. He looks individually at each one of the points and applies this to the local church where he leads. He makes copious notes. He knows that God is still in control, and that God still wants the local church to touch people with the gospel. Despite all the negatives in all these trends, he sees some powerful ways the church can reach this audience. He is excited about the future of the church after he analyzes all of this material and plans a leadership retreat to brainstorm. The leaders usually come out of the retreat with some great ideas, but they face an enormous obstacle: HOW DO WE MAKE THESE NEEDED CHANGES WITHOUT ROCKING THE BOAT?

> The big question is: how do we make needed changes without rocking the boat?

Now that we see that change is inevitable, let's look at some good ways to implement change. Dr. Lynn Anderson has a complete book I would like to recommend on this topic called *Navigating the Winds of Change*. Here are some suggestions I would like to share after being a "change implementer" in the local church for the last thirty years.

1. Get the leadership on their knees praying. Have them study things like the ten changes in today's world we have just shared. Have them brainstorm ways this applies to the church.

2. Get the membership on its knees praying for the future of the church. Pray that we might always have a biblically centered church which our children and grandchildren will attend.

3. Have a series of pulpit sermons and possibly adult Bible school lessons about changes in today's world. Have the classes and other members apply this to the church and offer suggestions.

4. Establish close relationships with your members. The closer you are to someone, the more you can communicate and

How do you feel about these suggestions for implementing change?

191

effect change. It is especially important for elders, ministers, deacons, ministry leaders and teachers to have a flock they are close to.

5. Meet individually with ministry leaders where change needs to be effected. Develop a game plan and a PERT chart.

6. Make sure that every elder is supportive of this game plan. I have never known a church to split unless the eldership is divided!

7. Make sure all the people involved in the ministry area you are wanting to change are supportive. The idea might be to start a second service which would be more contemporary, and you are meeting with the worship ministry about this.

8. Clearly communicate your goals, purposes and objectives to the congregation. Define clearly where you are going.

9. Present a series of biblical lessons about the need for this change. Unless our theology backs up the change, we do not need to do it. I sometimes teach a series on legalism from the book of Galatians, and it really helps people become receptive to change. I first define a legalist as "a person who thinks that he can gain God's approval by outward conformity to a list of rules, and who minimizes the importance of motives, the work of Christ, faith, and the dynamic role of the Holy Spirit in daily living."

How does legalism keep us from implementing change?

> Unless our theology backs up the change, we do not need to do it.

I ask for the people to answer five major questions.

a. *Am I self-sufficient?* This is a major problem if I like to do everything with my own power and might. We cannot leave God out of our planning and we cannot quench people's spirits by putting a lid on God. We cannot be self-made people interested in doing our own thing. We cannot leave God and others out of the planning and out of the process.

b. *Am I self-serving?* This is a problem if I just want things done the way I want them to be done. It's a problem if I want the worship services, Bible classes and ministries of the church to only be done for me or for the way I want them done.

c. *Am I shallow?* This is a problem if I want a quick easy answer or solution to everything. Life in today's world is too complex for this. We need to be driven to our knees in prayer and probe deeply into the word of God. A trite answer such as "we have always done it this way" will not suffice in today's world.

d. *Am I law bound?* This is a problem if I want a legalistic set of rules for everything I do or do not do. The Bible is a message of grace and presents beautiful Christian principles of how to live and what to do. It is not nearly as specific and detailed as some in this category would like, and they have a tendency to develop an additional set of "church rules."

e. *Am I hypersensitive?* This is a problem if I have a small comfort zone of tolerance for other people. I need to allow others freedom in Christ if it is biblical. This is a problem if we are more bound to tradition than we are to the Bible. This is a problem if it bothers me for people to worship differently than I do when there is nothing biblically wrong with it.

How does hypersensitivity prevent us from making neded changes?

The greatest difficulty in being hypersensitive usually centers around the area of tradition. Our major problems in the church today are usually not over whether or not something is biblically wrong.

> # There are good and bad traditions in the church.

Let's look at tradition for a moment. We have many good and probably some bad traditions in the church. A tradition can be good or bad, right or wrong. Tradition becomes a problem when we make it our creed of right or wrong. Let's look at some traditions I have seen in the church. They are not wrong unless we count them as biblical law, say they cannot be changed, and they keep us from reaching a new generation of people who might otherwise be receptive to the gospel.

  a. A church building.
  b. A song leader.
  c. Three songs and a prayer.
  d. A communion table at the front.
  e. A communion table with a white cloth.
  f. "This do in remembrance of me" carved into the communion table.
  g. A closing song.
  h. An invitation song.

I could give many other illustrations, but I think you get the point. We have many good things which are traditions. They are not wrong, but they can become wrong if we say it cannot be done any other way. They are not the biblical law and the gospel. This series on Legalism using the book of Galatians as our textbook can really speak to church members today. It can cause them to meditate, reflect, pray and be open to "weightier matters." It is always fun and useful to have people brainstorm in class about good and bad traditions in the church.

What are some traditions that hinder change?

Don't hassle over unimportant details.

---

10. Teach some principles about change from the book of Acts. Look at the early church in the book of Acts and see how they handled change.

  a. **Have initial success.** Religious changes were dramatic after the death of Jesus. He has now ascended to heaven, and the world will never be the same after Pentecost in Acts 2. By any measure, the beginning of the church on Pentecost Sunday was a tremendous success with 3,000 additions to the Kingdom!

  b. **Have convictions about change you are willing to die**

for. Stephen in Acts 7 gave his life trying to bring about change.

c. **Don't hassle over unimportant details.** This was the spirit of the Jerusalem conference in Acts 15 as they nailed down only the essentials. Have a giving spirit on as many points as possible. That's the reason Paul circumcised Timothy in Acts 16 even though he did not have to.

d. **Give everyone the opportunity for open discussion.** Notice how the church handled a major problem in Acts 6 by doing this. The solution arrived at "pleased the whole group."

> ## Give everyone a chance for input.

e. **Write things down to convince the analytically-minded group.** The Jerusalem Conference of Acts 15 wrote down a formal statement.

f. **Share stories with the "feelers" and those not as interested in logical reasons.** Peter shared an emotional story about the conversion of Cornelius, the first Gentile convert in Acts 11.

g. **Be as open as possible.** Look at Paul's candor at the Jerusalem Conference in Acts 15.

h. **Get ready for opposition to change.** Paul had many stripes on his body to prove this.

i. **Use confrontation when you need to.** This is difficult, but important. Galatians 2 tells us Paul even had to confront Peter.

j. **Concentrate on God's major priority for the local church.** Critics throughout the book of Acts tried to discredit Paul and keep him from preaching the word. But, he kept right on doing his job. People will follow a leadership and respect a church which keeps its major priorities before the people and follows them. An example

from the book of Acts might be:
    (1) A commitment to Scripture (Acts 2:4).
    (2) A commitment to one another (Acts 2:42-46).
    (3) A commitment to prayer (Acts 2:42).
    (4) A commitment to praise and worship
        (Acts 2:43-47).
    (5) A commitment to outreach (Acts 2:45-47).

k. **Meet the needs of the people.** They met the widows' needs in Acts 6 and took care of them.

l. **Do your best to please God.** Acts 24:16 from *The Message* says: "Believe me, I do my level best to keep a clear conscience before God and my neighbors in everything I do."

11. Get feedback from the congregation. Get input from them concerning the best ways to meet the needs of the church and the community. Identify some of the problems to them, and let them share possible solutions. Small group meetings, congregational suggestion boxes, or response cards completed following a sermon or lesson on this topic can be beneficial.

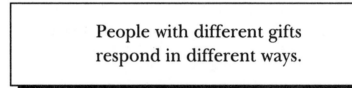

People with different gifts
respond in different ways.

12. Understand the diverse gifts God has given the people in your congregation. Design a balanced program to meet all of these needs.

In what areas are people most interested, according to their spiritual gifts?

These gifts are a gift from God so we certainly do not want to be critical of him. These diverse gifts enable us to build a balanced church which meets the needs of the people in the church and community. Let's look at how people with different gifts see things. As you read about each gift study the chart in illustration 39.

    a. The evangelist is interested in a lot of sermons on "first principles." He wants a lot of conversions and a lot of responses.

    b. The **prophet** likes to point out the wrongs in the church

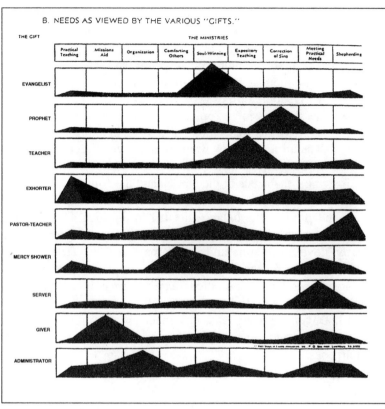

Illustration 39

and the community. He likes sermons and campaigns against pornography, abortion, drinking, drugs, etc.

c. The **teacher** is interested in in-depth Bible lessons and Bible study.

d. The **exhorter** wants to encourage everyone and he is not interested in a heavy, deep Bible lesson. He is a hugger and a feeler.

e. The **pastor-teacher** likes to listen to people and help them with their problems. He likes to shepherd the people and get them back closer to God.

f. The **mercy shower** likes to comfort others. He laughs and cries with people.

g. The **server** wants to get the job done. He is willing to do

197

anything to help someone else. He just likes to serve. He believes we spend too much time talking about doing things and not enough time doing them.

h. The **giver** is interested in giving and wants more to be said about it from the pulpit. He does not understand why people do not give more. He wants to give to successful mission efforts and to significant ministries that successfully make a real difference in today's world.

i. The **administrator** wants to organize all of these gifts to effectively work together for the glory of God as they meet the needs of the church and the community.

Proper response to this sheet will help implement needed change and provide the balance needed in the local church. This chart is an awesome tool for preachers, teachers and elders as you strive to develop lessons and programs TO FEED THE ENTIRE FLOCK. Material for the gift chart was developed by Larry Gilbert and comes from his book entitled *Team Ministry*. It will be a very useful book for you to study as he takes this to much more detail.

13. Develop programs which meet the individual needs of your members and community as they relate to your overall goals and purposes.

> It takes eighteen miles for an oil tanker to make a U-turn.

14. Be patient. It takes eighteen miles for an oil tanker to make a U-turn. The most fuel used in a missile is used just getting it off the ground.

What can you do to cause the congregation to see the need for change?

a. Change will not come until the group sees the need. They will ask:
   (1) Why change?
   (2) Will it help?
   (3) Is it scriptural?
b. Change will not come without resistance.
c. Changes will not come without trust which grows out of

relationships. I know of one servant minister in a small church who fixes breakfast for the leadership once a month. It has developed trust and relationships which facilitate change.

d. Change will not come without ownership by those being asked to change.

e. Change is more successful if options are presented and allowed.

f. Change usually will not come immediately.

g. Change will not last without maintenance.

(1) Review why you made the change.

(2) Evaluate whether or not you are successfully meeting your objectives.

(3) Provide options as needed.

(4) Set boundaries.

(5) Set new goals as needed.

h. Total change will probably not take place.

(1) Because of human nature.

(2) Because of personnel turnover.

(3) Because of resistance to change.

(4) Because of changing times and cultures.

i. The harder you push, the harder the system pushes back.

> Why will change usually not last without maintenance?

There are five major responses to change.

---

j. There are five major responses to change.

(1) Avoid it at all costs and do not deal with it.

(2) Accommodate the people wanting to make the change. You give the people what they want because you do not feel it is worth getting upset over.

(3) Compete with the group wanting to make the change. Let them know you are dead set against it, and that there is a better way.

(4) Compromise by giving a little to get a little.

(5) Collaborate by putting the problem on the table, get-

ting both groups together, praying about it, and agreeing we have a problem. We decide we are going to put our heads together and solve it. It's amazing how God uses strong spiritual leaders to work things out. Thirty minutes of prayer on our knees with strong spiritual leaders can provide "miracles" when diverse groups meet together. I have seen this happen over and over again!

> ## Take advantage of the best times for change.

15. Take advantage of the best times for change. It's usually when you have a new preacher, appoint new elders or select new deacons. It can come when a church is struggling or facing a major crisis. You can use teaching, programs, and experiences to create a church culture which will be more receptive to change.

16. Expose people to situations where they see the need for change.

17. Give honest, spiritual, dependable people the important responsibility of making needed changes. The situation should not be we vs. they, but a competent team working together implementing what God wants implemented.

Why will even necessary changes usually cause you to lose some people?

18. Change will cause you to lose some people. I know it is difficult for you to accept this, but it is necessary. You are losing people all the time. You know why some are leaving, but most just leave. We do not want to lose anyone, but it will happen. If we do not make needed changes, we will not be a church of the future which is vibrantly reaching the community with the gospel. It will not be a church where our children and grandchildren will attend without needed changes. We can lose a few people because we make changes, but we can gain hundreds of people when we make needed changes!

19. Build family boundaries on togetherness by focusing on the great commandment and the great commission.

"Love the Lord your God with all your heart and with all your soul and with all your mind. . . . Love your neighbor as yourself (Matt. 22:37-40).

"Go and make disciples of all nations, baptizing them in the name of the Father and of the Son and of the Holy Spirit, and teaching them to obey everything I have commanded you" (Matt. 28:19-20).

> # Leadership's example and enthusiasm for change is necessary.

20. Leadership's example and enthusiasm for change is imperative. They must all stick together and support one another. A church is just as strong as its weakest leadership link. This weak link can be one of the greatest problems in church leadership. Don't let Satan divide you! United together with Christ, you can accomplish all things together for him.

This leadership principle is so important I would like to take you with me to visit an elders meeting in Garden Grove, California, which is something I did many years ago. A friend of mine invited me to sit over in a corner at this meeting. Here are the points which spiritually impressed me that I would like to pass on to you.

a. Each elder carries a Bible to the meeting. When proposals or discussion is made, each person gives a biblical answer as to whether or not they should approve something. It was inspirational to hear them quote Scripture for their answers or to say that Jesus, John, Peter, Paul or someone else said some point in the Bible. When any proposal is made, the elders first ask, "Is it scriptural?"

b. There is a vacant chair at the head of the elders table. I noticed that each elder would look at this vacant chair before they voted. I asked my friend who was missing from the meeting because each elder was always looking at that empty chair. I was told that the chair was always empty to remind them that Jesus is head of this organization and that he is the chairman of the board! This reminds

Do you need an "empty chair" in your leadership meetings?

them that where "two or three are gathered" together, he is in their midst. They feel that his presence is always with them. They not only want to vote from Scripture the way Jesus would have them vote, but they also want to communicate with the same spirit that Jesus would communicate with. They said that their elders meetings changed dramatically when they realized he was there with them. It eliminates the bickering and harsh things said. Each person tries to communicate modeling the fruits of the spirit with the attitude of Christ.

> # Is there a need for the change, and is it within God's revealed purpose?

c. They are never allowed the first meeting in which anything is proposed to say anything about money. They are not allowed to ask, "How much will this cost?" or state, "It costs too much." They ask, "Is it scriptural?" "What would Jesus do?" They would discuss this with the spirit of Jesus.

d. They would then decide whether or not the proposal filled a valid need in the church or the community. If the proposal passes to this point, it is assigned to a task force. The task force develops a PERT chart to find out the cost, personnel needed, best way to implement and schedule for the PERT chart. They do not bring this proposal back to the elders until after their homework is done.

e. They always take two votes on each proposal. I was there when the first vote was 11 to 1 and the next vote was 12 to 0. There was another vote which was 9 to 3 and then 12 to 0. I didn't have to be there long until I realized that the second vote is always unanimous. So, I asked my friend why they always take two votes. He explained to me that there is absolutely no power or authority in one elder. He pointed out that the Bible teaches that God doesn't want any one-man shows, but that he wants a plurality of elders to lead

> ## 95% of leadership disagreements are over matters of opinion.

his local church! My friend told me that each elder has an agreement to go along with the majority or he will not serve as an elder. The only exception to this is a biblical disagreement. In that case, they would have an elders retreat and reach a biblical conclusion. My friend pointed out that 95% or more of their disagreements were over matters of opinion. He further pointed out why unity and togetherness of the eldership are so very important. He said in the early days they had a proposal where the vote was 11 to 1. When they left the elders meeting, a woman caught the elder who had voted in the minority in the foyer. She began to "let him have it"! He began to defend the proposal as strongly as if he had originated it. The woman stepped back and said, "Well, if you are going to support it, that's good enough for me!" But if this man had said, "I am against it, but the other elders are for it," you have just begun to split a church! I hope you will always remember this elders meeting as a valuable model for the implementation of change.

How do you feel about the Garden Grove elders meeting?

This chapter on change is very, very important. We have covered a lot of material which should prove valuable to you. May God bless you as you implement needed change. The following questions for you to ask should also be valuable to all church leaders.

1. What is the context of the change?
2. What will never change?
3. What are the psychological and logical aspects of this change?
4. What are the advantages of the change?
5. Am I changing too much too fast?
6. Should I allow this change?
7. Should I allow this change now?

8. Is this change temporary or permanent?
9. Is my attitude toward change right?
10. Do I have the right appreciation for this change?
11. What negative aspects of this change need creative problem solving?
12. Is this what God wants me to do?

God Blesses the Servant-Driven Churches

Servant-driven churches are dedicated to ten major principles for the 21st century as they strive to reach the community with the gospel.

1. Leaders and members can clearly express the purpose of the church. Although it is difficult, programs which are not related to the mission of the church are avoided. Programs which cease to be relevant are dropped.

2. Choices for celebrative, worship services are offered. The servant-driven church wants to reach all the people so they will have traditional services, contemporary services and seeker services. Some will be very casual and informal with upbeat contemporary music.

3. Positive leaders communicate a strong sense of purpose and vision. They are leaders of personal integrity, openness, and competence. They are people of faith who want to have the kind of church that God wants them to lead.

4. Inspirational, relevant biblical preaching is provided. People of all ages will respond to this message. Personal stories mixed with God's word related to today's needs touch lives in a powerful way.

> ## Churches need to constantly look at themselves through the eyes of visitors.

5. Members constantly look at themselves through the eyes of visitors. They are sensitive to the suggestions of visitors and will do everything they can to meet their needs.

Do you agree with these ten principles?

6. The organization of the church has a very simple operating structure. People today hate red tape and many are wary of "organized religion." The servant-driven church will have a ministry system which coordinates activities with the simplest structure possible.

7. Servant-driven churches make attendance convenient for the people in the community. They will offer multiple services, abundant parking, friendly ushers, quality children's programs, clean restrooms, professional nursery care, good facilities and one-hour services to meet the needs of the larger portion of the community. Those who desire deeper study and closer relationships will be provided these opportunities through small groups, Bible classes and special programs.

Servant-driven churches are user friendly.

---

8. The church will provide a chance to build meaningful relationships. Many singles and young couples are especially starved for meaningful relationships. Servant-driven churches will provide as many opportunities as possible to meet this need.

9. The leadership should demonstrate innovative approaches to ministry. These churches look to the present and the future, rather than tradition. Diversity is tolerated and appreciated. Emphasis is placed upon being in harmony with the church's philosophy of ministry.

Why is the Involvement Ministry the key ministry to help members identify their gifts and use them?

10. Most importantly, the church must encourage active ministry for lay persons. The servant-driven church wants every member to use his gifts to meet the needs of the church and the community for the glory of God. Lay persons are encouraged to get involved and lead. The Involvement Ministry becomes the key ministry to help members identify their gifts and use them. Membership information classes are held in multiple sessions to explain doctrine and benefits of being active members in the local church family. They are challenged to be a part of a volunteer team who will make a significant difference in today's world.

God Blesses the Servant-Driven Churches

God blesses servant-driven churches such as the Broadway Church of Christ in Lubbock, Texas. That church grew in worship attendance from 1400 to 3000 from 1968 to 1978! Contributions grew from $5,000 to $16,000 a week and a special Sunday morning contribution of $863,000 was taken up. One of the major contributing factors of this was a devastating tornado that hit Lubbock and the Broadway building in 1970. This developed a group of servants who really got in touch with the needs of the people in the community.

> ## The servant tries to find a need and fill it.

God blesses servant-driven churches such as the Richland Hills Church of Christ in Fort Worth. Worship attendance grew from 900 to 2900 and contributions from $6,000 a week to $60,000 a week! Membership grew from 1000 to 4100. This happened in the years from 1978 to 1991. Catalyst for this growth was a man who walked into the church offices during the week, held his guns on staff members and secretaries, and then killed himself in the church foyer. The man was going through a divorce and had already shot his wife nine times earlier that day. God used Jon Jones to preach some powerful sermons about this and the Richland Hills Church developed a counseling center that counseled over 1,000 people a month with eight counselors, and they developed a benevolent center which fed over 2,000 people a month. They twice raised over $8,000,000 on a single Sunday!

God blesses servant-driven churches like the Central Church of Christ in Amarillo. They were devastated by a financial depression and nearly had to close the doors of the church building. But in the last five years attendance has grown from 1200 to nearly 1700 and giving has grown from $21,000 to $27,000 a week. Major reasons for this were the servant attitudes of the elders and the minister, Dick Marcear. The elders said there was no way they could make payments on the $6 million debt. They started getting on their knees and praying. They turned the problem over to God and a small group of men outside the eldership, and God provided

What was the "miracle" God provided?

207

a "miracle." Dick Marcear is a pulpit servant at Central who has been serving the Central family for over 20 years. Dick will do anything for anybody, and his servant spirit is contagious. He is surrounded by a team of shepherds, ministers, deacons, secretaries, teachers, women ministry leaders and custodians who serve with great servant attitudes.

> # God blesses servant-driven churches who practice the work ethic of Nehemiah.

God blesses servant-driven churches who practice the work ethic of Nehemiah in the first seven chapters of Nehemiah. These chapters are great models for servants at work.

1. Nehemiah learns of a great need — the "wall of Jerusalem is broken down" (Neh. 1:3, NASB, also the following quotations).

2. He has a strong feeling to do something about the need — "sat down and wept and mourned" (Neh. 1:4).

3. He recognizes the importance of prayer — "prayed day and night" (Neh. 1:4-11).

4. He arranged for adequate materials to do the job — "timber to make beams for the gates" (Neh. 2:8); leaders and people gave over $350,000 to the work (Neh. 7:70-72).

Does Nehemiah teach some valuable lessons to your congregation?

5. He motivated the people to build the wall — "You see the trouble we are in, how Jerusalem lies in ruins. . .let us build the wall. . .the hand of God is upon me for good. . . . They said, 'Let us rise up and build'" (Neh. 2:17-18).

6. Preparation is made — ". . .they strengthened their hands for the good work" (Neh. 2:18).

7. He overcame the critics and opposition — "they derided us and despised us. . . then I replied, 'The God of heaven will make us prosper'" (Neh. 2:19-20).

8. People were workers, not shirkers — "the people had a mind to work" (Neh. 4:6).

9. The Israelites didn't allow interruptions to stop them — "Enemies sent messages trying to get him to interrupt the work, but

Nehemiah replied: 'I am doing a great work and cannot come down'" (Neh. 6:3).

10. The work was a success — "wall was finished in 52 days" (Neh. 6:15).

11. Around 50,000 gathered to worship and listen to Ezra read to them from the Word of God (Neh. chapters 8 and 9).

The servant wants to build a Christ-centered church for the 21st century. He yearns for a church dedicated to lifting up CHRIST in the church and in the community.

> ## The servant-driven church lifts up Christ.

THE SERVANT'S CHURCH

C aring. This church genuinely cares about people and their needs.

H earing. This church listens to people. You are interested in people and you take the time to listen.

R elating. This church forms close relationships with people and helps them find "a place to call home" with friends in the family of God.

I nvesting. This church is willing to pay the price to be the church which God wants it to be in the 21st century.

S haring. This church not only wants to share the message of Christ, but they also want to share the heart and spirit of Christ. You want to share your talents to meet the needs of others because you may be the only Bible people initially view.

T eaching. This church is filled with dedicated teachers who want to use every available soul for Jesus CHRIST. These teachers are dedicated to teaching a changeless gospel with the newest exciting methods in a constantly changing world.

As it relates to the acrostic on Christ, is your congregation adequately fulfilling these principles?

The servant's definition of hell: If God were ever to show me what I could have accomplished if I had more FAITH!

THE SERVANT BELIEVES

The **self-centered** person has to grow in **unselfishness**
before God says, "GO."
The **cautious** person must grow in **courage**
before God will say, "GO."
The **reckless** person must grow in **carefulness**
before God will say, "GO."
The **timid** person must grow in **confidence**
before God will say, "GO."
The **self-belittling** person must grow in **self-love**
before God will say, "GO."
The **dominating** person must grow in **sensitivity**
before God will say, "GO."
The **critical** person must grow in **tolerance**
before God will say, "GO."
The **negative** person must grow in **positive attitude**
before God will say, "GO."
The **power-hungry** person must grow in **kindness and gentleness**
before God will say, "GO."
The **pleasure-seeking** person must grow in **compassion for suffering people**
before God will say, "GO."
And the **God-ignoring** soul must become a **God-adoring** soul
before God will say, "GO."

When the idea is not right —
God says, "NO!"
When the time is not right —
God says, "SLOW!"
When you are not right —
God says, "GROW!"
When everything is right —
God says, "GO!"
Then GREAT THINGS HAPPEN!

A teacher prepares a child for eternity!
A Bible school becomes a soul winning factory!
A doubter becomes as a child in his belief!

A great church rises out of an old downtown area!

A torn up home responds to God's message and healing begins.

The door to your dream. . .suddenly swings open. . .

And there stands God saying to his SERVANTS, "GO! GO! GO!"

Edited and adapted by Ray Fulenwider
from material by Dr. Robert Schuller.

THE SERVANT-DRIVEN CHURCH — spiritual and numerical growth by releasing every member for ministry.

The servant-driven church believes God will bless them.

Purpose Statement

The church exists to love and save the world through Jesus Christ.

This means that our purpose is to change lives. This occurs when a person centers his life around Jesus Christ. Our responsibility, then, is to preach and model the life-changing power of Jesus to our community and the world.

We make this our purpose because this is what God would do and did do in Jesus Christ. The more we know our God, the more we desire to honor Him whom we want all the world to know.

This is the shared purpose of the community of believers. We place a priority on biblical teaching and nurturing relationships, because the healthier we are as a church family, the more effective we are at impacting the world.

The Church — *because people matter to God.*

If we fulfill our purpose, then:

1. Each member must *know God's purpose for this church.*

2. Each member must *be willing to serve.*

3. Each member must *know his/her unique contribution.*

Question: If the Richland Hills Church ceased to exist, what would this community miss?

A. Saving

B. Caring

Knowing God's Purpose

Matthew 28:16-20 (NASB — version used throughout this appendix): "But the eleven disciples proceeded to Galilee, to the mountain which Jesus had designated. And when they saw Him, they worshiped Him; but some were doubtful. And Jesus came up and spoke to them saying, "All authority has been given to Me in heaven and earth. Go therefore and make disciples of all the nations, baptizing them in the name of the Father and the Son and the Holy Spirit, teaching them to observe all that I commanded you; and lo, I am with you always, even to the end of the age."
Discussion Time: The text says, "but some were doubtful." What was the source of their concern?

♦ He gave them purpose.

When you don't have a purpose, doubts arise.

♦ He promised His presence.

God's Purposes Include Me

1. We Must Know Our Purpose.

Jeremiah 29:11: "'For I know the plans that I have for you,' declares the Lord, "plans for welfare and not for calamity to give you a future and a hope.'"

Discussion Time: How important is it that we know our purpose?

2. We Must Have Faith in His Presence.

". . . I am with you always, even to the end of the age" (Matt. 28:20).

Discussion Time: What helps you to acknowledge the presence of God in your life?

3. We Must Be Willing to Worship through Service

Serving reluctantly or with wrong motives does not honor God.

	Servility (Honor Me)	Servanthood (Honor God)
Service is done out of a sense of	obligation	obedience
Priorities are established by a	me-first mindset	Father-first mindset
Motivated to serve by	fear of men	fellowship with God
Attitude reflects	not my job	whatever it takes
Approaches ministry out of	fullness which becomes emptiness	emptiness which becomes fullness
Results are	self-seeking	God-glorifying
A spirit of	pride	humility

1 Corinthians 3:10-15: "According to the grace of God which was given to me, as a wise master builder I laid a foundation, and another is building upon it. But let each man be careful how he builds upon it. For no man can lay a foundation other than the one which is laid, which is Jesus Christ. Now if any man builds upon the foundation with gold, silver, precious stones, wood, hay, straw, each man's work will become evident; for the day will show it, because it is to be revealed with fire; and the fire itself will test the quality of each man's work. If any man's work which he has built upon it remains, he shall receive a reward. If any man's work is burned up, he shall suffer loss; but he himself shall be saved, yet so as through fire."

Notes:

Discussion Time: Why is it important for every member to serve with God-honoring attitude and motivation?

Requires:

Proper Perspective

Philippians 2:1-11

We need to see as Christ sees. "Have this attitude in yourselves which was also in Christ Jesus" (Philippians 2:5). This is not an option for believers, but an imperative.

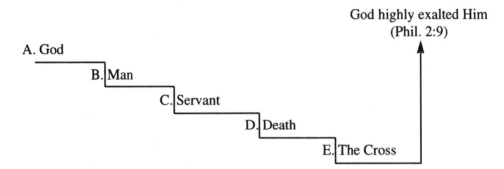

God highly exalted Him
(Phil. 2:9)

A. God

B. Man

C. Servant

D. Death

E. The Cross

This mind set provides practical principles for a proper perspective on serving.

1. We are called to serve *people.*

    A. "Through love, serve one another"
        (Galatians 5:13).

    B. "The Son of Man did not come to be served, but to serve"
        (Matthew 20:28).

2. Serving *people* is actually serving *Christ.*

    A. "Whatever you do in word or deed, do all in the name of the Lord Jesus. . . do your work heartily as for the Lord rather than for men. . . . It is the Lord Christ whom you serve" (Colossians 3:17, 23, 24).

    B. **Jesus negatively states:** To the extent that you did not feed, give drink to, visit, clothe and lodge one of the least of these, you did not do it to me. . . . (Matt. 25:45).

    C. **Jesus positively states:** To the extent that you fed, gave drink to, visited, clothed, and lodged one of these brothers of mine, even the least of them, you did it to me (Matt. 25:40).

3. Serving Christ is an act of *obedience* and *worship.*

   A. Obedience: "Serve one another" (Galatians 5:13).

   B. Worship: "Present your bodies a living and holy sacrifice, acceptable to God, which is your spiritual service of worship" (Romans 12:1).

Review:

1. We must **corporately** know God's purpose for this church.

2. We must **individually** be willing to serve with the right attitude and motivation.

Discovering What God Is Making in and through You

Ephesians 1:18-19: "I pray that the eyes of your heart may be enlightened, so that you may know what is the hope of His calling, what are the riches of the glory of His inheritance in the saints, and what is the surpassing greatness of His power toward us who believe. These are in accordance with the working of the strength of His might."

Ephesians 3:14-16: "For this reason, I bow my knees before the Father, from whom every family in heaven and on earth derives its name, that He would grant you, according to the riches of His glory, to be strengthened with power through His Spirit in the inner man."

Ephesians 4:11-16: "And He gave some as apostles, and some as prophets and some as evangelists, and some as pastors and teachers, for the equipping of the saints for the work of service, to the building up of the body of Christ; until we all attain to the unity of the faith, and of the knowledge of the Son of God, to a mature man, to the measure of the stature which belongs to the fullness of Christ. As a result, we are no longer to be children tossed here and there by waves, and carried about by every wind of doctrine, by the trickery of men, by craftiness in deceitful scheming; but speaking the truth in love, we are to grow up in all aspects into Him, who is the head, even Christ, from whom the whole body, being fitted and held together by that which every joint supplies, according to the proper working of each individual part, causes the growth of the body for the building up of itself in love."

I pray you may be able to see:

1. Your Hope
2. Your Riches
3. Your Power

God has equipped the Saints for service in His kingdom.

Ephesians 2:10-13: "For we are His workmanship, created in Christ Jesus for good works, which God prepared beforehand, that we should walk in them. Therefore remember, that formerly you, the Gentiles in the flesh, who are called "Uncircumcision" by the so-called "Circumcision," which is performed in the flesh by human hands — remember that you were at that time separate from Christ, excluded from the commonwealth of Israel, and strangers to the covenants of promise, having no hope and without God in the world."

In Christ we have:

1. Hope
2. A Place
3. Power

Outside of Christ we have:

1. No Hope
2. No Place
3. No Power

Why Study Spiritual Gifts?

1. **I want you to be *aware* of spiritual gifts.**
   "Now concerning spiritual gifts, brethren, I do not want you to be unaware" (1 Cor. 12:1).

2. **Do not *neglect* the spiritual gift within you.**
   "Do not neglect the spiritual gift within you, which was bestowed upon you through prophetic utterance with the laying on of hands by the presbytery" (1 Tim. 4:14).

3. **We are to be good *stewards* of the spiritual gifts God has bestowed by His grace.**

"As each one has received a special gift, employ it in serving one another, as good stewards of the manifold grace of God" (1 Peter 4:10).

4. **We will learn about God's *will* for our lives. We will discover our spiritual *job description*.**

"I urge you therefore, brethren, by the mercies of God, to present your bodies a living and holy sacrifice, acceptable to God, which is your spiritual service of worship. And do not be conformed to this world, but be transformed by the renewing of your mind, that you may prove what the will of God is, that which is good and acceptable and perfect" (Rom. 12:1-2).

Verses 3-6 explain the "how to" for verses 1 and 2. We prove God's will as we understand our particular gift and its function within the body, and then use that gift accordingly.

5. **The results of God-glorifying service are *fruitfulness* and *fulfillment*.**

"By this is My Father glorified, that you bear much fruit, and so prove to be My disciples. . . .If you keep My commandments, you will abide in My love; just as I have kept My Father's commandments, and abide in His love. These things I have spoken to you, that My joy may be in you, and that your joy may be made full" (John 15:8, 10, 11). Fulfillment is defined as having a sense of accomplishment in a way that is not self-gratification.

6. **God's choice of organization for the church is *the body*.**

(1 Cor. 12:12-27). The body is an organism with Christ as the head and each member functioning with a spiritual gift.

7. **The church will benefit because there will be more *unity of the faith* and *unity of knowledge of the Son of God*.**

"And He gave some as apostles, and some as prophets, and some as evangelists, and some as pastors and teachers, for the equipping of the saints for the work of service, to the building up of the body of Christ; until we all attain the unity of the faith, and of the knowledge of the Son of God, to a mature man, to the measure of the stature which belongs to the fullness of Christ" (Eph. 4:11-13).

8. **The whole body will be *mature*.**

"As a result, we are no longer to be children, tossed here and there by waves, and carried about by every wind of doctrine, by the trickery of men, by craftiness in deceitful scheming; but speaking the truth in love, we are to grow up in all aspects into Him, who is the head, even Christ" (Eph. 4:14-16).

9. **The church will** *grow.*

"For the equipping of the saints for the work of service, to the building up of the body of Christ . . . from whom the whole body, being fitted and held together by that which every joint supplies, according to the proper working of each individual part, causes the growth of the body for the building up of itself in love" (Eph. 4:12, 16).

10. **God will be** *glorified.*

"As each one has received a special gift, employ it in serving one another, as good stewards of the manifold grace of God. Whoever speaks, let him speak, as it were, the utterances of God; whoever serves, let him do so as by the strength which God supplies; so that in all things God may be glorified through Jesus Christ, to whom belongs the glory and dominion forever and ever. Amen" (1 Pet. 4:10, 11).

Deacon Nomination Form

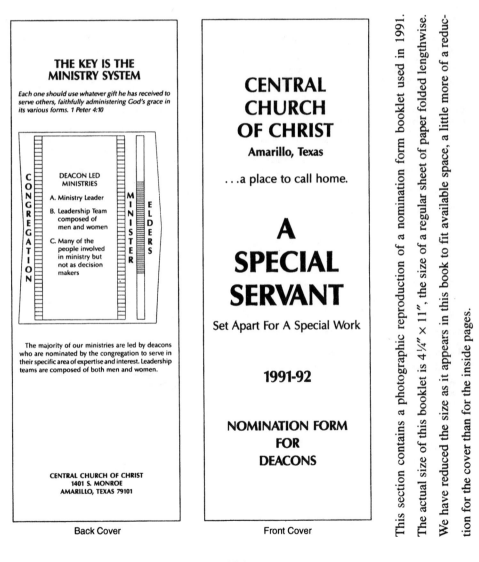

THE KEY IS THE MINISTRY SYSTEM

Each one should use whatever gift he has received to serve others, faithfully administering God's grace in its various forms. 1 Peter 4:10

CONGREGATION

DEACON LED MINISTRIES

A. Ministry Leader

B. Leadership Team composed of men and women

C. Many of the people involved in ministry but not as decision makers

MINISTER

ELDERS

The majority of our ministries are led by deacons who are nominated by the congregation to serve in their specific area of expertise and interest. Leadership teams are composed of both men and women.

CENTRAL CHURCH OF CHRIST
1401 S. MONROE
AMARILLO, TEXAS 79101

Back Cover

CENTRAL
CHURCH
OF CHRIST

Amarillo, Texas

...a place to call home.

A
SPECIAL
SERVANT

Set Apart For A Special Work

1991-92

**NOMINATION FORM
FOR
DEACONS**

Front Cover

This section contains a photographic reproduction of a nomination form booklet used in 1991. The actual size of this booklet is 4¼″ × 11″, the size of a regular sheet of paper folded lengthwise. We have reduced the size as it appears in this book to fit available space, a little more of a reduction for the cover than for the inside pages.

221

A MESSAGE FROM THE ELDERS...

To Members of Our Spiritual Family,

We're calling on every family member to call on God's power and wisdom as we launch our deacon selection process with 40 Days of Prayer. 1992 is going to be an exciting year. In fact, we see evidence that the Lord is already causing remarkable progress and growth in our congregation.

In the early years of the church, growth created the need to select special servants called "deacons" to help carry out the church's responsibilities. According to the Bible, these men had proven to be spiritual leaders in their private lives. Because so many people are becoming involved in the Central church's ministry and because we are reaching out farther into our community and the world every day, we believe that God has provided us with many men qualified to serve as deacons in this church.

We want you to be involved in the process of identifying spiritual men in this congregation who could serve as special servants. On the next three pages you will find the Biblical qualifications for the role, the tasks for which deacons are needed, and places for you to recommend individual men.

■ Prayerfully consider the qualifications of deacons as you search the congregation for men to serve.

■ Suggest men for specific roles. It's fine if you can't fill in all the blanks or if you recommend the same man for several roles.

■ Even though you've received only one nomination form, we encourage you to pick up one for every Christian in your family. Extra copies are available at the church building at the foyer tables.

■ Only forms with signatures will be considered.

■ Return the forms to the church building on or before Sunday night, October 20.

So you will be informed about the process involved, you should know:

Deacons will have specific assignments and be expected to:

1) involve as many other people as possible in the area of their responsibility

2) report regularly to the elders

3) carry out their responsibilities effectively

Deacons will serve for 12 months and then be given the opportunity to:

1) serve another year in that role

2) move to another responsibility

3) step out of a deacon role altogether

All men currently serving as deacons are being given these same options before the new deacons are added.

We will personally meet with the nominated men to explain their responsibilities and verify, to the best of our ability, the spiritual qualifications of each man.

Thank you for caring about the progress of this church and about the lives we can touch. Because of your concern for the service this church renders to the world and to its own, the light of Jesus Christ can shine brighter.

In His love,
The Elders

INSTRUCTIONS

1. Carefully read each job description.

2. Place the name of those you recommend in the blanks following each description of an area of special work.

3. The persons you recommend should meet the level of maturity set forth in I Timothy 3:1-13.

4. Recommend only those people you know personally and feel they can adequately fulfill that area of special ministry. You are not expected to complete each blank.

WHAT WE EXPECT FROM DEACONS

1. A time when you let the Father talk to you daily from His word.

2. A time when you talk to Him daily through prayer about your ministry, the people in your ministry, this church, and the servant model leadership role of you and your family.

3. A demonstrated love for this church.

4. A commitment to reach the community as we meet various needs.

5. A giving of your time, talents, gifts and money as God has blessed you.

6. A time to think and dream weekly about two different ministries — the one you have now and the one you dream of having.

7. The assembly of a leadership team of people including men and women to serve as the decision makers for your ministry.

8. To assign each member of your leadership team to an individual task in your ministry.

9. To gather your ministry once a month to evaluate what is happening and complete the Ministry Communication Form to be sent to the elders.

10. To use the staff contact assigned to your ministry as a resource person and communication tool to express your needs to the church office, ministers and elders.

11. To call the chairman of the elders or the church office by noon Tuesday if you would like to be on the Wednesday night elders' agenda.

12. To get information to the church office by noon Tuesday if you would like for this information to be in the elders' reading file on Wednesday night.

13. To contact each person who expresses an interest in working in your ministry.

14. To involve every person you can in your ministry. This includes present membership as well as new members God will send us.

15. To utilize training programs and retreats designed to help your ministry.

16. To help the elders with an undershepherding program.

17. To formulate a ministry program for your team. To listen to and get input from everyone in your ministry. Example: The education leadership team needs to get input from all the teachers.

18. To formulate a budget with input from everyone in your ministry.

19. To stay within your budget.

20. To get a purchase order from the office for expenditures.

21. To decorate and man a booth at a Ministry Fair each year. To explain your ministry and encourage as many people as possible to be a part of your ministry.

22. To help with the church seminars and workshops as needed.

23. To be a warm, spirit-filled person who reaches out to visitors and fellow members in this congregation with love and care.

WHAT WE PROVIDE FOR DEACONS

1. A specific ministry in which to serve to utilize your gifts for the glory of God.

2. People for you to interview to serve on your leadership team.

3. New people for you to involve in your ministry.

4. Ministry Communication Forms for you to use in your meeting to provide a monthly evaluation of your ministry.

5. Staff contacts to serve as resource people for you.

6. Newsletter articles, Bulletin communications and other publicity help for your ministry as you notify the church office.

7. Office help for your ministry as you coordinate a work assignment through your staff contact.

8. The counsel of elders as needed through individual counseling or a meeting with all the elders as scheduled on Wednesday night.

9. An opportunity to place communication in the elders' reading files each week.

10. Church office secretary to schedule all your events on the church calendar. She also schedules rooms as you need them for various meetings and functions.

11. Training to better equip you to serve in your ministry.

12. Men's retreats.

13. Training seminars and workshops to furnish training for you and opportunities to exchange ideas with people in similar ministries throughout the nation.

14. The opportunity for you and your ministry to plan your program and budget.

15. Freedom and trust to allow responsible people like yourself to develop your ministry.

16. Exciting, uplifting worship assemblies.

17. Quality Bible classes.

18. Groups in which to be involved.

19. Library for the use of books and tapes.

20. Visitors for you to reach out to with love on a weekly basis.

21. A philosophy dedicated to meeting the needs of people in this community and church through ministry.

22. People to help you with your ministry upon your request.

23. A brochure listing all the leaders in your ministry to be given to every member of this congregation to enhance the communication process.

PRESENT DEACONS

Alex Bell	Tim McMenamy
Everett Blanton	Cal Morgan
Alford Blount	John Noyes
Tom Burdett	A.F. Pyeatt
Steve Cearley	Jim Reid
Benny Dement	John Richardson
Gary Douglass	Mike Robertson
Chester Dunavin	Steve Rogers
Kelly Forehand	Warren Sanders
Don Glenn	Dale Scott
Jim Hollifield	Richard Smith
Grady Jackson	Eldon Stapp
Lee Kendle	Bill Team
David Kilpatrick	Kelly Utsinger
Ernie King	Tim Vachon
Max Ladd	Johnny Weems
Harry Lisle	Steve Wood
	Bob Wright

DEACON SELECTION

Deacons, likewise, are to be men worthy of respect, sincere, not indulging in much wine, and not pursuing dishonest gain. They must keep hold of the deep truths of the faith with a clear conscience. They must first be tested, and then if there is nothing against them, let them serve as deacons. In the same way, their wives are to be women worthy of respect, not malicious talkers but temperate and trustworthy in everything. A deacon must be the husband of but one wife and must manage his children and his household well. Those who have served well gain an excellent standing and great assurance in their faith in Christ Jesus.

I Timothy 3:8-13

As we select deacons, we feel convicted by God that an increasing level of spiritual maturity should be evident in those who serve in leadership roles in this church. We, as elders, state our personal commitment to a deeper level of spiritual growth here at Central.

We propose that the role of deacon be enhanced as one of greater spiritual awareness and responsibility. We are convicted by the words of I Timothy 3:8-13, and the responsibilities they imply. In our congregation these words could have the meaning...

■ Men, increasingly aware of their influence in this church and community as leaders, abstaining from drinking and dishonesty in all their dealings.

■ Men, joyfully and unselfishly giving their money, time and other resources.

■ Men, feeling compelled to be supportive of all programs, outreach, meetings and activities of the church family.

■ Men, committing to give additional time to serve in this role as special leaders.

■ Men, being convicted of their roles as spiritual leaders in their families.

■ Men, realizing the significance of an ever-growing and maturing relationship with Jesus Christ.

Because of our current emphasis on spiritual growth in this family, our pledge to lift up Christ and in light of scripture, we therefore urge you to '...select from among you men full of wisdom and the Holy Spirit...' Acts 6:3-4

Ministries of the Central Church of Christ

1. ADULT RECREATION
Provide recreational activities to draw people together and reach out to nonmembers.

1. _____
2. _____
3. _____
4. _____

2. ALCOHOL AND DRUGS
Provides prevention and training programs. Provides support groups.

1. _____
2. _____
3. _____
4. _____

3. ASSEMBLY PLANNING
This ministry works closely with the minister in planning what happens during our assemblies. Will select and work with those who are to read scriptures and give prayers at all worship services.

1. _____
2. _____
3. _____
4. _____

4. BAPTISMAL ASSISTANCE
Assist the preacher in all baptisms. Provides clothing for individuals being baptized. Arranges for ladies to assist women during baptisms at all services. Responsible for seeing the baptismal garments, towels, etc., are properly taken care of following baptisms.

1. _____
2. _____
3. _____
4. _____

5. BARNABAS
Writes, calls or visits all people who respond at our services.

1. _____
2. _____
3. _____
4. _____

6. BIBLE HOUR
Coordinates the activities relative to Children's Bible Hour both morning and evening including materials, teachers, workers, etc.

1. _____
2. _____
3. _____
4. _____

7. BUILDING MAINTENANCE
Checks existing physical structure for maintenance such as need for painting, carpenter work, electrical work or plumbing repair. Furnishes task force to move walls in fellowship area.

1. _____
2. _____
3. _____
4. _____

8. CALLING & CARING
This is a ministry of caring, love and concern. The purpose is to prevent people from becoming inactive and to restore dropouts.

1. _____
2. _____
3. _____
4. _____

9. CHILDREN'S SINGING AND DRAMA
Develops children's singing, puppet, and drama groups.

1. _____
2. _____
3. _____
4. _____

10. CHRISTIAN CAMPS AND RETREATS
Encourages our youth and adults to participate in this. Helps coordinate activities in this area.

1. _____
2. _____
3. _____
4. _____

11. CHURCH BUILDING AND CLASSROOM DIRECTORIES
Provide classroom directories at building entrance. Will keep directories up to date. Will provide direction signs throughout the building.

1. _____
2. _____
3. _____
4. _____

12. CHURCH GROWTH

What makes a church grow? This ministry was created for the purpose of researching all facets of church growth. It will eventually serve as a resource for many of the other ministries.

1. _____
2. _____
3. _____
4. _____

13. COMMUNICATIONS

This ministry's function is to communicate through every means possible — newspaper, brochures, billboards, posters, radio, television — what Christianity is all about at Central.

1. _____
2. _____
3. _____
4. _____

14. COMMUNITY CARE

Provides food and clothing for needy. Involves church in events such as "Sack Sunday". Works with High Plains Food Bank. Works to provide Blood Bank reserve.

1. _____
2. _____
3. _____
4. _____

15. COMMUNITY OUTREACH

This ministry seeks to create an atmosphere at Central which leads to the involvement of each member in leading people to Christ. They are responsible for home Bible studies.

1. _____
2. _____
3. _____
4. _____

16. COUNSELING

Provides support for our counseling program, working closely with our counselor. Provides Family Enrichment classes, seminars, and retreats.

1. _____
2. _____
3. _____
4. _____

17. CONTRIBUTION

In charge of contributions and special funds at all services. Appoints assistants in order that money may be counted after each service. Deposits money in bank.

1. _____
2. _____
3. _____
4. _____

18. DORCAS & TIMOTHY

Provides leadership training for our children.

1. _____
2. _____
3. _____
4. _____

19. EDUCATION — ADULT

Works with education director to coordinate and develop the adult education program.

1. _____
2. _____
3. _____
4. _____

20. EDUCATION — CHILDREN

Works with education director and supervisors to develop the children's education program.

1. _____
2. _____
3. _____
4. _____

21. EDUCATION — YOUTH

Works with the youth minister and supervisors to develop the youth education program.

1. _____
2. _____
3. _____
4. _____

22. FAMILY CARE

This ministry is responsible for financial support of all those under the oversight of our elders, ensuring that we have "no needy" among us. This ministry advises and assists family members in times of emergency. It also recruits, "Good Samaritans", and helps with employment.

1. _____
2. _____
3. _____
4. _____

23. FAMILY LIFE GROUPS

Responsible for our once a month small group Bible studies in homes. Integrates new people into groups and works with our shepherding program.

1. _____
2. _____
3. _____
4. _____

24. FELLOWSHIP DINNERS

Wednesday Roundup — Coordinates all activities: menu, food purchase, setting up room, food preparation, serving of food, clean up, and record keeping. Congregational Fellowships — Plan and coordinate all activities: Year End — Date, time, menu, food, serving, place, decorations, clean up, ticket sales, entertainment and any other details.

1. _____
2. _____
3. _____
4. _____

25. FINANCE

This ministry coordinates our annual budget preparation. It also monitors our financial progress throughout the year and insures financial responsibility.

1. _____
2. _____
3. _____
4. _____

26. GREETERS

Arrives at the assigned services 15 minutes prior to the beginning of the worship hour. Arranges for a minimum of three people to greet at each worship service. Secures substitutes for absentees. Greets each individual by name, if possible, at the assigned entrance. Greeter must be alert for new members and visitors. Distributes "order of worship" sheets at morning services. At the end of the service, attempts to contact "potential new members" and invite them to return. Counts auditorium attendance and records on the sheet provided. Staff information booth in lobby area.

1. _____
2. _____
3. _____
4. _____

27. GRIEF RECOVERY

Contacts those who have lost loved ones, and provides grief recovery seminars.

1. _____
2. _____
3. _____
4. _____

28. GROUND MAINTENANCE

Cares for plants in and around the building as well as plants along streets, alleys and property lines of parking lots. Is responsible for weed control and maintenance of parking stripes on the lots. Responsible to see that sidewalks and entrances are free of ice and snow during winter storms.

1. _____
2. _____
3. _____
4. _____

29. HALL MONITORS

Assigns workers to monitor the halls during worship and Bible classes. Assists in directing members and visitors to classes.

1. _____
2. _____
3. _____
4. _____

30. HIGH PLAINS CHILDREN'S HOME

Works with children's home group attending Central to provide support for houseparents and maximum spiritual growth for youth.

1. _____
2. _____
3. _____
4. _____

31. HOSPITAL VISITATION

Provides a team to visit people in our local hospitals. Report family needs to proper source.

1. _____
2. _____
3. _____
4. _____

32. INVOLVEMENT

This ministry strives to identify the interests and talents and gifts of our members and match them with an appropriate ministry. They are dedicated to the principle of helping everyone find their place in the body. This responsibility includes the assimilation of new members.

1. _____
2. _____
3. _____
4. _____

33. JAIL MINISTRY

Shares the Gospel with those in prison and jails. Provides emotional and counseling support for families. Works with new state prison ministry. Provides Bible lessons for inmates.

1. _____
2. _____
3. _____
4. _____

34. LIBRARY

The Library Ministry is responsible for the purchase of new books and categorizing of these and other incoming volumes.

1. _____
2. _____
3. _____
4. _____

35. LIGHTING AND SOUND

Operates lighting and sound for assemblies and special events.

1. _____
2. _____
3. _____
4. _____

36. LORD'S TABLE SERVICE

Selects men to serve the Lord's Supper. Obtains substitutes for those not present. Keeps records pertaining to those willing to serve and those who have served. Appoints individuals in charge for each service to line up volunteers and select substitutes. Oversees the preparation and clean up for communion.

1. _____
2. _____
3. _____
4. _____

37. MEDIA

Provide media equipment and personnel for media presentations.

1. _____
2. _____
3. _____
4. _____

38. MISSIONS

Coordinates our World Bible School and Mission activities. Keeps congregation informed about our mission program.

1. _____
2. _____
3. _____
4. _____

39. NEW MEMBER ASSIMILATION

Keeps rosters of new members to ensure their assimilation into the Central body. Uses a key couple or single individual to assist the new member by providing friendship, companionship and an understanding of any problems. Finds out if new members are potential Bible class teachers or are experienced in any other phase of the work. Provide a special welcome to all new members by hosting new members in their homes for meals.

1. _____
2. _____
3. _____
4. _____

40. NURSERY AND CHILD CARE

Develops and maintains a quality childcare program.

1. _____
2. _____
3. _____
4. _____

41. PARKING AND TRAFFIC

Directs those who are seeking a parking place. Encourages those trying to park in the immediate church lot not to use those facilities which are reserved for handicapped and elderly people. Assigns young people to help by opening doors, carrying babies, etc.

1. _____
2. _____
3. _____
4. _____

42. PERSONAL FINANCE

Provides free counseling to members needing financial advice.

1. _____
2. _____
3. _____
4. _____

43. PRAYER

Encourages Central family to spend more time in prayer.

1. _____
2. _____
3. _____
4. _____

44. SINGLES AND COLLEGE PROGRAMS

This ministry will coodinate all phases of the singles and college programs such as: organizational structure, spiritual growth, class activities, Bible study, fellowship activities, visitation program, retreats and development of leadership. Provides Divorce Recovery Seminars.

1. _____
2. _____
3. _____
4. _____

45. SPECIAL EVENTS

Works with staff coordinator in the coordination of special events for the Central Church family.

1. _____
2. _____
3. _____
4. _____

46. SPECIAL MUSIC

Furnishes singers for weddings and funerals. Develops special groups and provides special training.

1. _____
2. _____
3. _____
4. _____

47. SUNSHINERS

Establish a committee of approximately 20 people to plan, develop and execute programs for members 65 and over. Have special programs designed to meet the physical and spiritual needs for their members. Develops programs for regular sunshiner dinners. Encourages involvement in church affairs, including visitation of shut-ins, social affairs and Bible study.

1. _____
2. _____
3. _____
4. _____

48. SUPPORT GROUPS

Works with the Support Groups which are organized through the adult Bible classes — to help each member of the Central family to belong and find support for their faith and Christian life.

1. _____
2. _____
3. _____
4. _____

49. TAPE MINISTRY

Tapes services, duplicates and sends out weekly to shut-ins and people throughout the country who request tapes. Keeps supply of tapes on hand for use. Orders special tapes to be kept in media room.

1. _____
2. _____
3. _____
4. _____

50. TRANSPORTATION

Provides rides to church services and activities.

1. _____
2. _____
3. _____
4. _____

51. USHERS

Help people find seats during our services. Also provide a way to recognize and greet visitors.

1. _____
2. _____
3. _____
4. _____

52. VISITATION
Coordinates visitation program. Calls, visits, or writes all visitors.

1. _____
2. _____
3. _____
4. _____

53. VISITATION SPECIAL
Monitors and coordinates activities involved in an active visitation program for Central shut-ins. Coordinates this activity with the Sunshiners group. Works in the hospital visitation program.

1. _____
2. _____
3. _____
4. _____

54. WELCOME HOME
Utilizes supper clubs to invite new members into homes.

1. _____
2. _____
3. _____
4. _____

55. YOUTH
Works with youth minister to develop Huddle groups and the youth program.

1. _____
2. _____
3. _____
4. _____

A BIBLICAL PLAN TO INVOLVE EVERY MEMBER

We're in the people business at the Central Church of Christ. We strive in every way possible to let Christ work through us so our Lord can be magnified. We've developed a unique Biblical structure called the Ministry System which features a plan to involve every member. Ministries are led by ministry leaders and a leadership team of men and women who are the decision makers. They strive to involve everyone in the congregation who is interested in their particular ministry. Everyone is someone special in the Central family.

EPHESIANS 4

WHO: God chose you to be His people. (vs 1)
WHAT: Christ gave each one of us a special gift. (vs 7)
WHY: Christ gave those gifts to prepare God's Holy people for the work of serving. (vs 12)
WHEN: Each part does its own work. (vs 12)
RESULTS: This makes the whole body grow and be strong with love. (vs 16)
MESSAGE: Say what people need . . . words that will help others become stronger. (vs 29)

SPECIAL NOTE TO ALL MEMBERS

The elders will be adding new ministries to take care of the needs of our fast-growing family.

1. Please list below areas of additional work needed in this church family.

_____
_____
_____

2. List the major areas in which you are currently involved:

_____
_____
_____
_____

3. List any new area in which you would like to be included:

_____
_____
_____
_____

Your name: _____
Address: _____
City/Zip: _____
Phone: _____
Signature: _____

Task Force Goal Sheets

#1

TASK FORCE GOAL SHEET*

"If we aim at nothing, we will achieve it with remarkable accuracy." — unknown

Strategy: Service (helping each member discover his or her spiritual gift)

Task Force Leader: Peter Stone

Task Force Members: John Boarges, Jim Boarges, Lydia Philips, Mary Madagen, Joanna King, Simon Battle, Mark Peterson

- State the goal in "SMART" format, using one goal sheet per goal. ("SMART" — specific, measurable, attainable, realistic, timed.)

TEACH ABOUT SPIRITUAL GIFT DISCOVERY

- What steps will be required to complete the goal?

Action	Time Required	Start	Complete
	one quarter (or longer)	January	end of first quarter

1. Pulpit Minister Sermons (emphasize discovery of spiritual gifts)
2. Include Testimonials, beginning with our own elders, from people who have "discovered" their spiritual gifts, as well as people who struggled to find their spiritual gift for years and only after many prayers, attempts, etc., were able to do so.
3. This study on spiritual gift discovery could expand/deepen through Sunday morning/Wednesday night studies or small groups (for example, Charles Swindoll's <u>Improving Your Serve</u>).

* Modified from Worsham Strategic Resources, Inc. Goal Sheet

Page 2

Strategy: Service (helping each member discover his or her spiritual gift)

Goal: #1 Teach About Spiritual Gift Discovery

- What are the primary risks (obstacles) to accomplishment?
  What controls will be utilized (how do you plan to overcome the obstacles)? What risks will be accepted?

Risk (Obstacle)	Control (Plan)
people relying on "works" for their relationship with God or for their salvation (<u>doing</u> service vs. <u>being</u> a servant)	encourage the church to develop and deepen their personal relationship with Christ through daily quiet time (prayer, meditation on Scripture, asking God to guide our lives and reveal His will for us)

- How will progress be measured?

  Is individual growing in his/her personal relationship with Christ?

  Is he/she seeking communion with other believers?

  Is his/her life bearing fruit?

- How will progress be tracked and noted?

  By having Involvement Minister stay in touch with the ministry leaders and <u>mentoring team</u> (see goal #4)

- What are the benefits to accomplishing this goal — to the church collectively and to individuals?

  The benefits are that members understand the Biblical basis for "discovering" spiritual gifts. As God manifests these gifts in a member, he/she finds spiritual and personal fulfillment in operating within his/her gifts, plugs into ministry matching that gift, matures in the faith, builds and strengthens the church.

#2

TASK FORCE GOAL SHEET*

"If we aim at nothing, we will achieve it with remarkable accuracy." — unknown

Strategy: Service (helping each member discover his or her spiritual gift)

Task Force Leader: Peter Stone

Task Force Members: John Boarges, Jim Boarges, Lydia Philips, Mary Madagen, Joanna King, Simon Battle, Mark Peterson

- State the goal in "SMART" format, using one goal sheet per goal. ("SMART" — specific, measurable, attainable, realistic, timed.)

DISCOVERY OF SPIRITUAL GIFTS BY EACH INDIVIDUAL

- What steps will be required to complete the goal?

Action	Time Required	Start	Complete

one or two Sundays a year
We could have the "fair" in the foyer in lieu of
Bible class on those Sundays.

1. Ministry Fairs to expose members to exciting ministries to match gifts/service opportunities.
2. Begin a "sponsor" program where a member of the church would "adopt" a new member for six months. The sponsor would stay in contact with the new member, help the individual or family fill out the "Personal Information Questionnaire," answer questions about the congregation, and put the new member in touch with other members who have similar interests, etc.
3. Spiritual Gifts Assessment — Have members complete a spiritual gifts survey if they do not know their spiritual gift(s).
4. As new members come in after the church has completed the quarter (or longer) of teaching and assessing spiritual gifts, the Involvement Minister could be responsible for having new members take the gifts assessment, or this could be done in the New Member Orientation Classes or small groups.

* Modified from Worsham Strategic Resources, Inc. Goal Sheet

Page 2

Strategy: Service (helping each member discover his or her spiritual gift)

Goal: DISCOVERY OF SPIRITUAL GIFTS BY EACH INDIVIDUAL

- What are the primary risks (obstacles) to accomplishment? What controls will be utilized (how do you plan to overcome the obstacles)? What risks will be accepted?

Risk (Obstacle)	Control (Plan)
making sure we follow through and make this a natural part of our process in plugging in new members	ongoing New Member Orientation Classes; sponsor program; small groups
assessments should not be used by themselves as a "paper only" experience	mentors (see goal #4), members of an individual's small group, and especially seeking God with an open heart and teachable spirit — all help one find his/her gifts

- How will progress be measured?

  If the Ministry Fair is planned and executed; if the sponsor program begins; if the spiritual gifts assessment is given to the members and to new members (on a continual basis)

- How will progress be tracked and noted?

  Sponsor program leader may report to the Involvement Minister; along with the results of the "Personal Information Questionnaire," the results of the spiritual gifts assessment and the ministries that each member signs up for after the Ministry Fair can be entered into the computer

- What are the benefits to accomplishing this goal — to the church collectively and to individuals?

  By implementing the sponsor program, new members will have someone encouraging them to fill out the "Personal Information Questionnaire," inviting them to special events, answering questions, and just making sure they do not "fall through the cracks." The Ministry Fair and gifts assessment will help to encourage current and new members to find their spiritual gifts and put them to use as they mature in the faith and grow spiritually through Christ-centered service.

#3

TASK FORCE GOAL SHEET*

"If we aim at nothing, we will achieve it with remarkable accuracy." — unknown

Strategy: Service (helping each member discover his or her spiritual gift)

Task Force Leader: Peter Stone

Task Force Members: John Boarges, Jim Boarges, Lydia Philips, Mary Madagen, Joanna King, Simon Battle, Mark Peterson

- State the goal in "SMART" format, using one goal sheet per goal. ("SMART" — specific, measurable, attainable, realistic, timed.)

ACTIVATE - SELECT AN AREA OF MINISTRY

- What steps will be required to complete the goal?

Action	Time Required	Start	Complete

Select one or two areas of ministry and commit to a six-month period of time to be involved in it. After the six months, a person could reevaluate and decide to continue in the same ministry, or he/she could try a different ministry area. The key is to continue to try areas until a person feels he/she has identified an area of ministry that is right for him/her.

The ministry leader (or someone he/she appoints) should give on-the-job training and hands-on shepherding to personalized ministry. Current members who are trying out new ministries for themselves and new members need nurturing, support, and affirmation.

Perhaps an existing area of ministry does not match the talents of a person in which case a new area should be developed.

* Modified from Worsham Strategic Resources, Inc. Goal Sheet

Page 2

Strategy: Service (helping each member discover his or her spiritual gift)

Goal: ACTIVATE — SELECT AN AREA OF MINISTRY

- What are the primary risks (obstacles) to accomplishment? What controls will be utilized (how do you plan to overcome the obstacles)? What risks will be accepted?

Risk (Obstacle)	Control (Plan)
member tries an area of ministry; does not like it and does not initiate finding another area to use his/her gifts and becomes discouraged	have Involvement Minister (or someone he appoints) to conduct an interview with the member, putting emphasis first on the person as a child of God and then placing the person in ministry — there is a place for everyone in the body of Christ

- How will progress be measured?

  computerized system we have now or a system the Involvement Minister and team devise to monitor the overall system, watching for members who are misplaced, evaluate the level of member involvement and spiritual growth through ministry, and build in accountability and feedback

- How will progress be tracked and noted?

  Believers flourish in service to Christ when they are serving in their areas of giftedness — someone must be designated to make sure this happens. The involvement Minister may need to train a team such as a Lay Ministry Committee (or could be called advisory team, task force, etc.).

- What are the benefits to accomplishing this goal — to the church collectively and to individuals?

  After members are inspired toward growth by preaching and study, hopefully they are ready for "next step" in their journey. As we grow spiritually in serving those both within and outside the walls of the building itself, ministry will, ideally, become a part of the daily life of a Christian. Needs will be met, relationships will strengthen, and we will develop more and more a real sense of community...a "family" that will reach out to the unchurched and help them to find meaning, practical help, and relevancy in their day-to-day lives. Serving others in love and compassion puts our faith into action...in that process we and those around us are transformed into the likeness of Christ.

#4

TASK FORCE GOAL SHEET*

"If we aim at nothing, we will achieve it with remarkable accuracy." — unknown

Strategy: Service (helping each member discover his or her spiritual gift)

Task Force Leader: Peter Stone

Task Force Members: John Boarges, Jim Boarges, Lydia Philips, Mary Madagen, Joanna King, Simon Battle, Mark Peterson

- State the goal in "SMART" format, using one goal sheet per goal. ("SMART" — specific, measurable, attainable, realistic, timed.)

DEVELOP A CORE OF TRAINED MINISTRY MENTORS

- What steps will be required to complete the goal?

Action	Time Required	Start	Complete

1. Look for those people who have a pastor's heart, spiritual maturity, and wisdom...a desire to help people and meet needs. This position could be used to help people grow spiritually through guiding them to a place of service that fits their gifts...a discipler...an ability to listen well...an ability to ask good questions...an ability to see a person's potential and encourage him/her...ability to link person's gifts and the available opportunities for service...willingness to make the time to invest in the lives of other people.

2. A trained and developed centralized talent bank of ministry mentors could also learn about gifts assessment, matching and placement and could serve as "consultants" to members, new members, or small groups.

* Modified from Worsham Strategic Resources, Inc. Goal Sheet

Page 2

Strategy: Service (helping each member discover his or her

spiritual gift)

Goal: DEVELOP A CORE OF TRAINED MINISTRY MENTORS

- What are the primary risks (obstacles) to accomplishment?
  What controls will be utilized (how do you plan to overcome the obstacles)? What risks will be accepted?

Risk (Obstacle)	Control (Plan)
Finding the spiritually qualified people who are willing to serve.	Pray for God to raise up the right people for this task.

- How will progress be measured?

  Our own elders and ministers could do the training, mentoring, and apprenticeship. If time does not permit this, there are Leadership Network and Stephen Ministry materials available.

- How will progress be tracked and noted?

  More people involved at a deeper level.

- What are the benefits to accomplishing this goal — to the church collectively and to individuals?

  The work of the church would be more spread out, giving more people opportunities to serve, and relieving some of the load of the others.

Talent Interest Profile

TALENT INTEREST PROFILE (TIP)

(This is your <u>TIP</u> to us concerning how you would best like to use
your talents and interest to the glory of God.

Name _____ Phone _____

Address _____ Date _____

City - Zip _____ Year placed membership _____

Occupation _____ Favorite pastime _____

Circle one number for each statement. Your interest, talent, and desire to become involved will be indicated by the *higher number circled*.

EXAMPLE:

20	Very interested	5 Very interested
15	Interested	4 Interested
10	About 50-50	3 About 50-50
5	Not very interested	2 Not very interested
1	Definitely not interested	1 Definitely not interested

AGAPE

(20-15-10-5-1) 1. Work with spiritually weaker members.
(5-4-3-2-1)   2. Visit hospitals and shut-ins.
(5-4-3-2-1)   3. Prepare food for funerals.
(5-4-3-2-1)   4. Check Bible School attendance.
(5-4-3-2-1)   5. Follow up on absentees.

BENEVOLENT

(20-15-10-5-1) 1. Help people with financial and physical needs.
(5-4-3-2-1) 2. Work in clothing room.
(5-4-3-2-1) 3. Interview people seeking help.
(5-4-3-2-1) 4. Repair furniture and appliances.
(5-4-3-2-1) 5. Provide food for needy families.

CARPENTER'S CHILDREN

(20-15-10-5-1) 1. Help teach children by using television.
(5-4-3-2-1) 2. Research and plan TV lesson.
(5-4-3-2-1) 3. Use puppets on TV.
(5-4-3-2-1) 4. Help with Carpenter's Children notebook.
(5-4-3-2-1) 5. Follow up on TV requests.

CHRIST'S HAVEN

(20-15-10-5-1) 1. Work with homeless children.
(5-4-3-2-1) 2. Keep children from broken homes on weekend.
(5-4-3-2-1) 3. Visit children's home.
(5-4-3-2-1) 4. Provide special programs for homeless children.
(5-4-3-2-1) 5. Help with physical needs of homeless children.

CHURCH GROWTH

(20-15-10-5-1) 1. Help promote the physical growth of the church.
(5-4-3-2-1) 2. Research reasons for church growth.
(5-4-3-2-1) 3. Implement programs for growth.
(5-4-3-2-1) 4. Provide seminars for those interested in church growth.
(5-4-3-2-1) 5. Research needs of people in community.

COMMUNICATION

(20-15-10-5-1) 1. Help communicate what is happening at the church.
(5-4-3-2-1) 2. Write newspaper articles.
(5-4-3-2-1) 3. Design brochures.
(5-4-3-2-1) 4. Take pictures.
(5-4-3-2-1) 5. Provide publicity for congregation.

CHRISTIAN EDUCATION

(20-15-10-5-1)   1. Teach students in Bible school.
(5-4-3-2-1)   2. Prepare Bible school visuals and materials.
(5-4-3-2-1)   3. Help students grow spiritually closer to God and each other.
(5-4-3-2-1)   4. Daily Bible Reader.
(5-4-3-2-1)   5. Love to teach.

FACILITY MANAGEMENT

(20-15-10-5-1)   1. Provide for the needs of the facility.
(5-4-3-2-1)   2. Help with building repairs.
(5-4-3-2-1)   3. Coordinate work day for building maintenance.
(5-4-3-2-1)   4. Oversee repairs done by outsiders.
(5-4-3-2-1)   5. Look for new ways to improve facility.

FAMILY LIFE MINISTRY

(20-15-10-5-1)   1. Coordinate activities of the Family Life Center.
(5-4-3-2-1)   2. Provide fellowship activities.
(5-4-3-2-1)   3. Supervise athletic activities.
(5-4-3-2-1)   4. Plan special family events.
(5-4-3-2-1)   5. Research Single and Family needs.

FAMILY FINANCIAL COUNSELING MINISTRY

(20-15-10-5-1)   1. Help families wisely plan finances.
(5-4-3-2-1)   2. Train others in family financial management.
(5-4-3-2-1)   3. Interested in helping others in financial planning.
(5-4-3-2-1)   4. Conduct classes on family finances.
(5-4-3-2-1)   5. Evaluate family's financial needs.

FELLOWSHIP MINISTRY

(20-15-10-5-1)   1. Provide fellowship activities for church.
(5-4-3-2-1)   2. Help with churchwide dinners.
(5-4-3-2-1)   3. Provide "welcome home" dinners for new members.
(5-4-3-2-1)   4. Set up tables and chairs for fellowship activities.
(5-4-3-2-1)   5. Arrange special fellowship activities.

FINANCE MINISTRY

(20-15-10-5-1)   1. Accumulate and disperse church funds.
(5-4-3-2-1)   2. Coordinate material for church budget.
(5-4-3-2-1)   3. Prepare financial statements.
(5-4-3-2-1)   4. Keep people informed about financial needs of church.
(5-4-3-2-1)   5. Count money.

FOUR SEASONS MINISTRY

(20-15-10-5-1)   1. Provide service to those in convalescent homes.
(5-4-3-2-1)   2. Help with services in convalescent homes.
(5-4-3-2-1)   3. Write cards to those in convalescent homes.
(5-4-3-2-1)   4. Visit convalescent homes.
(5-4-3-2-1)   5. Strive to meet needs of those in convalescent homes.

INFORMATION AND ASSISTANCE

(20-15-10-5-1)   1. Provide helpful information and friendly atmosphere for visitors and members.
(5-4-3-2-1)   2. Greet new people in foyer.
(5-4-3-2-1)   3. Usher.
(5-4-3-2-1)   4. Provide name tags.
(5-4-3-2-1)   5. Serve at information booth.

INVOLVEMENT MINISTRY

(20-15-10-5-1)   1. Involve people in the work of the church.
(5-4-3-2-1)   2. Interview new members.
(5-4-3-2-1)   3. Identify talents of new members.
(5-4-3-2-1)   4. Find place for members in one of our ministries.
(5-4-3-2-1)   5. Start new ministries to meet needs of people.

LIBRARY MINISTRY

(20-15-10-5-1)   1. Coordinate church library.
(5-4-3-2-1)   2. Purchase new library books.
(5-4-3-2-1)   3. Assist with library newsletter.
(5-4-3-2-1)   4. Catalog library books.
(5-4-3-2-1)   5. Promote new library programs.

MISSION MINISTRY

(20-15-10-5-1) 1. Take gospel outside our area.
(5-4-3-2-1)   2. Make congregation mission-minded.
(5-4-3-2-1)   3. Research and evaluate mission fields.
(5-4-3-2-1)   4. Maintain correspondence with missionaries.
(5-4-3-2-1)   5. Mail lesson materials and benevolent packages to mission fields.

NURSERY MINISTRY

(20-15-10-5-1) 1. Provide adequate care for babies.
(5-4-3-2-1)   2. Work in nursery.
(5-4-3-2-1)   3. Recruit nursery workers.
(5-4-3-2-1)   4. Provide nursery for all major church activities.
(5-4-3-2-1)   5. Encourage nursery workers.

OUTREACH MINISTRY

(20-15-10-5-1) 1. Reach people with the Gospel in our community.
(5-4-3-2-1)   2. Be part of visitation team.
(5-4-3-2-1)   3. Teach home Bible studies.
(5-4-3-2-1)   4. Be part of Share Your Faith class.
(5-4-3-2-1)   5. Grade correspondence courses.

RETREAT MINISTRY

(20-15-10-5-1) 1. Coordinate retreat activities.
(5-4-3-2-1)   2. Develop 25-acre retreat center.
(5-4-3-2-1)   3. Organize class retreats.
(5-4-3-2-1)   4. Plan ways retreat site can spiritually help this church.
(5-4-3-2-1)   5. Clean up and repair present retreat site.

SOUND AND TAPE MINISTRY

(20-15-10-5-1) 1. Provide adequate sound system for services and classes.
(5-4-3-2-1)   2. Knowledge of sound equipment.
(5-4-3-2-1)   3. Provide adequate sound system for classes.
(5-4-3-2-1)   4. Work in sound booth.
(5-4-3-2-1)   5. Fulfill tape requests.

SINGLES
(Both couples and singles needed to help)

(20-15-10-5-1)   1. Provide program for singles that draws them closer to God and one another.
(5-4-3-2-1)   2. Plan special functions for singles.
(5-4-3-2-1)   3. Teach in singles program.
(5-4-3-2-1)   4. Open home for gathering of singles.
(5-4-3-2-1)   5. Help meet counseling needs of singles.

39ers MINISTRY

(20-15-10-5-1)   1. Provide activities for the elderly.
(5-4-3-2-1)   2. Enjoy working with elderly.
(5-4-3-2-1)   3. Suggest special speakers and programs.
(5-4-3-2-1)   4. Send cards to sick.
(5-4-3-2-1)   5. Special care for widows and widowers.

WORSHIP

(20-15-10-5-1)   1. Plan meaningful worship experiences.
(5-4-3-2-1)   2. Select communion servers.
(5-4-3-2-1)   3. Select prayer leaders.
(5-4-3-2-1)   4. Assist with baptismal garments.
(5-4-3-2-1)   5. Preparation of communion materials.

YOUTH

(20-15-10-5-1)   1. Plan spiritual and social development of youth.
(5-4-3-2-1)   2. Plan fellowships.
(5-4-3-2-1)   3. Participate in youth retreats.
(5-4-3-2-1)   4. Help with youth devotionals.
(5-4-3-2-1)   5. Teach in youth program.

CHURCH OFFICE

(20-15-10-5-1)   1. Do volunteer office work at the church office.
(5-4-3-2-1)   2. Type.
(5-4-3-2-1)   3. File and research.
(5-4-3-2-1)   4. Help with mailings.
(5-4-3-2-1)   5. Run errands.

Appendix D: Talent Interest Profile

0 5 10 15 20 25 30 35 40

| Agape |
| Benevolent |
| Christ's Haven |
| Carpenter's Children |
| Church Growth |
| Communication |
| Christian Education |
| Facility Management |
| Family Life |
| Family Financial Counseling |
| Fellowship |
| Finance |
| Four Seasons |
| Information and Assistance |
| Involvement |
| Library |
| Mission |
| Nursery |
| Outreach |
| Retreat |
| Singles |
| Sound and Tape |
| 39ers |
| Worship |
| Youth |
| Church Office |

App E Spiritual Gifts Survey

Church Name Here

SPIRITUAL GIFTS SURVEY

People Matter to God

Front Cover of 8½×11 booklet
Rear cover is blank except for church
name, address, and telephone numbers

246

SPIRITUAL GIFTS SURVEY

Involvement Ministry

INSTRUCTIONS:

Mark each statement to the extent that it reflects your life and/or your feelings. Enter the appropriate number in the unshaded box according to the following scale:

0 - Not at all
1 - Little
2 - Some
3 - Much

Example:

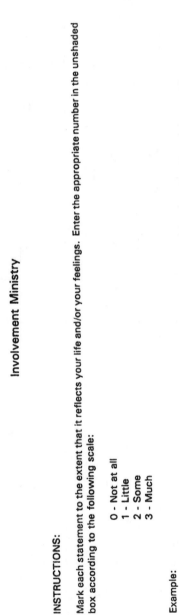

| I pray knowing that God hears and is already active in providing an answer. | 3 |

After you have answered the questions, add each column and enter the total of each column at the end of the survey. Each column represents a different spiritual gift.

247

STATEMENT — Page 1	A	B	C	D	E	F	G	H	I	J	K	L	M	N	O	P
I am direct, frank, passionate, and persuasive in speaking about God's message.	□															
I find that I identify with the downtrodden of society more than most.						□										
I often assume the leadership in a group where others are not assigned to lead.								□								
I am willing to spend large amounts of time in prayer for others.			□													
I enjoy getting to know new people at church and helping them to get acquainted with others.				□												
I have the capacity to identify, define, and hate evil.	□															
I have a strong sense of evil and good in today's world.															□	
I feel most fulfilled when I am able to serve in an area of need no matter the task.						□										
I am accepting and sensitive toward others who are troubled or in crisis.							□									
When a group of Christians gets together for relaxation and fellowship, I want to sing hymns, devotional songs or contemporary Christian songs.									□							
When a person is confronted with a problem, I can usually guide them in the best biblical solution.					□											
Telling others what Christ has done for me is one of the greatest joys in my life.																
On many occasions I have trusted in God to provide an answer or solution when things looked impossible.																
I seem to have the ability to clarify different biblical concepts in a way that people understand them and are motivated to study them more.								□								
I have enjoyed long-term relationships with varied groups of people, sharing personally in their successes and failures as they share in mine.																
I can accurately recognize spiritual gift(s) that others have or don't have.															□	
I usually have a strong sense of where I am going and can influence others in that direction.																□

STATEMENT (Page 2)	A	B	C	D	E	F	G	H	I	J	K	L	M	N	O	P
I view my house as a very important tool in my ministry to others and enjoy having others use it whenever there is a need.			X													
I hurt for others who are poverty-stricken, physically sick, lonely or imprisoned.																
Once I know the goal I can't help but think of plans and strategies to achieve it.													X			
Others affirm me in my ability to explain clearly what it means for Jesus Christ to be savior.									X							
Others tell me that I have helped them understand important facts in scripture.					X											
When alone, I continually find myself singing or listening to Christian music.							X									
I enjoy giving my money and possessions without expecting anything in return.																
I willingly do a variety of odd jobs around the church to practically meet the needs of others.																
Others tell me that I have an unusual ability to trust in the presence of God to lead and take care of me.											X					
I am comfortable pressing for a decision when sharing Christ with a lost person.			X													
Spending time with visitors in order to help them feel welcomed and cared for is very important to me.												X				
Guiding people to specific scriptures and then praying with them about important lessons they can learn about maturing in Christ is a big part of how I view ministry in my own life.					X											
I have the ability to motivate others.																
I enjoy assuming the responsibility for the spiritual well-being of a particular group of Christians.		X														
I enjoy organizing ideas, people and events.																
Normally, my Christian character, lifestyle and behavior seem to motivate others to follow me.								X								
I have a desire to help those who are suffering or undeserving and feel I do well in such a ministry.						X										

STATEMENT — Page 3	A	B	C	D	E	F	G	H	I	J	K	L	M	N	O	P
Wanting to relate to unbelievers so that I can share my faith is a top priority to me.																X
I am willing to suffer or have others suffer if it yields a more obedient or faithful walk with God.	X															
I have confidence in God that even in difficult times I can accomplish great things for Him.				X												
I have a strong concern to relate biblical truth to life.										X						
Finding things that need to be done and doing them without being asked is typical of me.																
I am able to adjust my leadership style so that it is appropriate for the maturity of those working with me.								X								
When making important decisions, I place great importance on determining God's will for my life.														X		
I enjoy having people in my home even though the house may not be totally presentable.			X													
I am a good manager of money and possessions without expecting anything in return.							X									
I enjoy leading or directing others in singing songs of praise to God.											X					
Spending time with those who are ignored by most people is a pattern of behavior for me.						X										
I feel at ease when sharing Christ as my Savior and Lord.			X													
I pray knowing that God hears and is already active in providing an answer.																
I am easily frustrated when I hear people violate the context of scripture.									X							
Evaluating results from studies of the effectiveness of a major church program is a task I accomplish with ease.															X	
I can see through a phony before it is clearly evident to others.												X				
Teaching that is not practical upsets me.													X			
I am able to communicate a leadership goal clearly, then organize people and resources to achieve it.												X				

STATEMENT — Page 4	A	B	C	D	E	F	G	H	I	J	K	L	M	N	O	P
I successfully and routinely solve problems by using biblical principles.															X	
It is hard for me to say "No" when I see so many things that need to be done.														X		
I like to greet, welcome, and create a warm, friendly atmosphere for those who attend functions of this church.					X											
When I teach, I feel comfortable responding to questions.			X													
One of my greatest joys has been giving anonymously to help fulfill an individual's or ministry's need.												X				
Other people might perceive me as being weak because of my patience and lack of firmness with some people.						X										
I enjoy and place great emphasis on the study of scripture.		X														
I am impatient with the wrong actions and wrong motives of others.								X								
I get frustrated when others don't share their faith with unbelievers as much as I do.						X										
I am confident of God's daily presence and move boldly in His power.									X							
I can easily recognize when a person is being led by the Spirit of God.							X									
Delegation of important responsibilities is something I do well.														X		
I can effectively motivate others to get involved in ministry when it is needed.												X				
It is evident to me that others experience strong emotions, like joy and sorrow, as I share my thoughts and feelings through meaningful songs.													X			
Others recognize my biblical approach to problem solving and often ask me for workable ideas or alternatives to their problems.								X								
Paul's concern (Col. 1:10) that I be "increasing in the knowledge of God" is something I take and apply seriously.										X						
I usually have a readiness to help if there is a job that needs to be done.																X

STATEMENT — Page 5	A	B	C	D	E	F	G	H	I	J	K	L	M	N	O	P
I am willing to exert energy to persuade and organize others to move toward biblical objectives.																
Christians have told me that I have helped them understand biblical truths that make a difference in the way they presently live.																
Many people have told me that when we host them in our house they "feel at home" with us.																
I can recognize whether a person's teaching is of God, of Satan, or of human origin.																
I feel deeply moved when made aware of the urgent financial needs of a ministry in the Lord's work.																
People look to me to help those who are going through a difficult time.																
In my conversations with unbelievers, I will often bring up spiritual matters.																
Others have told me how much they appreciated my continued support and concern for them.																
Understanding and retaining large amounts of biblical truth is easy for me.																
I am able to recognize the spiritual gifts in others and put them to work in appropriate areas that express that gift.																
I can easily delegate responsibilities to others, even when the ultimate goal is of utmost importance to me.																
I make what appears to be correct decisions for my life.																
Having to routinely practice songs to enhance the worship of others is not a burden but is one of the great joys of ministry to me.																
I believe the teaching-learning process is vital to local church growth.																
When I speak to a group, my message usually deals with topics, not verse by verse studies.																
I am always looking for better ways to share my faith.																
I have an abiding peace knowing that God will work all things for good.																

STATEMENT — Page 6	A	B	C	D	E	F	G	H	I	J	K	L	M	N	O	P
I know that I have a knack for making strangers feel comfortable and at home.															X	
I am not afraid to warn a person or a group of people that they are parting with God's truth on a matter.															X	
I am satisfied to contribute my skills by helping others in charge.										X						
I have a compassionate need to protect wandering believers.		X														
I study and read quite a bit in order to learn new biblical truths.											X					
My greatest fulfillment comes from giving to the Lord, even if it means maintaining a lower standard of living.					X											
I feel compelled to expose sin in the culture, church or an individual's life in order to have them walk consistently in the truth.	X															
I enjoy helping others resolve complicated problems in their lives.																
I am motivated by people more than by tasks.														X		
People say that they learn a lot when I teach because I make the lessons easy to understand and motivate them to apply the truths.																X
Bearing the responsibility of the success of a particular task in my church is not a great burden to me.									X							
I enjoy giving my time, energy, and insights to young or straying Christians even if it means that I am inconvenienced.								X								
I am able to identify that which is false to Christ's teachings.																
I understand the emotional and spiritual swings of those going through painful experiences and am able to patiently support them.						X										
I have the ability to discover new truths for myself through reading or observing situations first hand.													X			
I give cheerfully because I love God and want to see His work extended and helped.						X										
I feel joy in persisting in prayer for specific needs even when an answer is not yet apparent.					X											

253

STATEMENT — Page 7	A	B	C	D	E	F	G	H	I	J	K	L	M	N	O	P
When strangers stay in my home, I sense a feeling of enjoyment and satisfaction.																X
The people I select for leadership positions in the church often prove to be good selections.			X													
I am content to perform jobs that are considered unimportant by other people.				X												
I rely on and use scripture to validate my arguments.	X															
I am willing to study whatever is necessary in order to feed those I am teaching and in relationship with.														X		
People tend to say they feel good when they are around me.									X							
I often feel a burden in ministry that compels me to organize a group of people to achieve a goal or fix what is perceived to be a problem.													X			
I have a concern for details in the scriptures.												X				
Others tell me that my singing has been a source of spiritual strength and encouragement for them.							X									
I enjoy working with facts and figures in order to help a ministry complete its task.															X	
I am able to identify ideas, plans or activities that are not true to the Bible.											X					
I feel a great need to expose sin to others even if it means being considered by others as narrow-minded.	X															
I am concerned that interpersonal relationships are peaceable, reasonable, and without hypocrisy or partiality.														X		
I measure my own and others' spirituality by the ability and willingness to give.																
Being a teacher's aide or an usher, helping set up or clean up, or doing some other supporting task suits me well.										X						
Teaching adults and/or children about God's word and how it applies to everyday life is enjoyable and energizing to me.						X										
One of the most effective ways I can teach others about God's salvation, grace, and the joy of being a Christian is through song.																X

STATEMENT	Page 8	A	B	C	D	E	F	G	H	I	J	K	L	M	N	O	P
I tend to be a verbal encourager to those who are unsure of themselves, discouraged, or troubled.													☐				
People have told me that I get too personally and emotionally involved in helping others with needs.							☐										
I regularly see the activity of God in my affairs as well as in the affairs of others.						☐											
I am not afraid to give spiritual guidance and direction in a group of Christians, even if I must be patient but firm.			☐														
When working with an unorganized group, I tend to step in and help find ways to complete the task more efficiently.										☐							
One of my strongest motivations is in wanting to create an appropriate atmosphere through songs in assemblies or fellowships.								☐									
I give myself, things and money liberally to the Lord's work.												☐					
I speak the truth of God's Word even when it is unpopular and difficult for others to accept.		☐															
TOTALS FOR EACH COLUMN		A	B	C	D	E	F	G	H	I	J	K	L	M	N	O	P

____ A Prophecy

____ B Pastor

____ C Hospitality

____ D Evangelism

____ E Faith

____ F Mercy

____ G Music Vocal

____ H Leadership

____ I Administration/Organization

____ J Helps

____ K Giving

____ L Encouragement/Exhortation

____ M Knowledge

____ N Wisdom

____ O Discernment of Spirits

____ P Teaching

DEFINITIONS OF SPIRITUAL GIFTS

ADMINISTRATION/ORGANIZATION: The God-empowered ability to understand what makes an organization function and what is required to work with and through fellow disciples to plan and achieve biblical goals and organizational objectives.

DISCERNMENT OF SPIRITS: The God-empowered ability to distinguish between truth and error, being able to use this information to caution those in the body, resulting in continued spiritual health.

ENCOURAGEMENT/EXHORTATION: The God-empowered ability to comfort, reassure, strengthen, affirm, and challenge, doing it in such a way that spirits are lifted, helped and healed.

EVANGELISM: The God-empowered ability to be a productive communicator of God's *Good News* about Christ to unbelievers.

FAITH: The God-empowered ability to see the Lord's will clearly and to act upon it in great confidence in spite of all worldly evidence to the contrary.

GIVING: The God-empowered ability to contribute yourself, money, time and material resources to the work of the Lord with cheerfulness and liberality.

HELPS: The God-empowered ability to provide physical labor for the accomplishment of tasks within the body of Christ, thus enabling others to increase the effectiveness of their own spiritual gifts.

HOSPITALITY: The God-empowered ability to provide in your own home, as well as other settings, an open house with an atmosphere of acceptance and love to those in need of food, lodging or fellowship.

KNOWLEDGE: The God-empowered ability to discover, accumulate, analyze, clarify, organize and communicate the Word of God so that the author's intended meaning is seen in its original context.

LEADERSHIP: The God-empowered ability to set goals in accordance with God's purpose and to motivate others in the body of Christ to voluntarily and harmoniously work together to accomplish those goals for the glory of God.

MERCY: The God-empowered ability to identify with the hurting, causing you to respond in an appropriate way with comfort, aid, understanding, and cheerfulness.

MUSIC VOCAL: The God-empowered ability to use one's voice in singing so that it honors God and blesses others, causing them to be strengthened to worship in a submitted and authentic way.

PASTOR: The God-empowered ability to lead, nurture, instruct, and care for individuals or groups in the body on a long-term basis so that their relationship with Christ is deepened and faith is developed.

PROPHECY: The God-empowered ability and urgent need to communicate God's truths with power and clarity in such a way that brings correction, repentance, edification, and comfort.

TEACHING: The God-empowered ability to understand, communicate and apply the Word of God in such a way that the teacher and listeners will learn and be motivated to have a deeper relationship with Jesus Christ.

WISDOM: The God-empowered ability to know how to apply God's truth to contemporary problems, combining an understanding of life situations with a perception of what to do and how to do it.

Central's 1992 Budget Program and Presentation

App F

BUDGET INVOLVEMENT PROGRAM

Nov. 17	- Deacon installation and training
	Challenged to plan program and budget
Dec. 3, 10, 17	- Finance Ministry Meetings
Dec. 8	- Budget Forms given to deacons
Dec. 18	- Staff Meeting on Budget
Dec. 18	- Elders Meeting on Budget
Dec. 22	- Budgets due to be returned
Jan. 5	- Noon meal and meeting. Elders, ministers, deacons, adult teachers, Bible school supervisors and mates.
Jan. 15	- Train Budget Group Leaders for Family Life Groups that night.
Jan. 19	- Audio Visual Presentation Sunday Morning
	Budget envelopes ready in pews
	Budgets discussed in Family Life Groups that night
Jan. 22	- Ministry Fair Meeting
Jan. 26	- Sermon on "Why I'm Excited about the Future of Our Church"
Jan. 26	- Ministry Fair
Jan. 5, 12, 19, 26	- Brief testimonies from individuals on Sunday morning
Feb. 2	- Sunday Morning Sermon - "Moses - Mighty in the Lord: God's Purpose for Stewardship," Lesson 5

WHY DO PEOPLE GIVE TO LOCAL CHURCH BUDGETS

1. Feel they "ought" to give to God (Christian duty).
2. "Taught" to give.
3. Because of a particular ministry or ministries.
4. Feel good about goals and direction of local church and what's happening in the life of the church. (A place to call home or exciting.)
5. Spirit of giving is "caught" from example of others (testimonies).
6. Because of a perceived need (crisis giving).
7. Because their needs are met.

ALL MEMBERS ARE ENCOURAGED TO INCREASE GIVING 2% OR MORE

Income	2% Wkly	4% Wkly	6% Wkly	8% Wkly	10% Wkly
$ 10,000	$ 3.85	$ 7.70	$ 11.55	$ 15.40	$ 19.25
20,000	7.70	15.40	23.10	30.80	38.50
30,000	11.55	23.10	34.65	46.20	57.75
40,000	15.40	30.80	46.20	61.60	77.00
50,000	19.25	38.50	57.75	77.00	96.25
60,000	23.10	46.20	69.30	92.40	115.50
70,000	26.95	53.90	80.85	107.80	134.75
80,000	30.80	61.60	92.40	123.20	154.00
90,000	34.65	69.30	103.95	138.60	173.25
100,000	38.50	77.00	115.50	154.00	192.50

1992
"A LOVING HOME SEES THE NEED"

(SONG: 1st verse of "A Place to Call Home")

Our church is truly a place to call home. It's been mine and my wife's for many years. It's been home to some of you for over 25 years. Because of our recent growth, it's a brand new home for many of you. In fact, the 1,704 people we had in our assembly worship Sunday, and our 1,465 in attendance for Bible school was our largest crowd at the building in nearly eight years.

A loving home sees the need:
- TO EVANGELIZE THE COMMUNITY
- TO ENERGIZE THE CHURCH
- TO MOBILIZE FOR SERVICE
- TO NEUTRALIZE THE DEBT

I. EVANGELIZE THE COMMUNITY

Our 1992 budget is dedicating over $105,000 toward evangelizing the community. Many special events are planned as this church family strives to touch Amarillo with the love of Christ. We're planning a "Friend's Day" on April 12, when we will reach out to family, friends and neighbors. A special Easter service is planned for April 19. And a giant Community Teachers Appreciation Night is planned for May 20.

The Community Care Ministry continues to feed and clothe hundreds each year. Hundreds of sacks of groceries were donated to us during our "Sack Sunday" food drive.

The local Jail Ministry continues to baptize over 60 people each year.

We continue to expand our Missions Ministry with our support of the Continent of Great Cities Program. This includes help for our missionaries ELLIS LONG, ALAOR LEITE, GARY SORRELLS, and BOB WALDRON. Central has been the sponsoring congregation for this great mission effort for 30 years. This ministry has established 18 new congregations and 4,377 baptisms in the past six years. There are now 99 congregations and 102 full-time missionaries in Brazil. The majority of these missionaries have been recruited and trained by Central's stateside missionaries. The Central church is also trying to raise an additional $100,000 outside the budget to help continue this great effort.

(SONG: 2nd verse of "A Place to Call Home")

A loving home sees the need to:

II. ENERGIZE THE CHURCH

This portion of our budget calls for $241,532. The church has already been energized as each home participated in the "40 Days of Prayer" devotionals. This climaxed with the installation of 58 new deacons. These deacons have expanded their ministries and involved many different members in the preparation of this budget. The first major activity of all the new deacons was a "Family Reunion Day." The hard-working ministries successfully brought a spiritual feast to over 1,660 who were in attendance that day.

Our Communications Ministry plans to tell what the Central Family is all about in 1992. They hope to use radio, billboards, newspapers and bumper stickers to let the community know that "Central is a place to call home."

The Cradle Roll department is the first "handshake" of the church, and many new babies are finding a new "Second Home" here. High-quality childcare is a necessity and a priority for all the young children God has blessed us with.

The Central Church has one of the largest Bible class attendances in our brotherhood. This is largely due to the quality programs led by our Children's Supervisors.

(SONG: "We're All Part of the Family" - Children's Voices)

You can see how much these children are enjoying class; take notice of the evidence of the hours teachers spend in preparation.

A Sunday Night Children's Bible Hour is the latest addition to our Children's Education Program.

The large and exciting Youth Ministry has many special activities to bring our young people closer to the Lord. Sunday morning classes, Wednesday night Huddles, retreats, parties, trips, and "Eyes for Him" all bring these youth closer to God and to one another. Almost 2,000 area youth came to our building to enjoy the Acappella concert we hosted on January 12th.

The quality Adult Education Ministry is growing at a rapid pace. Intensive Bible study is mixed with food, fun, fellowship and special projects. A special "90-Day Experience" will begin February 2, whereby each member will be given a plan to read the complete New Testament in 90 days.

Rapid expansion is planned for the Singles and College Ministries in the near future, as we strive to better meet these needs.

Our Family Life Groups will begin meeting in homes on the 2ND SUNDAY of each month, starting in February. A unique video series entitled "In His Steps" will be shown and discussed in our homes beginning in February. It will strive to deepen each family member's spiritual faith and cause us soberly to ask: "What Would Jesus Do?" as we face all the great challenges of life.

Our Music Ministry adds so much to our praise service. A musical presentation called "A Man after God's Own Heart" will be presented on Wednesday evening, May 27th. Carlie Burdett's writing of the song "A Place to Call Home" has done so much to enhance our services.

Praise to God and encouragement of one another is so evident in our exciting assemblies. Inspirational singing, dynamic lessons, encouraging one another and spiritual communion are all important ingredients to our worship assemblies.

Dick Marcear and Ray Fulenwider have begun a new Sunday evening series where they dialogue — teach on "Families of the Bible." Friendly greeters, dedicated sound people and a hard-working Fellowship Ministry all energize fellow Christians. Great interest has been shown in bringing back the Wednesday Night Round-Up Dinners.

(SONG: 3rd verse of "A Place to Call Home")

A LOVING HOME SEES THE NEED TO:

III. MOBILIZE FOR SERVICE

This portion of the budget calls for $483,985. The Involvement Ministry wants each person to find his place and use his gifts to the glory of God. Many of you may want to check ministries listed on the card in your envelope. You can be sure this will be followed up — we want you to be involved! This ministry is also responsible for ministry training.

The New Member Assimilation Ministry strives to help each new member find his place at the church. All new members are invited to attend a six-week class taught by the senior minister, which culminates with a dinner at the home of the senior minister and his wife.

The Barnabas Ministry plans to furnish a host for every new member to encourage them and help them find their place in the family.

Our active Women's Ministries provide ladies classes each Wednesday morning, assist with weddings, host area-wide retreats, help with Meals on Wheels, hospital visitation, wedding and baby showers, and provide special services to High Plains Children's Home.

Our maintenance ministry does everything they can to take care of this beautiful facility, which can be such a useful tool for reaching our community with the gospel.

Family Enrichment Ministry provides counseling, seminars, retreats, and lessons to improve marital, parental and basic human relationships. People come from many miles to attend some of these sessions. A wonderful new class taught by Everett and Peggy Blanton on Wednesday night draws around 200 people.

Family Care is our "Good Samaritan" Program. Many of our members give generously to a designated fund outside the budget to meet the financial needs of others.

The Service Center is the real name for the Church Office. It is truly a service center for this church and community. Pat, Karen, Robin, Janie, Dorothy, Alice & Glenna all do a great job.

Sunshiners are important to the church family. To let them know just how much they mean to us, we've designated the month of February as a time to show appreciation to these special people.

There are many other volunteers and ministries who mobilize for service. We will be having a special Volunteer Appreciation Day on March 1 to let these people know how vital they are to our church family.

(SONG: "Leaning on the Everlasting Arms")

IV. NEUTRALIZE THE DEBT ($569,300)

(Dick, tell in your own words, briefly . . .)
        *Excitement about building the new auditorium, etc.
        *Financial problems

*Financial miracle

*"I'm excited about the future of our church. . ."

1. Been here 16 years — believe this will be our greatest
2. Have great elders to lead us — men of vision and prayer
3. Have great staff team
   a) EVERETT BLANTON (Part-time) — "Calling & Caring"; encourager; former elder at Southwest
   b) PEGGY BLANTON — Counselor; family programs
   c) PAUL SNEED — loved by all; hospitals; funerals
   d) CHAD HAMMOND — New Youth Minister; great gifts and spiritual depth
   e) RAY FULENWIDER — Education & Involvement; loves to see churches grow and develop spiritually; Broadway grew from 1200 to 3200 members while he was there; Richland grew from 900 to 4100 members while he was there.
   f) Elders, deacons, ministers, staff, congregation all work together as a team for the "Family of God"

(SONG: "We're All Part of the Family")

Our 1992 budget calls for $26,923 a week, which is a ten percent increase over last year's giving.

I see a new sunrise for this church. I believe God wants to raise up a great lighthouse for our brotherhood. "Who knows, but that we have been called to the Kingdom for such a time as this" (Esth. 4:14).

CENTRAL CHURCH OF CHRIST
"A Place To Call Home"
"A Loving Home Sees the Need"

1. To Evangelize the Community ($105,183)

Baptismal Assistance	High Plains Children's Home	Community Outreach	Community Care
Missions	Special Events	Visitation	Jail Ministry
Church Growth			

2. To Energize the Church ($241,532)

Lord's Table Service	Calling & Caring	Family Life Groups	Education-Adult
Education-Children	Christian Camps & Retreats	Greeters & Ushers	Lighting & Sound
Education-Youth	Nursery	Singles	Library
Youth	Huddles	Fellowship Dinners	Tape
Prayer	Support Groups	Adult Recreation	Dorcas & Timothy
Communications	Music		

3. To Mobilize for Service ($483,985)

Barnabas	Family Care	Finance	Contribution
Involvement	Maintenance-Building	Welcome Home	Parking & Traffic
Women's Ministry	Service Center	Hospital Visitation	Transportation
New Member Assimilation	Grief Recovery	Building & Classroom	Personal Financial
Ground Maintenance	Visitation, Special	Directories	Counseling
Family Enrichment	Sunshiners	Hall Monitors	

4. To Neutralize the Debt ($569,300)

Building Debt Service

Weekly Proposed Budget — $26,923
Annual Proposed Budget — $1,400,000
"Not Equal Gifts, But Equal Love"

Budget Publicity Materials

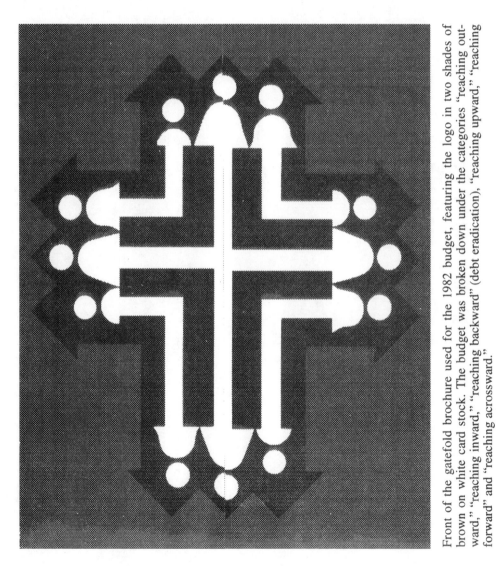

Front of the gatefold brochure used for the 1982 budget, featuring the logo in two shades of brown on white card stock. The budget was broken down under the categories "reaching outward," "reaching inward," "reaching backward" (debt eradication), "reaching upward," "reaching forward" and "reaching acrossward."

264

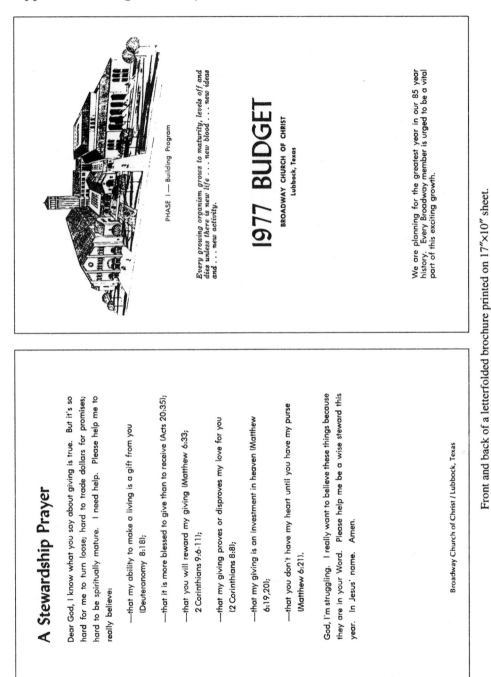

PHASE I — Building Program

Every growing organism grows to maturity, levels off and dies unless there is new life . . . new blood . . . new ideas and . . . new activity.

1977 BUDGET

BROADWAY CHURCH OF CHRIST
Lubbock, Texas

We are planning for the greatest year in our 85 year history. Every Broadway member is urged to be a vital part of this exciting growth.

A Stewardship Prayer

Dear God, I know what you say about giving is true. But it's so hard for me to turn loose; hard to trade dollars for promises; hard to be spiritually mature. I need help. Please help me to really believe:

—that my ability to make a living is a gift from you (Deuteronomy 8:18);

—that it is more blessed to give than to receive (Acts 20:35);

—that you will reward my giving (Matthew 6:33; 2 Corinthians 9:6-11);

—that my giving proves or disproves my love for you (2 Corinthians 8:8);

—that my giving is an investment in heaven (Matthew 6:19,20);

—that you don't have my heart until you have my purse (Matthew 6:21).

God, I'm struggling. I really want to believe these things because they are in your Word. Please help me be a wise steward this year. In Jesus' name. Amen.

Broadway Church of Christ / Lubbock, Texas

Front and back of a letterfolded brochure printed on 17"×10" sheet.

1977 BUDGET

1. PREACHING THE GOSPEL **$531,643**

In Lubbock—Radio and Television, Advertising, Meetings, Buses, Salaries, Thursday School, Tracts, Youth Outreach, Spanish Program, Deaf Program, Personal Evangelism, College Program.

In the United States—Las Vegas, N.M.; Espanola, N.M.; Buena Vista, Colo.; Vancouver, Wash.; New York City; Herald of Truth.

Around the World—Frankfurt, Essen and Heidelberg, Germany; Regina and Port Coquitlam, Canada; Glenrothes, Scotland, Liverpool, England; Belfast, Northern Ireland; Barcelona, Spain.

2. EDIFYING THE CHURCH **$155,760**

Educational Program, Library, Equipment and Supplies, Printing, Church Bulletin, Communion Supplies, Fellowship and Visitation, Hymn Books, Building Maintenance.

3. MINISTERING TO THE NEEDY .... **$ 42,380**

Children's Homes: Lubbock, Boles, Medina, High Plains, Sunny Glen, Tipton, Foster. Homes for the Aged: Houston, Gunter. Smithlawn Maternity Home. Local Benevolence.

4. PLANNING FOR GROWTH AND SERVICE .... **$ 77,412**

Property Acquisition, Property Improvement, Debt Service.

TOTAL **$807,295**

WEEKLY CONTRIBUTION NEEDED **$15,524.90**

In addition to the regular operational Budget, there will be at least two Special Contributions during the year: MISSIONS (May), CHILDREN'S HOME (December).

Of special importance will be our financial involvement in the new building program. This will require the most sacrificial gifts ever asked of our people.

When I Give

WHEN I GIVE NOTHING:
I cast a vote to close the church.
I take a "free ride" on the gifts and services of others.

WHEN I GIVE LESS THAN LAST YEAR:
I have experienced a decrease in income — or —
I have changed my priorities — or —
I question the need for the work the church is doing.

WHEN I GIVE LESS THAN ONE-TENTH OF MY INCOME:
I do less than what was required of the poorest of the Jews.

WHEN I GIVE GRUDGINGLY:
I find no joy in my giving.
I am a disappointment to the Lord, for God loves a cheerful giver (2 Corinthians 9:7).

WHEN I REFUSE TO PURPOSE IN ADVANCE:
I fail to follow God's plan (2 Corinthians 9:7).
I make it difficult for the elders to make plans for the year.

WHEN I GIVE WEEKLY:
I help fulfill the planned programs of the church.
I make it much easier for myself by avoiding the accumulation of my stewardship obligation.
I find joy and satisfaction in my giving.
I follow the God-given plan (1 Corinthians 16:2).

WHEN I GIVE PROPORTIONATELY:
I shall be blessed in my giving and will be enriched in every way (2 Corinthians 9:11).
I shall increase my gifts as my income increases.

Stewardship Test

1. In view of what God has done for me, my giving reflects fairness with Him. ☐ Yes ☐ No
2. I believe God deserves at least 10% of my income. ☐ Yes ☐ No
3. I believe ninety cents will go farther with God's blessing than a dollar without His blessing. ☐ Yes ☐ No
4. I have grown in the grace of giving during the past year. ☐ Yes ☐ No
5. I believe God is pleased with the level of my giving. ☐ Yes ☐ No
6. Because of what God has done for me I find real joy in giving. ☐ Yes ☐ No
7. My giving shows that God has first place in my heart. ☐ Yes ☐ No

Consider giving at least 10%

An increasing number of our people are giving 10% or more of their income to the church. Please consider giving a minimum of this amount for the most important work in the world.

Calculated on the basis of 50 weeks per year, 10% amounts to $2 per week for every $1,000 per year earned.

If your annual income is:

$1,000—the weekly offering of a 10% giver is	$ 2.00
$5,000—the weekly offering of a 10% giver is	$ 10.00
$10,000—the weekly offering of a 10% giver is	$ 20.00
$15,000—the weekly offering of a 10% giver is	$ 30.00
$20,000—the weekly offering of a 10% giver is	$ 40.00
$30,000—the weekly offering of a 10% giver is	$ 60.00
$50,000—the weekly offering of a 10% giver is	$ 100.00
$75,000—the weekly offering of a 10% giver is	$ 150.00
$100,000—the weekly offering of a 10% giver is	$ 200.00

Inside spread of the 1977 budget booklet

Money Back Guarantee

If the Broadway church were to give you a written guarantee to return everything you give this year if you did not benefit from generous giving . . . would you increase your giving? You have a much better promise. It comes from God.

GUARANTEED RETURN

"Bring the full tithes into the storehouse . . . and thereby put me to the test, says the Lord of hosts, if I will not open the windows of heaven for you and pour down for you an overflowing blessing." (Malachi 3:10).

"Give, and it will be given to you; good measure, pressed down, shaken together, running over, will be put into your lap. For the measure you give will be the measure you get back" (Luke 6:38).

"He who sows sparingly will also reap sparingly, and he who sows bountifully will also reap bountifully . . . And God is able to provide you with every blessing in abundance, so that you may always have enough of everything and may provide in abundance for every good work. . . . He who supplies seed to the sower and bread for food will supply and multiply your resources . . . You will be enriched in every way for great generosity . . ." (2 Corinthians 9:6, 8, 10, 11).

There is God's promise. Let us pray that it will be matched by our faith.

Foldout flap from the 1977 budget booklet

"Money Back Guarantee" was the budget theme for 1977,
but this same guarantee stamement was used in other later brochures as well.

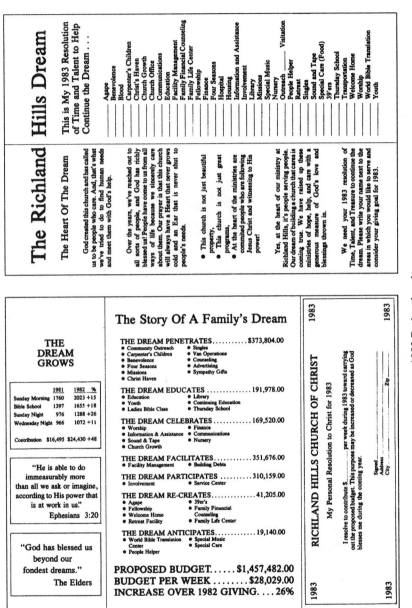

1983 Budget brochure

Shown are the front (two flaps fold out) and the inside spread. The Back of the brochure had the words to the song "To Dream the Impossible Dream."

Money Back Guarantee

If the Richland Hills church were to give you a written guarantee to return everything you give this year if you did not benefit from generous giving...would you increase your giving?

You have a much better promise. It comes from God.

GUARANTEED RETURN

"Bring the whole tithe into the storehouse.... Test me in this," says the Lord Almighty, "and see if I will not throw open the floodgates of heaven and pour out so much blessing that you will not have room enough for it." (Malachi 3:10)

"Give, and it will be given to you. A good measure, pressed down, shaken together and running over, will be poured into your lap. For with the measure you use, it will be measured to you." (Luke 6:38)

"Remember this: Whoever sows sparingly will also reap sparingly, and whoever sows generously will also reap generously.... And God is able to make all grace abound to you, so that in all things at all times, having all that you need, you will abound in ever good work.... Now he who supplies seed to the sower and bread for food will also supply and increase your store of seed and will enlarge the harvest of your righteousness. You will be made rich in ever way so that you can be generous on ever occasion, and through us your generosity will result in thanksgiving to God.

(2 Corinthians 9:6, 8, 10, 11)

There is God's promise. Let us pray that it will be matched by our faith.

RICHLAND HILLS
CHURCH OF CHRIST
6720 N. E. Loop 820 76118

RICHLAND HILLS CHURCH OF CHRIST

THE STORY OF A FAMILY'S FAITH

II Corinthians 5:7..."We walk by faith, not by sight." NAS

1984 was an incredible year for the Richland Hills Family.

- Over $8 million committed by this congregation for Building to Serve.
- Purchased 54 acres on Loop 820 for new facilities.
- Had ground breaking for $10,000,000 facilities to be ready in the summer of 1986.
- Membership reached 2900.
- Gave over $1,800,000 in regular contribution.
- Added 4 new missionaries.
- Launched 15 new ministries.
- Hosted 1300 church leaders from all over the nation in two Church Growth Seminars.
- Bread for A Hungry World collected more than $1,000,000 to feed hungry people all over the world.

Back and front of the 1985 budget brochure

Inside pages of the 1985 budget brochure

The brochures for 1984 (not shown) and 1985 were 8½×11" sheets folded once. Note how the theme for the year's budget is carried through in the divisions listed.

MOUNTAIN MOVING FAITH

Matthew 17:20 — Jesus answered..."your faith is too small. I tell you the truth. If your faith is as big as a mustard seed, you can say to this mountain, 'Move from here to there,' and the mountain will move. All things will be possible for you."

RICHLAND HILLS FAMILY GIVING REPORT

* All families will be mailed Progress Giving Reports in 1985 for IRS records.

Year	Amount
76	6,190
77	7,216
78	8,104
79	8,940
80	11,991
81	16,465
82	22,153
83	25,393
84	30,000
85	39,689

FAITH CARES			**$264,969**
FAITH CARES			**$264,969**
• Benevolence	• Church Growth		
• Christ's Haven	• Singles		
• Four Seasons	• Visitation		
• Video	• Discipling		
FAITH SHARES			**$293,374**
• Missions	• World Bible Translation Center		
FAITH PROVIDES			**$313,889**
• Facility Planning	• Maintenance - Exterior		
• Maintenance - Building	• Maintenance - Mechanical		
FAITH CELEBRATES			**$166,039**
• Assembly Management	• Nursery		
• Assembly Planning	• Sound and Tape		
• Information and Assistance	• Special Music		
FAITH LOVES			**$106,133**
• Fellowship	• 39ers		
• Hospitals - Shut-ins	• Family Care		
• Special Care	• Calling and Caring		
• Family Life Center	• Communications		
FAITH EDUCATES			**$300,383**
• Education - Adult	• Ladies' Bible Class		
• Education - Children	• Youth - Junior High		
• Young Children's World	• Youth - Senior High		
• Library			
FAITH SERVES			**$423,823**
• Involvement	• Service Center		
• Welcome Home			
FAITH GROWS			**$195,437**
• Building to Serve	• Transportation		
• Real Estate Management	• Employment and Financial Counseling		
• Finance	• People Helpers		
• Life After Drugs	• Bread for A Hungry World		
1985 PROPOSED BUDGET			**$2,063,847**
BUDGET PER WEEK			**$39,689**
INCREASE OVER 1984 BUDGET			**17%**

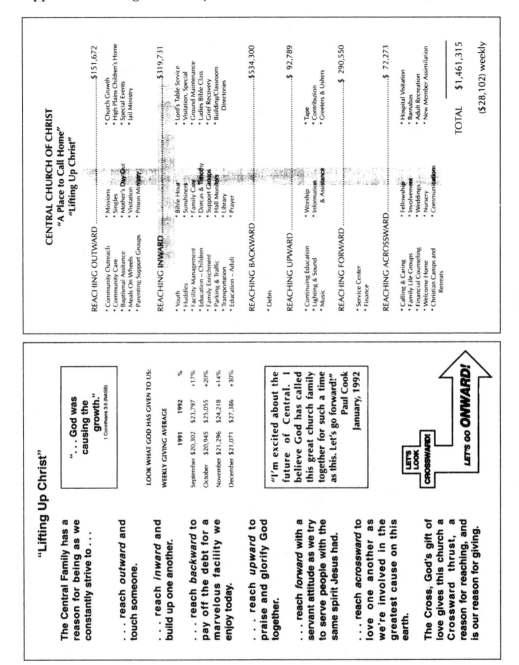

CENTRAL CHURCH OF CHRIST
"A Place to Call Home"
"Lifting Up Christ"

REACHING OUTWARD $151,672
- Community Outreach
- Community Care
- Baptismal Assistance
- Meals On Wheels
- Parenting/Support Groups
- Missions
- Singles
- Mother's Day Out
- Visitation
- Prison Ministry
- Church Growth
- High Plains Children's Home
- Special Events
- Jail Ministry

REACHING INWARD $319,731
- Youth
- Huddles
- Facility Management
- Education – Children
- Family Enrichment
- Parking & Traffic
- Transportation
- Education – Adult
- Bible Hour
- Sunshiners
- Family Care
- Dorcas & Timothy
- Support Groups
- Hall Monitors
- Library
- Prayer
- Lord's Table Service
- Visitation, Special
- Ground Maintenance
- Ladies Bible Class
- Grief Recovery
- Building/Classroom Directories

REACHING BACKWARD $534,300
- Debts

REACHING UPWARD ....$ 92,789
- Continuing Education
- Lighting & Sound
- Music
- Worship
- Information & Assistance
- Tape
- Contribution
- Greeters & Ushers

REACHING FORWARD ....$ 290,550
- Service Center
- Finance

REACHING ACROSSWARD ....$ 72,273
- Calling & Caring
- Family Life Groups
- Financial Counseling
- Welcome Home
- Christian Camps and Retreats
- Fellowship
- Involvement
- Weddings
- Nursery
- Communications
- Hospital Visitation
- Barnabas
- Adult Recreation
- New Member Assimilation

TOTAL $1,461,315

($28,102) weekly

"Lifting Up Christ"

The Central Family has a reason for being as we constantly strive to . . .

". . . God was causing the growth."
1 Corinthians 3:6 (NASB)

. . . reach *outward* and touch someone.

LOOK WHAT GOD HAS GIVEN TO US:

WEEKLY GIVING AVERAGE

	1991	1992	%
September	$20,302	$23,797	+17%
October	$20,945	$25,055	+20%
November	$21,296	$24,218	+14%
December	$21,071	$27,386	+30%

. . . reach *inward* and build up one another.

. . . reach *backward* to pay off the debt for a marvelous facility we enjoy today.

". . . reach *upward* to praise and glorify God together.

"I'm excited about the future of Central. I believe God has called this great church family together for such a time as this. Let's go forward!"
Paul Cook
January, 1992

. . . reach *forward* with a servant attitude as we try to serve people with the same spirit Jesus had.

. . . reach *acrossward* to love one another as we're involved in the greatest cause on this earth.

The Cross, God's gift of love gives this church a Crossward thrust, a reason for reaching, and is our reason for giving.

LET'S LOOK CROSSWARD!

LET'S GO ONWARD!

Front and back of a 5½×8½″ card included in the packet (6×9″ envelope) of materials for 1993

1993   **1993**

"Lifting Up Christ"

CENTRAL CHURCH OF CHRIST
My Personal Resolution to Christ for 1993

I resolve to contribute $_____ per week during 1993 toward carrying out the proposed budget. This purpose may be to increased or decreased as God blesses me during the coming year. If this is an increase, this represents an increase of _____ per week over my 1992 contribution.

Name (Please Print) _____

Address _____

City_____ Zip _____

COUNT ON ME–
"to lift up Christ"
John 3:14

1993   **1993**

Monetary pledge card (4×6″) from the 1993 packet. Volunteering of time to various ministries was on another card, a 5×7½″ postcard (reproduced on the next page) preaddressed to the church's Involvement Ministry.

COMING SPECIAL EVENTS

Jan. 17	Ted Stewart teaches combined class of all adults in the auditorium on "New Discoveries Confirm Great Bible Miracles."
Jan. 17	Stewart continues series on Sunday night
Jan. 24	Ministry Fair
	Stewart series continues on Sunday night
Jan. 31	Stewart series continues on Sunday night
	Nomination for additional elders begins
Feb.	Shepherding Series in Adult Classes
Feb. 28	Police & Fireman Appreciation Night
Mar. 28-May 16	Ministry Leaders: Nomination, Selection, Affirmation, Training
April 4	Friends Day
April 11	Easter and Special Outreach Service
May 5	Central Teachers Appreciation
May 9	Mother's Day
May 12	Community Teachers Appreciation
May 23	Senior's Appreciation Service

Front and back of a schedule of events reminder card.

Central Church of Christ
A Place to call Home
MINISTRY FAIR SUNDAY
(January 24)

"If anyone serves, he should do it with the strength God provides, so that in all things God may be praised through Jesus Christ."
I Pet. 4:11

8:30 a.m. "Why I'm Excited About the Future of Central" Dick Marcear

9:45 a.m. Bible Classes for all Ages

11:00 a.m. "Why I'm Excited About the Future of Central"
Dick Marcear (Chapel)

11:00 - 2:00 p.m. Lunch provided for every person in Basement
Fellowship Area. Tours of Ministry Fair Displays

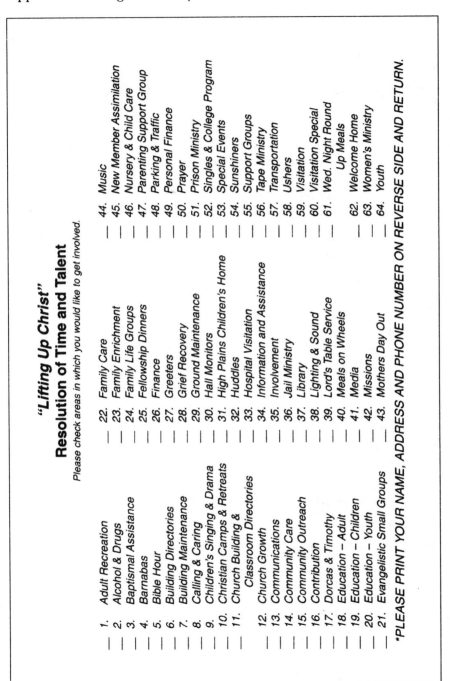

"Lifting Up Christ"
Resolution of Time and Talent

Please check areas in which you would like to get involved.

1.	Adult Recreation	22.	Family Care
2.	Alcohol & Drugs	23.	Family Enrichment
3.	Baptismal Assistance	24.	Family Life Groups
4.	Barnabas	25.	Fellowship Dinners
5.	Bible Hour	26.	Finance
6.	Building Directories	27.	Greeters
7.	Building Maintenance	28.	Grief Recovery
8.	Calling & Caring	29.	Ground Maintenance
9.	Children's Singing & Drama	30.	Hall Monitors
10.	Christian Camps & Retreats	31.	High Plains Children's Home
11.	Church Building &	32.	Huddles
	Classroom Directories	33.	Hospital Visitation
12.	Church Growth	34.	Information and Assistance
13.	Communications	35.	Involvement
14.	Community Care	36.	Jail Ministry
15.	Community Outreach	37.	Library
16.	Contribution	38.	Lighting & Sound
17.	Dorcas & Timothy	39.	Lord's Table Service
18.	Education – Adult	40.	Meals on Wheels
19.	Education – Children	41.	Media
20.	Education – Youth	42.	Missions
21.	Evangelistic Small Groups	43.	Mothers Day Out

44.	Music		
45.	New Member Assimilation		
46.	Nursery & Child Care		
47.	Parenting Support Group		
48.	Parking & Traffic		
49.	Personal Finance		
50.	Prayer		
51.	Prison Ministry		
52.	Singles & College Program		
53.	Special Events		
54.	Sunshiners		
55.	Support Groups		
56.	Tape Ministry		
57.	Transportation		
58.	Ushers		
59.	Visitation		
60.	Visitation Special		
61.	Wed. Night Round		
	Up Meals		
62.	Welcome Home		
63.	Women's Ministry		
64.	Youth		

*PLEASE PRINT YOUR NAME, ADDRESS AND PHONE NUMBER ON REVERSE SIDE AND RETURN.

Budgets and Fund Raising

NEW THOUGHTS ON FUND RAISING

I. BEST COMMUNICATION WORDS

   A. Care or caregiver or compassion

   B. Dream or vision

   C. Promise, promise keeper, accountability

   D. Purpose
      1. Who we are
      2. Whose we are
      3. Where we are
      4. Where we are going
      5. How we are going to get there

   E. Significant — What can I give or do that will make a significant difference?

   F. Involvement — How can my family and I get involved?

   G. Something for everybody — in regular contributions
      1. Large goal — includes something for everybody to feel good about going to
      2. Special efforts for individual parts of the large goal.

   H. Team — joyful praise or celebration to God by all.

   I. Constant "Seed Planting" is an imperative in long-term fund raising.

II. Specific information about the under-40 age group

   A. Have not been major givers, but can be

   B. Need to know older group really CARES about their needs

   C. Open communication with them

   D. Peer to peer communication is best for pledges and fund raising.

   E. Promise Keeper accountability groups and class good for teaching. (Promise Keepers encourage each man to give 10% to his local church.)

F. What's in it for me?

G. Where are we going?

H. What's really significant?

I. Underwritten motive — What will bring praise and glory to God? What can I do that will help this world, community or church be significantly better?

J. What kind of world or church will my children have?

K. Open doors for women to get involved is a major factor in giving in this age group.

III. Singles (including widows) can be significant givers percentage-wise.

A. Key word is CARE.

B. Do you really want us here, care about us and desire to meet our needs?

IV. Biggest factor in giving is a person's model or example.

A. Family, friend or peer

B. People moving into a congregation normally give about what the friend who got them to come gives — but it takes from two to three years to reach this level. (Unwritten expectation level).

C. Involvement is important: People who attend church regularly and are involved in ministry give three times more than those who only attend once a month.

D. Average contribution per member who attends Sunday school regularly is $20 in Southern Baptist churches. For those who only attend worship service, it's 50 cents a person.

E. Average giving per income for all members of churches has dropped to less than 2%. Our church's is around 4%.

F. Success produces more success. A friendly church takes pride in being friendly. A giving church is internally motivated to give more and more. Morale and motivation are very important.

G. Younger people need to know of past victories and that it can be done today.
1978 — Broadway in Lubbock — $2.0 million
1980 — Central in Amarillo — $2.2 million
1984 — Richland Hills — $8 million
1988 — Richland Hills — $8 million

JOURNEY TO THE HEART OF GOD IMPLEMENTATION

1. Faulkner Film Series on Sunday Nights beginning July 30

   "Being a Success at Work and Having a Successful Family"

2. "40 Days of Prayer" as we are having deacon selection.

3. "Walk Thru the Bible" seminar on Sunday nights, Sept. 17, 24, Oct. 1

4. Adult class lesson series on this theme.

5. Cards printed for kids to give to parents asking them to lead them on a "Journey to the Heart of God."

6. JOG — Journey of God program to meet with all members in groups 100 at a time on Sunday nights beginning Oct. 8. Get input on what and how they are doing on their journey. Get suggestions from them on how we can help everyone on this "Journey." Get input from congregation on needs, how we are doing, how can we improve, suggestions for 1996 program, needs and budget.

7. Do a survey in Sunday morning classes to find major reasons people are coming to our church.

8. One month devotional guide on theme with a personal commitment page.

9. Put some specific Wednesday night courses in the program to implement the theme.

10. Use the new song Carlie Burdett wrote, "Journey to the Heart of God."

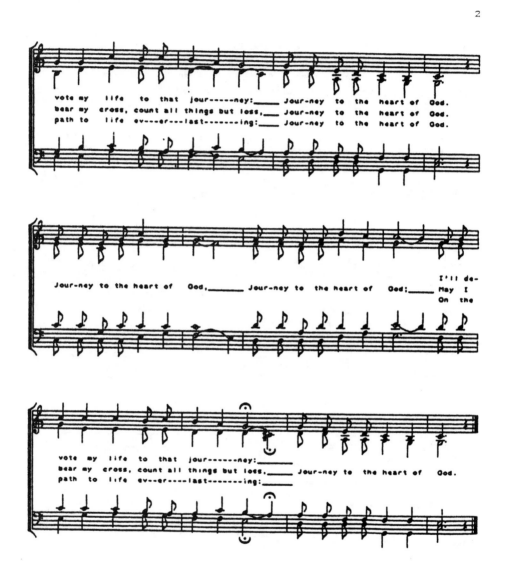

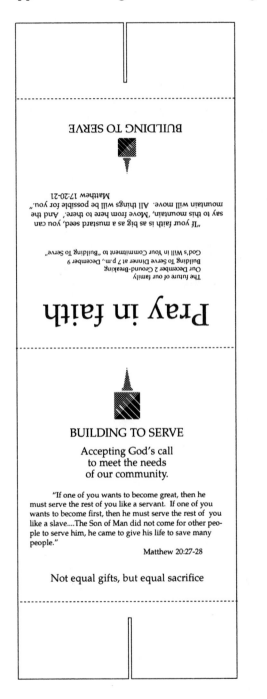

BUILDING TO SERVE

Matthew 17:20-21

"If your faith is as big as a mustard seed, you can say to this mountain, 'Move from here to there.' And the mountain will move. All things will be possible for you."

The future of our family
Our December 2 Ground-breaking
Building To Serve Dinner at 7 p.m., December 9
God's Will in Your Commitment to "Building To Serve"

Pray in faith

BUILDING TO SERVE

Accepting God's call
to meet the needs
of our community.

"If one of you wants to become great, then he must serve the rest of you like a servant. If one of you wants to become first, then he must serve the rest of you like a slave....The Son of Man did not come for other people to serve him, he came to give his life to save many people."

Matthew 20:27-28

Not equal gifts, but equal sacrifice

Prayer reminder for the building program

50-Day Spiritual Walk

"The Church You've Always Longed For"
"What You Can Do To Make It Happen"

Jan. 26	**Announce Deacon Nominations**
Feb. 2	**"Works at Being a Caring Family"** (Turn in Deacon's Nominations in class.)
Feb. 9	**"Captures the Heart of the Community"** (Turn in Deacon's Nominations in class.)
Feb. 16	**"Welcomes All People"** (Turn in Deacon's Nominations in class.)
Feb. 23	**"Empowers Each Individual"** (Elders interview potential deacons.)
March 2	**"Models Integrity"** (Elders interview potential deacons.)
March 9	**"Serves a Broken World"** (Elders interview potential deacons.)
March 16	**"Encounters the Living God"** (Potential deacons names before the congregation.)
March 23	**"Anticipates a Great Future"** (Deacons installed and trained.)

- Please use this prayer and study guide daily for the next 50 days.
- You will have an incredible spiritual adventure.
- Pray for God to give us men of faith with servant's hearts for additional deacons.

Feb. 4 *Work at Caring for Your Church Family*

Read: Romans 12:9-16
Living Message: "Don't just pretend that you love others. Really love them." Rom. 12:9
Scripture Meditation: Which of Paul's instructions do you follow well?

Prayer Requests: _____

Prayers Answered:
Table Prayer: We do not know the name of the many people who shared in growing, harvesting and preparing this food, but we are thankful for it. Help us share love, a fruit of the spirit, with others. In Jesus name. Amen

Feb. 5 *Work at Caring for Your Church Family*

Read: 1 John 4:7-12
Living Message: "If we love each other, God lives in us, and his love has been brought to full expression through us." I John 4:12
Scripture Meditation: Would a visitor be able to recognize that love is important to your congregation? Why?

Prayer Requests: _____

Prayers Answered:
Table Prayer: We know that Jesus Christ is the Bread of Life, and we ask you to feed our souls with love so that we might be spiritually nourished to share your love with others. In Jesus name. Amen

"THE CHURCH YOU'VE ALWAYS LONGED FOR"
"What You Can Do To Make It Happen!!"

Feb. 2 *Work at Caring for Your Church Family*

Read: Acts 2:42-47 and 4:32-35
Living Message: "All the believers were of one heart and mind, and they felt that what they owned was not their own; they shared everything they had." Acts 4:32
Scripture Meditation: As you read these passages, what do you like about the early church?

Prayer Request: _____

Prayers Answered:
Table Prayer: As the scattered grains of field have been gathered into a loaf of bread, so are we drawn together, dear Lord. In Jesus name. Amen

Feb. 3 *Work at Caring for Your Church Family*

Read: Mark 10:46-52
Living Message: "What do you want me to do for you?" Jesus asked." Mark 10:51
Scripture Meditation: What can we do that will make us more sensitive to the needs of others?

Prayer Requests: _____

Prayers Answered:
Table Prayer: Father, help us not only feed food to others, but help us also share spiritual food with them. In Jesus name. Amen

Feb. 8 *Capture the Heart of Your Community*

Read: Acts 5:12-16

Living Message: "More and more people believed and were brought to the Lord - crowds of both men and women." Acts 5:14

Scripture Meditation: What good things happening at Central might interest someone in your community? Who could you tell about these things this week?

Prayer Requests: _____

Prayers Answered: _____

Table Prayer: May this food bring health to our bodies and may you use us to bring renewal to our community. In Jesus name. Amen

Feb. 9 *Capture the Heart of Your Community*

Read: Luke 5:29-32

Living Message: "Healthy people don't need a doctor - sick people do." Luke 5:31

Scripture Meditation: How is the Central Church like a hospital?

Something I did that brought joy to someone else today. (example: inviting them to lunch)

Prayer Requests: _____

Prayers Answered: _____

Table Prayer: May we eat this food in cheerfulness and may the Great Physician relieve all of our hearts from their burdens. In Jesus name. Amen

Feb. 6 *Work at Caring for Your Church Family*

Read: II Samuel 9:1-13

Living Message: "I want to show God's kindness to them in any way I can." II Samuel 9:3

Scripture Meditation: Describe a time at church or in your own life when an incredible act of kindness was shown.

Prayer Requests: _____

Prayers Answered: _____

Table Prayer: Father, help us weep with those who weep. As we sit at this table, we cherish the memories of those whose chairs are empty and who are now at your right hand at the heavenly table. In Jesus name. Amen

Feb. 7 *Work at Caring for Your Church Family*

Read: Philippians 2:1-4

Living Message: "Don't think only about your own affairs, but be interested in others, too, and what they are doing."
Philippians 2:4

Scripture Meditation: "If we practiced these principles toward others in the church, how would they respond?"

Prayer Requests: _____

Prayers Answered: _____

Table Prayer: Father, help us consider the needs of others before we seek to satisfy only the hunger of our own bodies and the cravings of our own hearts. In Jesus name. Amen

Feb. 10 *Capture the Heart of Your Community*

Read: Matt. 5:13-16
Living Message: "Let your good deeds shine out for all to
  see, so that everyone will praise your heavenly Father."
  Matt. 5:16
Scripture Meditation: What can you do for others that will
  bring praise to God?

Prayer Requests: _____

Prayers Answered: _____
Table Prayer: May the salt at this meal remind us that we are
  salt of the world. Please use us to bring others to praise
  and glorify God. In Jesus name. Amen

Feb. 11 *Capture the Heart of Your Community*

Read: Acts 9:36-43
Living Message: "The news raced through the whole town, and
  many believed in the Lord." Acts 9:42
Scripture Meditation: How often do you share with others the
  good things God is doing in the church, as well as, how
  God is working in your life?

Prayer Requests: _____

Prayers Answered: _____
Table Prayer: Father, as we hold hands at this table and bow in
  your presence, may all we say and do at this table and
  abroad in the world be a witness for you. In Jesus name.
  Amen

Feb. 12 *Capture the Heart of Your Community*

Read: Philip. 2:12-18
Living Message: "Let your lives shine brightly before them."
  Philip. 2:15
Scripture Meditation: What kind of responses do you get
  when you say good things about the Central Church?

Prayer Requests: _____

Prayers Answered: _____
Table Prayer: As these lights shine brightly over our table,
  help us shine brightly before others for you in this
  community. In Jesus name. Amen

Feb. 13 *Capture the Heart of Your Community*

Read: John 4:1-42
Living Message: "Please sir," the woman said, "give me
  some of that water!" John 4:15
Scripture Meditation: How did the woman persuade the
  rest of the community to come and see Jesus?

Prayer Requests: _____

Prayers Answered: _____
Table Prayer: As we drink water at this meal, may we remember there are many people in this community who need
  the 'living water' of life. In Jesus name. Amen

Feb. 16 *Welcome All People*

Read: John 6:35-40; Heb. 13:2
Living Message: "Those the Father has given me will come to me, and I will never reject them." John 6:37
Scripture Meditation: What can we do to make all visitors feel welcome?

Something I did that brought joy to someone else today.
_____

Prayer Requests: _____

Prayers Answered:
Table Prayer: Father, may this meal be lit by the light of love and may everyone be warmly welcomed with the flame of fellowship. In Jesus name. Amen.

Feb. 17 *Welcome All People*

Read: Leviticus 19:32-34; I Tim. 4:12
Living Message: "Love foreigners or visitors as much as you love yourself." Leviticus 19:34
Scripture Meditation: How did you feel when you visited a church or place and didn't feel welcome?

Prayer Requests: _____

Prayers Answered:
Table Prayer: Even though we might have foreign visitors with us at our table, love is an international language which we all understand. In Jesus name. Amen

Feb. 14 *Capture the Heart of the Community*

Read: II Kings 5:1-15
Living Message: "Sir, if the prophet had told you to do some great thing, wouldn't you have done it? So you should certainly obey him when he says simply to go and wash." II Kings 5:13
Scripture Meditation: What are some "small" things we might do in obedience to God's command to reach our community with the gospel?

Prayer Requests: _____

Prayers Answered:
Table Prayer: Thank you for those who carefully followed directions in the preparation of this food. Help us obey your simple commandments and may we be more interested in being servants than stars. In Jesus name. Amen

Feb. 15 *Welcome All People*

Read: Acts 10:1-35
Living Message: Then Peter replied. "I see very clearly that God doesn't show partiality. In every nation he accepts those who fear him and do what is right." Acts 10:34-35
Scripture Meditation: "What are some benefits of having a church that welcomes all people from many different backgrounds?

Prayer Requests: _____

Prayers Answered:
Table Prayer: Help us not waste food and may we not want more than we truly need in a world where many would gladly accept crumbs from our table. In Jesus name. Amen

Feb. 20 *Welcome All People*

Read: Acts 9:19-20
Living Message: "When Saul arrived in Jerusalem, he tried to meet with the believers, but they were all afraid of him?" Acts 9:26
Scripture Meditation: Why were the Christians afraid of Saul? What kinds of people are churches afraid of welcoming today?

Prayer Requests: _____

Prayers Answered: _____
Table Prayer: Father, we thank you for foods that we like and enjoy. Help us not be afraid to bring new foods to our table which are good for us. In Jesus name. Amen

Feb. 21 *Welcome All People*

Read: Revelation 7:9-10
Living Message: "I saw a vast crowd, too great to count, from every nation and tribe and people and language... And they were shouting with a mighty shout, 'Salvation comes from our God...!'" Revelation 7:9-10
Scripture Meditation: What would we have to do for our worship services today to be like this?

Prayer Requests: _____

Prayers Answered: _____
Table Prayer: May our table never be too crowded for friends who are looking for God. In Jesus name. Amen

Feb. 18 *Welcome All People*

Read: James 2:1-9
Living Message: "If you give special attention and a good seat to the rich person, but you say to the poor one, "You stand over there, or else sit on the floor - well. doesn't this discrimination show that you are guided by the wrong motives?" James 2:3-4
Scripture Meditation: According to James, why should we not show favoritism?

Prayer Requests: _____

Prayers Answered: _____
Table Prayer: As we leave this meal and wipe on a towel, may we never forget that Jesus washed the disciples feet, dried them with a towel. and taught that the person who would be the greatest must become the greatest servant. In Jesus name. Amen

Feb. 19 *Welcome All People*

Read: Romans 14:1-12
Living Message: "Why do you look down on another Christian?" Romans 14:10
Scripture Meditation: What are some things which might cause us to look down on another Christian which are a matter of tradition and not a matter of Bible doctrine?

Prayer Requests: _____

Prayers Answered: _____
Table Prayer: We thank you for all the food at this table. We don't all like the same food, but we thank you for providing food for all of us. In Jesus name. Amen

283

Feb. 24 *Empower Individuals*

Read: Matthew 9:9-13

Living Message: "Why does your teacher eat with such scum?" Matthew 9:11

Scripture Meditation: Do you think you would have seen Matthew's potential like Jesus did?

Prayer Requests: _____

Prayers Answered: _____

Table Prayer: Father, the mustard at this meal reminds us of the great potential in a tiny mustard seed. In Jesus name. Amen

Feb. 25 *Empower Individuals*

Read: Philemon

Living Message: "Your kindness has so often refreshed the hearts of God's people." Philemon 1:7

Scripture Meditation: How could Paul's letter empower Philemon?

Prayer Requests: _____

Prayers Answered: _____

Table Prayer: Father, forgive us when we complain about our food, and help us to always be willing to forgive others. In Jesus name. Amen

Feb. 22 *Empower Individuals*

Read: Acts 18:24-28

Living Message: "They took him aside and explained the way of God more accurately." Acts 18:26.

Scripture Meditation: Who have you helped learn more about Jesus? Who have you helped develop their God given gifts to serve better?

Prayer Requests: _____

Prayers Answered: _____

Table Prayer: We thank you for this food bringing nourishment to our bodies. May we empower others by nourishing them with spiritual food. In Jesus name. Amen

Feb. 23 *Empower Individuals*

Read: Matt 4:18-22

Living Message: "Come, be my disciples, and I will show you how to fish for people!" Matthew 4:19

Scripture Meditation: How would you train someone to teach others about Jesus Christ and His Church?

Prayer Requests: _____

Prayers Answered: _____

Table Prayer: May our table be like that table in the upper room where you empowered your disciples to be special servants. In Jesus name. Amen

284

Feb. 28 *Empower Individuals*

Read: Acts 4:1-14

Living Message: "They recognized them as men who had been with Jesus." Acts 4:13

Scripture Meditation: How had being with Jesus changed their lives?

Prayer Requests: _____

Prayers Answered:

Table Prayer: Father, don't stand outside the door, we want you to come and be with us at this table. We want to be recognized as a family who has been with Jesus. In Jesus name. Amen

March 1 *Model Integrity*

Read: Acts 5:1-11 and Acts 20:17-38

Living Message: "How could you do a thing like this? You weren't lying to us, but to God." Acts 5:4

Scripture Meditation: Why do you think this couple lied?

Prayer Requests: _____

Prayers Answered:

Table Prayer: Father, help all in our family circle who sit together at this meal give priority to those things which are of eternal value. May we always put first things first. In Jesus name. Amen

Feb. 26 *Empower Individuals*

Read: Luke 8:1-3

Living Message: "Many others were contributing from their own resources to support Jesus and his disciples." Luke 8:3

Scripture Meditation: Can you think of some women at the Central Church who need to be thanked for what they do?

Prayer Requests: _____

Prayers Answered:

Table Prayer: Father, we thank you for Christian women, and we know there would be few cooked meals without them. In Jesus name. Amen

Feb. 27 *Empower Individuals*

Read: I Samuel 16:1-13

Living Message: "The Lord doesn't make decisions the way you do! People judge by outward appearance, but the Lord looks at a person's thoughts and intentions." I Samuel 16:7

Scripture Meditation: Who is a younger person at the Central Church whose gifts you could help develop?

Prayer Requests: _____

Prayers Answered:

Table Prayer: God, you taught us that growth comes first in the blade, then the ear and finally in the full corn in the ear. Help us not expect an overnight harvest of the fruits of spirit as we work patiently with others. In Jesus name. Amen

March 4 *Model Integrity*

Read: Psalms 15
Living Message: "God loves those who keep their promises even when it hurts." Psalms 15:4
Scripture Meditation: How would a church change if all of it's members obeyed this Psalm?

Prayer Requests: _____

Prayers Answered: _____
Table Prayer: Father, if after eating this meal we are called to do battle for righteousness, clothe us with your armor so we will be able to withstand any evil assault. In Jesus name. Amen

March 5 *Model Integrity*

Read: Genesis 35:1-5
Living Message: "Destroy your idols, wash yourselves, and put on clean clothing." Genesis 35:2
Scripture Meditation: What kind of "idols" are problems for God's people today?

Prayer Requests: _____

Prayers Answered: _____
Table Prayer: Father, sometimes we eat physical foods that are not healthy for our bodies. Forgive us when we pursue unhealthy activities which destroy us spiritually. In Jesus name. Amen

March 2 *Model Integrity*

Read: Genesis 39:1-10
Living Message: "How could I ever do such a wicked thing? It would be a great sin against God." Genesis 39:9
Scripture Meditation: What tactics did Potipher's wife use on Joseph?

Something I did that brought joy to someone else today?

Prayer Requests: _____

Prayers Answered: _____
Table Prayer: May our home and table where we break bread together encourage us to never break our promise to you concerning our spiritual character. In Jesus name. Amen

March 3 *Model Integrity*

Read: Mark 11:15-17 and II Chronicles 29:15-20
Living Message: "They purified the Temple of the Lord. They were careful to follow all the Lord's instructions in their work." II Chronicles 29:15
Scripture Meditation: Are there sins in your life that need God's cleansing?

Prayer Requests: _____

Prayers Answered: _____
Table Prayer: Father, after every meal we must wash the dirty dishes. Thank you for cleansing our lives. In Jesus name. Amen

March 6 Model Integrity

Read: Ephesians 4:22-32

Living Message: "There must be a spiritual renewal of your thoughts and attitudes." Ephesians 4:23

Scripture Meditation: How could following Paul's instructions in these verses help the church become what you long for it to be?

Prayer Requests: _____

Prayers Answered: _____

Table Prayer: Father, we come to this meal tired and hungry. Thank you for physical and spiritual renewal. In Jesus name. Amen

March 7 Model Integrity

Read: I Samuel 7: 2-13

Living Message: "He named it Ebenezer - "the stone of help" - for he said, "Up to this point the Lord has helped us." I Samuel 7:12

Scripture Meditation: Is it important for the church to know about spiritual victories in your life?

Prayer Requests: _____

Prayers Answered: _____

Table Prayer: Father, you are always the most Welcome Guest at every meal. May your love be the loom upon which we weave the tapestry of our lives today. In Jesus name. Amen

March 8 Serve A Broken World

Read: Acts 16:6-15

Living Message: He saw a man from Macedonia pleading with him, "Come over here and help us." Acts 16:9

Scripture Meditation: When is the last time you heard a cry for help? Did you respond?

Prayer Requests: _____

Prayers Answered: _____

Table Prayer: Father, you have promised that those who mourn will be comforted. We in faith claim this promise as we sit around this table. In Jesus name. Amen

March 9 Serve A Broken World

Read: Luke 4:16-21

Living Message: "This scripture has come true today before your very eyes." Luke 4:21

Scripture Meditation: What broken people today are saying to the church, "Come and help us."?

Something I did that brought joy to someone else today: _____

Prayer Requests: _____

Prayers Answered: _____

Table Prayer: Christ was born long ago in a stable because there was no room in the crowded inn. May we prepare a place for others at our table who are hurting and may we make room for your Spirit to fill our hearts. In Jesus name. Amen

March 10 *Serve A Broken World*

Read: Matthew 25:31-46
Living Message: "I assure you, when you did it to one of the least of these my brothers and sisters, you were doing it to me." Matthew 25:40
Scripture Meditation: How does this scripture challenge us to look at those in need?

Prayer Requests: _____

Prayers Answered: _____
Table Prayer: God, you created the first family and provided food for them. You have provided food for us and taught us to love. Create within our hearts a love for all your children. In Jesus name. Amen

March 11 *Serve A Broken World*

Read: Genesis 1:28-31
Living Message: "God looked over all he had made, and he saw that it was excellent in every way." Genesis 1:31
Scripture Meditation: What words would you use to describe the spiritual condition of Amarillo, Texas?

Prayer Requests: _____

Prayers Answered: _____
Table Prayer: Father, we thank those who prepared this meal. May we always have an attitude of gratitude and let them know this meal was excellent in every way. In Jesus name. Amen

March 12 *Serve A Broken World*

Read: Luke 14:12-14
Living Message: "At the resurrection of the godly, God will reward you for inviting those who could not repay you." Luke 14:14
Scripture Meditation: What does this passage have to do with the Central Church becoming all you long for it to be?

Prayer Requests: _____

Prayers Answered: _____
Table Prayer: Father, you invited us to your spiritual feast and we didn't even have to pay for it, because of your grace. May we invite others to our table who we would never expect to repay us. In Jesus name. Amen

March 13 *Serve A Broken World*

Read: Isaiah 58:6-11
Living Message: "the Lord will guide you continually, watering your life when you are dry and keeping you healthy, too. You will be like a well watered garden." Isaiah 58:11
Scripture Meditation: Has God ever blessed you when you reached out and helped someone who was hurting?

Prayer Requests: _____

Prayers Answered: _____
Table Prayer: We thank you for the vegetables at this meal and for a glass of cold water. We pray that these blessings will bring health to our bodies and cheerfulness to our lives. In Jesus name. Amen

March 16 *Encounter the Living God*

Read: Psalms 42:1-5

Living Message: "As the deer pants for streams of water, so I long for you, O God." Psalms 42:1

Scripture Meditation: What brings you closer to God than anything else?

Prayer Requests: _____

Prayers Answered: _____

Table Prayer: Father, we remember the miracle of Jesus turning water into wine. We thank you for the miraculous manner by which you transform food on this table into new strength and energy within our bodies. We thank you most of all for worship services which resurrect our dead spiritual bodies. In Jesus name. Amen

March 17 *Encounter the Living God*

Read: Mark 11:1-10

Living Message: "The crowds all around Him were shouting, "Praise God!" Mark 11:9

Scripture Meditation: How did the people of Jerusalem respond to their encounter with the Son of God?

Prayer Requests: _____

Prayers Answered: _____

Table Prayer: Father, we, along with the Psalmist, have never seen your righteous people forsaken nor their children begging bread. For this and immeasurable blessings, we praise you and thank you. In Jesus name. Amen

March 14 *Serve A Broken World*

Read: James 2:14-17

Living Message: "What's the use of saying you have faith if you don't prove it by your actions?" James 2:14

Scripture Meditation: In your own words, what is James main point in these passages?

Prayer Requests: _____

Prayers Answered: _____

Table Prayer: Father, we have faith that seed sown produced some of the food on this table. We also know that active faith which is pleasing to you allows you to produce a great harvest. In Jesus name. Amen

March 15 *Encounter the Living God*

Read: Acts 4:32-31

Living Message: "After this prayer, the building where they were meeting shook, and they were all filled with the Holy Spirit." Acts 4:31

Scripture Meditation: What church service in the past brought you closest to God?

Prayer Requests: _____

Prayer Answered: _____

Table Prayer: Father, with mighty power you raised Jesus from the grave. May we welcome Him to a place with us at this table and may we feel His power within us as we personally draw closer to Him. In Jesus name. Amen

March 20 *Anticipate a Great Future*

Read: Matthew 16:13-21

Living Message: "Upon this rock I will build my church, and all the powers of hell will not conquer it."
Matthew 16:18

Scripture Meditation: What perspective does this passage give on the future of the church as it battles the powers of evil?

_____

Prayer Requests: _____

Prayers Answered: _____

Table Prayer: Father, we anticipate great meals because we trust those loved ones who prepare them. Because we know who you are, we look to the future with confidence and joy. In Jesus name. Amen

---

March 21 *Anticipate A Great Future*

Read: Psalms 22

Living Message: "Future generations will also serve him. Our children will hear about the wonders of the Lord." Psalms 22:30

Scripture Meditation: What do you think the Central Church will be like ten years from now?

_____

Prayer Requests: _____

Prayers Answered: _____

Table Prayer: Father, as we bow in prayer at this table and anticipate a great future, may we always ask "What would Jesus say or do?". In Jesus name. Amen

---

March 18 *Encounter the Living God*

Read: Psalms 84

Living Message: "With my whole being, body and soul, I will shout joyfully to the living God." Psalms 84:2

Scripture Meditation: How can you help make the Central Church a place where people's longings for God are satisfied?

_____

Prayer Requests: _____

Prayers Answered: _____

Table Prayer: Father, we crave certain foods and greatly enjoy them. Help us have this same desire to be sensitive to what people are really saying. In Jesus name. Amen

---

March 19 *Encounter the Living God*

Read: I Timothy 3:14-16

Living Message: "This is the church of the living God, which is the pillar and support of the truth." I Timothy 3:15

Scripture Meditation: If someone was looking for the church of the living God, what would he look for?

_____

Prayer Requests: _____

Prayers Answered: _____

Table Prayer: May this family table and our home be a spiritual lighthouse for the church of the living God. In Jesus name. Amen

Appendix I: 50-Day Spiritual Walk

March 22 *Anticipate A Great Future*

Read: I Peter 1:3-9

Living Message: "There is wonderful joy ahead, even though it is necessary for you to endure many trials for awhile."
I Peter 1:6

Scripture Meditation: What is one way the 50 Day Spiritual Adventure has rekindled your hope for the church?

Prayer Requests: _____

Prayers Answered:

Table Prayer: Father, we thank you that this food is not contaminated and is good for us. We know that the prospects for the church are good when God's people daily prepare themselves for the Lord's return by confession of sin and a longing to be holy. In Jesus name. Amen

---

March 23 *Anticipate A Great Future*

Read: Acts 9:1-19

Living Message: "The Lord said, 'Go and do what I say.'"
Acts 9:15

Scripture Meditation: Do you long for a church that expects great things from God? How can you personally demonstrate that kind of attitude?

Prayer Requests: _____

Prayers Answered:

Table Prayer: Father, we pray for a family with good, healthy eating habits. And, we thank you for the spiritual habits we have developed in our 50 Day Spiritual Adventure. In Jesus name. Amen

A book on the servant-driven church could only creditably be written by a servant. Ray Fulenwider is one! He probably has more growth ideas and practical experience for building a great church than any man in our fellowship. Serving in the background rather than the pulpit, he has had a positive effect on thousands. *The Servant-Driven Church* is not a book about theology or doctrine. It is a guide to practical ministry. Some may disagree with some of Ray's conclusions, but anyone concerned about growing the church will find plenty they *can* agree with and enough good ideas to challenge them for years.

Truitt Adair
Director, Sunset International Bible Institute

Over the past thirty years it has been my privilege to observe Ray Fulenwider as he worked with three churches, teaching the principles that are found in this book. All three churches have shown tremendous growth . . . at Central I have observed firsthand these great teachings and over the past eighteen months our congregation has grown from 1400 to 1700 in attendance. I wholeheartedly recommend this book, *The Servant-Driven Church*.

Bill Johnson
Elder

Attention all churches! Ray Fulenwider has done it. This is the most comprehensive, powerful book on church development and success I've ever read! Maybe you've read Rick Warren's *The Purpose-Driven Church*! Maybe not! But this one is a must! It is biblically sound and culture-relevant. Churches that grow will do so along the lines prescribed in this book. Complete with charts, sources and addresses. Do your church a favor. Devour this book. Put it into practice. Watch things happen!

Marvin Phillips
Marvin Phillips Ministries

The Servant-Driven Church represents the heart of Ray Fulenwider. He has lived what he teaches. In the years I have known Ray there has been no better builder of churches than he. This book outlines the principles Ray has used in helping build three great churches . . . anyone who is interested in building a great church should read this book and follow its principles.

Dick Marcear
Minister

This is a wonderfully comprehensive treatise written by a true servant leader, who has successfully been in the trenches of Church life for many years. . . . *The Servant-Driven Church* is a practical "must-read" for every church leader.

Dr. Gary R. Beauchamp
Minister

The Servant-Driven Church is a constant dialogue between sound Biblical theology and practical, workable applications. This is a how-to manual in the truest sense of the word. Every chapter is chock full of effective, detailed guidance. For those who want to build a great church, this book is a God-send.

Mike Armour
Author, *Systems-Sensitive Leadership*

You will not need another supplementary text to implement Ray's plan for greater church involvement. Everything you need to know is right here in *The Servant-Driven Church*. I was relieved to discover how much can be implemented in the smaller congregation.

Jim McFarland
Minister of Involvement and Administration
Southeastern Church of Christ, Indianapolis

Ray Fulenwider is high-energy, high-faith, high-productivity. Wherever he goes, the church grows. Get this book. Thank me later.

Terry Rush
Minister

Congratulations on completing your book, *The Servant-Driven Church*. I know of few individuals who bring the wisdom, spirituality and leadership to such a volume as you. Your voice . . . has been one of influence for over three decades. Your theme of servant leadership certainly must be the emphasis for congregations in the 21st century. I appreciate the ways in which you have taken Warren's material and integrated it into language and concepts which will impact churches everywhere.

David W. Wray
Chairman, Undergraduate Bible and Ministry

The Servant-Driven Church will motivate and provide guidance and support for God's servants to build a Christ-centered church for the 21st century, a church dedicated to lifting up Christ in the church and in the community.

Frank Mullican
Elder

Ray Fulenwider has accumulated a lot of wisdom and experience when it comes to motivating Christians to service. By the examples of his life, and now through this informative and helpful book, Ray's circle of influence will be enhanced. To God be the glory!

Royce Money
Abilene Christian University

About the Author

Ray Fulenwider is the new Minister of Administration and Church Coordination for the Spring Woodlands Church of Christ in Houston, Texas, as of February 1, 2000. This 1100 member congregation plans major expansion for the next 10 years. The address is:

Spring Woodlands Church of Christ   Phone: 281-367-2304
1021 Sawdust Road   email: info@swcc.net
Spring, Texas 77380-2151

From 1991 to 2000 Ray Fulenwider has served as the Minister of Education and Involvement, Staff Coordinator and Office Manager at Central Church of Christ in Amarillo, Texas. Weekly attendance has grown from 1100 to 1750. Ray earned his BSE and MSE degrees from Abilene Christian University and has done graduate studies in New York, Tennessee and Texas. He received an Administration degree and counselors license from Texas Tech.

Ray began preaching at the age of twelve and has held ministries in churches of all sizes. In addition, he has worked in all types of jobs from pulling and chopping cotton to teaching at the university level (Pepperdine University, Oklahoma City College, Harding University, Lubbock Christian College, Abilene Christian University, The University of Texas and David Lipscomb University). He has been a principal and coach in the Texas public school system. He has directed workshops for Bible school teachers. For 25 years he was the coordinator for Church Growth and Involvement Seminars held semi-annually. These seminars have attracted over 12,000 people from 40 states and 5 foreign countries. He has also hosted a weekly cable television program entitled "Coping" and served as president of the American Cancer Society as well as being Executive Director of the Richland Hills Counseling Center and serving on the executive board of Texas Alcohol Narcotics Education.

When it comes to church growth, Ray speaks from experience. From 1968-1978 with the Broadway Church of Christ in Lubbock, Texas, and from 1978-1990 with the Richland Hills Church of Christ, he helped attendance in all services (already at the several hundred level) to double and even triple.

Ray has spoken throughout the United States and in two foreign countries. He has conducted over 350 leadership retreats for elders and deacons. He has written *How to Grow a Church through the Bible School* and has edited Bible school curricula and the magazines *Gospel Advocate* and *20th Century Christian*. He has also been a contributing editor to *Image Magazine*.

Ray is married to Ann and together they have four children: Deana, Jeana, Joel, and Jana. Ann has taught preschool and children's Bible classes for over 25 years.